T0206300

Communications
in Computer and Information Science 1155

Commenced Publication in 2007
Founding and Former Series Editors:
Phoebe Chen, Alfredo Cuzzocrea, Xiaoyong Du, Orhun Kara, Ting Liu,
Krishna M. Sivalingam, Dominik Ślęzak, Takashi Washio, Xiaokang Yang,
and Junsong Yuan

Leong Hou U · Jian Yang ·
Yi Cai · Kamalakar Karlapalem ·
An Liu · Xin Huang (Eds.)

Web Information Systems Engineering

WISE 2019 Workshop, Demo, and Tutorial
Hong Kong and Macau, China, January 19–22, 2020
Revised Selected Papers

 Springer

Editors
Leong Hou U
University of Macau
Macau, China

Yi Cai
South China University of Technology
Guangzhou, China

An Liu (iD)
Soochow University
Suzhou, China

Jian Yang (iD)
Macquarie University
Sydney, NSW, Australia

Kamalakar Karlapalem (iD)
International Institute
of Information Technology
Hyderabad, India

Xin Huang (iD)
Hong Kong Baptist University
Hong Kong, China

ISSN 1865-0929   ISSN 1865-0937 (electronic)
Communications in Computer and Information Science
ISBN 978-981-15-3280-1   ISBN 978-981-15-3281-8 (eBook)
https://doi.org/10.1007/978-981-15-3281-8

WISE 2019 has been postponed until January 2020 because of the problems in Hong Kong.

This Springer imprint is published by the registered company Springer Nature Singapore Pte Ltd.
The registered company address is: 152 Beach Road, #21-01/04 Gateway East, Singapore 189721, Singapore

Preface

Welcome to the proceedings of the 20th International Conference on Web Information Systems Engineering (WISE 2019), held in Hong Kong (and Macau), China, during January 19–22, 2020. It marks the 20th anniversary of the conference, which was first held in Hong Kong in 2000. The series of WISE conferences aims to provide an international forum for researchers, professionals, and industrial practitioners to share their knowledge in the rapidly growing area of web technologies, methodologies, and applications. The first WISE event took place in Hong Kong, China (2000). Then the trip continued to Kyoto, Japan (2001); Singapore (2002); Rome, Italy (2003); Brisbane, Australia (2004); New York, USA (2005); Wuhan, China (2006); Nancy, France (2007); Auckland, New Zealand (2008); Poznan, Poland (2009); Hong Kong, China (2010); Sydney, Australia (2011); Paphos, Cyprus (2012); Nanjing, China (2013); Thessaloniki, Greece (2014); Miami, USA (2015); Shanghai, China (2016); Puschino, Russia (2017); Dubai, UAE (2018); and this year, WISE 2019 returns to Hong Kong, China, supported by the Hong Kong Polytechnic University and City University of Hong Kong.

This volume contains the workshop, demo, and tutorial papers presented at WISE 2019. Specifically, the proceedings include seven workshop papers, five demo papers, and three tutorial papers. Each of the workshop papers and demo papers was reviewed by three reviewers.

Special thanks are due to the members of the international Program Committee and the external reviewers for a rigorous and robust reviewing process. We are also grateful to the Hong Kong Polytechnic University, City University of Hong Kong, Springer Nature Switzerland AG, and the International WISE Society for supporting this conference. The WISE Organizing Committee is also grateful to the workshop organizers for their great efforts to help promote web information system research to broader domains. Moreover, we are grateful to the University of Macau for supporting the workshop.

We expect that the ideas which emerged during WISE 2019 will result in the development of further innovations for the benefit of scientific, industrial, and social communities.

November 2019

Leong Hou U
Jian Yang
Yi Cai
Kamalakar Karlapalem
An Liu
Xin Huang

Organization

Executive Committee

Workshop Co-chairs

Leong Hou U	University of Macau, Macau, China
Jian Yang	Macquarie University, Australia

The International Workshop on Web Information Systems in the Era of AI

General Co-chairs

Mingjun Xiao	University of Science and Technology of China, China
Guanfeng Liu	Macquarie University, Australia
An Liu	Soochow University, China

Program Co-chairs

Detian Zhang	Soochow University, China
Shiting Wen	Zhejiang University (Ningbo Campus), China
Chaogang Tang	China University of Mining and Technology, China

Program Committee

Jianhua Li	Hefei University of Technology, China
Tao Yan	Jiangnan University, China
Liang Shi	East China Normal University, China
Jun Wang	Shanghai University, China
Fei Chen	Qingdao University, China
Xianglin Wei	National University of Defense Technology, China
Chunsheng Zhu	Southern University of Science and Technology, China
Yunjun Gao	Zhejiang University, China
Jianwen Tao	Zhejiang University (Ningbo Campus), China
Jinqiu Yang	Zhejiang University (Ningbo Campus), China
Liqun Deng	Huawei Central Research Institute, China
Yang Yang	Jiangsu University, China
Xuyun Zhang	The University of Auckland, New Zealand
Mehmet A. Orgun	Macquarie University, Australia

Contents

Tutorials

Knowledge Graph Data Management: Models, Methods, and Systems

Xin Wang[1,2](✉) and Weixue Chen[1,2]

[1] College of Intelligence and Computing, Tianjin University,
Tianjin 300350, China
wangx@tju.edu.cn
[2] Tianjin Key Laboratory of Cognitive Computing and Application,
Tianjin 300350, China

Abstract. With the rise of artificial intelligence, knowledge graphs have been widely considered as a cornerstone of AI. In recent years, an increasing number of large-scale knowledge graphs have been constructed and published, by both academic and industrial communities, such as DBpedia, YAGO, Wikidata, Google Knowledge Graph, Microsoft Satori, Facebook Entity Graph, and others. In fact, a knowledge graph is essentially a large network of entities, their properties, semantic relationships between entities, and ontologies the entities conform to. Such kind of graph-based knowledge data has been posing a great challenge to the traditional data management theories and technologies. In this paper, we introduce the state-of-the-art research on knowledge graph data management, which includes knowledge graph data models, query languages, storage schemes, query processing, and reasoning. We will also describe the latest development trends of various database management systems for knowledge graphs.

Keywords: Knowledge graph · Data management · Data model · Query language · Storage scheme

1 Introduction

Knowledge graphs, as the latest development of symbolism, has been widely regarded by academia and industry as an important cornerstone of artificial intelligence in recent years. At present, knowledge graphs with millions of vertices (10^6) and hundreds of millions of edges (10^8) are common. Linked Open Data (LOD) cloud released in March 2019 contains a great number of knowledge graphs with more than 1 billion triples [2], such as DBpedia (>3 billion triples) [1], LinkedGeoData (>3 billion triples) [3], UniProt (>13 billion triples) [6], and so on. The construction and release of large-scale knowledge graphs in various domains pose new challenges to knowledge graph data management.

Supported by the National Natural Science Foundation of China (61972275) and the Natural Science Foundation of Tianjin (17JCYBJC15400).

L. H. U et al. (Eds.): WISE 2019, CCIS 1155, pp. 3–12, 2020.
https://doi.org/10.1007/978-981-15-3281-8_1

On the one hand, knowledge graphs stored in the form of files obviously cannot meet the query, retrieval, reasoning, analysis and various application needs of high-level artificial intelligence tasks; on the other hand, there are significant differences between relational models of traditional databases and graph models of knowledge graphs, and relational databases cannot effectively manage large-scale knowledge graph data. In order to manage knowledge graphs more effectively, the Semantic Web community has developed triple stores that specifically store RDF graphs; the database community has developed graph databases for managing property graphs.

However, the biggest problem of knowledge graph data management is that the existing data models and query languages are not unified. There is no database system that is recognized as a mainstream knowledge graph database, while the emergence of large-scale knowledge graphs requires effective infrastructure for data management. The urgent needs of artificial intelligence tasks, such as learning, recognition, and prediction, to be supported by knowledge graphs is calling for the development of large-scale knowledge graph data management systems. In this context, theories and technologies of knowledge graph data management is not only an critical research topic in the database community, but also one of the foundational tasks for the development of next-generation AI.

In this paper, we comprehensively introduce the state-of-the-art research on knowledge graph data management, which consists of knowledge graph data models, query languages, storage schemes, query processing, and reasoning. We also describe the latest development trends of knowledge graph data management systems.

2   Data Models

A data model defines the logical structure of the data, operations and constraints on it, and determines the effective methods adopted for data management. Thus, a data model is essential for storage management, query processing, and query language design. Several early graph data models basically use the graph structure in graph theory (i.e., $G = (V, E)$, where V is the vertex set and E is the edge set) as the data structure [9]; knowledge graph data models can be considered as extensions of traditional graph data models. A knowledge graph data model is based on the graph structure, which uses vertices to represent entities, and edges to represent the relationships between entities. This general data representation can naturally describe broad connections of things in the real world.

Currently, there are two main types of knowledge graph data models: the RDF graph model and the property graph model.

RDF Graph Model. RDF (Resource Description Framework) is a standard data model for representing and exchanging machine-understandable information on the Semantic Web [12]. In an RDF graph, each resource has an HTTP URI as its unique identifier; An RDF graph is defined as a finite set of triples (s, p, o); each triple represents a statement, where s is the subject, p is the predicate, and o is the object; (s, p, o) indicates that there is a connection p between the resource s and o, or that s has a property p whose value is o.

Property Graph Model. Unlike RDF graph models, property graph models have intrinsic support for vertex attributes and edge attributes. Currently, the property graph model is widely adopted by the graph database industry, including the well-known graph database Neo4j [4]. More recently, the Linked Data Benchmark Council (LDBC), which is composed of members from both academia and industry in the field of graph databases, is also standardizing the graph data model and graph query language based on the property graph model [8].

3 Query Languages

A knowledge graph query language mainly implements query operations on a knowledge graph data model. At present, the query language on RDF graphs is SPARQL; the query languages on property graphs include Cypher, Gremlin, PGQL, and G-CORE. For the types of query languages, except that Gremlin is a procedural language, the others are all declarative languages.

SPARQL. SPARQL is a standard query language for RDF knowledge graphs developed by the W3C [14]. SPARQL borrows the syntax from SQL. The basic unit of a SPARQL query is a triple pattern. Multiple triple patterns can form a basic graph pattern. SPARQL supports multiple operators to extend a basic graph pattern into a complex graph pattern. The latest SPARQL 1.1 version also introduces a property path mechanism [15] to support navigational queries on RDF graphs.

Cypher. Cypher was originally a property graph query language implemented in Neo4j. Like SPARQL, Cypher is a declarative language. In 2015, Neo4j launched the open source project openCypher (https://www.opencypher.org), which aims to standardize Cypher and provide syntax and semantic reference standards for other implementers. A major feature of Cypher is the use of "ASCII art" syntax to express graph pattern matching.

Gremlin. Gremlin is a property graph query language provided by the Apache TinkerPop graph computation framework [5]. Apache TinkerPop is designed as a general API interface to access graph databases, and its role is similar to the JDBC interface on relational databases. Gremlin is a graph traversal language, and its execution mechanism is to navigate along the directed edges of the graph. This execution method determines that users need to specify navigation steps in Gremlin, so Gremlin is classified as a procedural language.

PGQL. PGQL is a declarative query language [18] on property graphs proposed by Oracle in 2016, which supports graph pattern matching queries and navigational queries. Unlike Cypher, PGQL fully supports the regular path query semantics; unlike SPARQL property paths, which only support regular paths consisting of edge labels, by defining path pattern expressions, PGQL also supports regular paths containing vertex label conditions and the vertex (or edge) attribute comparison. PGQL improves the expressiveness of regular path queries on property graphs while maintaining the evaluation complexity.

G-CORE. G-CORE is a property graph query language [8] designed by the LDBC Graph Query Language Task Force. The design goal of G-CORE is to fully draw on and integrate the advantages of various existing graph query languages, to find the best balance between query expressiveness and evaluation complexity. Compared with existing graph query languages, in G-CORE, (1) the input and output of a query are graphs, which completely implements the composability of the graph query language; (2) paths are treated as basic elements that are as important as vertices and edges in graph query processing. To this end, G-CORE extends the property graph model and defines the path property graph model.

4 Storage Schemes

The current knowledge graph storage schemes mainly include: relation-based knowledge graph storage and native knowledge graph storage.

4.1 Relation-Based Storage Schemes

A relational-database-based storage scheme is a major storage management method for knowledge graphs. Various relation-based knowledge graph storage schemes will be introduced in chronological order, including: triple table, property table, vertical partitioning, sextuple indexing, and DB2RDF.

Triple Table. A triple table is a table with three columns whose schema is $triple\_table(subject, predicate, object)$. Each triple in a knowledge graph is stored as a row in the triple table. Although the triple table scheme is simple and clear, the number of rows of a triple table is the same as the number of edges of a knowledge graph. The biggest problem is that there will be many self-joins of the triple table after translating a knowledge graph query into an SQL query. 3store is an early RDF triple store which implements the triple table scheme [13].

Property Table. The property table storage scheme stores subjects of the same type in the same table, and different types of subjects are divided into different tables. Although the property table overcomes the problem of self-joining of the triple table, the disadvantages of the property table are: (1) large real knowledge graphs may have thousands of subject types, which may exceed the limit of relational databases; (2) Even in the same property table, the set of predicates of different subjects may also be quite different, which will cause the null-value problem. Jena is a representative RDF triple store and library that uses the property table scheme [20].

Vertical Partitioning. This method creates a two-column table (*subject*, *object*) for each predicate. The table stores the subject and object values connected by the predicate. The total number of tables is the number of different predicates in a knowledge graph. The advantages of vertical partitioning are: (1) a predicate table stores only the triples that appear in a knowledge graph, which solves the null-value problem; (2) each predicate table is sorted by the value of the subject column, and a merge-sort join can be used to quickly perform a join operation of different predicate tables. However, the main disadvantage to the vertical partitioning is that the number of tables to be created is equal to the number of different predicates in a knowledge graph, which may incur additional overhead in a relational database for large-scale knowledge graphs. SW-Store is the first RDF database system that realizes the vertically divided scheme [7].

Sextuple Indexing. In this scheme, all six permutations of a triple are accordingly built into six tables, i.e., $spo(subject, predicate, object)$, $pos(predicate, object, subject)$, $osp(object, subject, predicate)$, $sop(subject, object, predicate)$, $pso(predicate, subject, object)$, and $ops(object, predicate, subject)$. The sextuple indexing not only alleviates the self-join problem of the triple table through the join operations of the six tables, but also accelerates the efficiency of some typical knowledge graph queries. However, the sextuple indexing requires 6 times the storage space overhead and the index maintenance cost. RDF-3X is a typical system that uses the sextuple indexing scheme [17].

DB2RDF. This scheme is a trade-off between previous RDF relational storage schemes. The advantage of a triple table is the flexibility in the "row dimension", that is, the storage schema does not change as the number of rows increases; DB2RDF introduces this flexibility to the "column dimension", where the columns of a table are used as storage locations for predicates and objects, without binding columns to predicates. When inserting triples, a predicate is dynamically mapped to a column; the scheme can ensure that the same predicate is mapped to the same set of columns. In DB2RDF, the mapping of predicates to columns is an important issue to be considered. Because the number of maximum columns in the relational table is fixed, the two optimization goals of the mapping are: (1) the number of columns used should not exceed a certain value m; (2) the allocation of two different predicates of the same subject to the same column should be minimized, thereby reducing spills which may cause self-joins. The DB2RDF scheme has been implemented in the latest IBM DB2 database system [10].

4.2 Native Storage Schemes

A native knowledge graph storage specifically designs the underlying storage management scheme for knowledge graphs.

Neo4j. Neo4j is currently one of the most popular property graph databases. The most significant feature of its native graph storage layer is the "index-free adjacency", which means that each vertex maintains direct references to its adjacent vertice [19]. Thus, each vertex can be regarded as a "local index" of its adjacent vertices, which can be used to look up neighbors of a vertex, saving a lot of time than using a global index. In Neo4j, the vertices, edges, and attributes of property graphs are stored separately in different files. It is this strategy of storing graph structure separately from graph attributes that makes Neo4j highly efficient in graph traversal.

gStore. The underlying store of gStore uses the signature graph corresponding to an RDF graph and establishes a VS-tree index structure to speed up query processing [21]. In gStore, each vertex and its neighbors are encoded into a binary bit string, and these bit strings are used as vertices to form a label graph G^* corresponding to the RDF graph G. The VS-tree index is actually a summary graph of the label graph G^*, which can be used to greatly reduce the search space of SPARQL queries.

5   Query Processing

Despite the variety of knowledge graph query languages, they mainly have two basic query mechanisms, i.e., subgraph matching and navigation. In addition, several knowledge graph databases also support analytical queries as built-in operations.

5.1   Subgraph Matching Queries

The subgraph matching query is one of the most fundamental types of knowledge graph query operations. Further, Basic Graph Pattern (BGP) matching is the core of subgraph matching query.

Basic Graph Pattern, BGP. Given a knowledge graph G, a BGP Q on it is defined as

$$\bigwedge_{1 \le i \le m} (s_i, p_i, o_i) \tag{1}$$

where (1) s_i, p_i, and o_i are constants or variables ($1 \le i \le m$); (2) (s_i, p_i, o_i) is a triple pattern; (3) $\wedge$ denotes logical conjunction. A BGP is actually the conjunction of triple patterns on the graph, so it is also called a conjunctive query. There are two semantic definitions of BGP matching queries, i.e., subgraph homomorphism and subgraph isomorphism.

Given a knowledge graph $G = (V, E)$ and BGP $Q = \wedge_{1 \le i \le m}(s_i, p_i, o_i)$ on it, let $\bar{s} = (s_i, \ldots, s_m), \bar{p} = (p_i, \ldots, p_m), \bar{o} = (o_i, \ldots, o_m)$, the subgraph homomorphism semantics for BGP matching is defined as: (1) let σ is a mapping from $\bar{s}, \bar{p}, \bar{o}$ to the vertex set V; (2) $(G, \sigma) \models Q$ if and only if $\forall i \in [1, m]$, $(\sigma(s_i), \sigma(p_i), \sigma(o_i)) \in E$; (3) $Q(G)$ is the set of σ that makes $(G, \sigma) \models Q$ true. The subgraph isomorphism semantics for BGP is more strict, which imposes restrictions on subgraph homomorphism so that the mapping in G maintains the structure of Q. Furthermore, a Complex Graph Pattern (CGP) is formed by extending other relation operations including projection, filtering (selection), join, intersection, difference, and optional (left outer join) based on BGP. It has been proven that BGP evaluation is NP-complete under various semantics. In terms of subgraph matching query evaluation algorithms, the database community has a long history of research on BGP and has accumulated a lot of work.

5.2   Navigational Queries

Navigational query is another important type of queries on knowledge graphs. The size of the matched paths cannot be determined in advance, and the navigation needs to be performed according to the underlying knowledge graphs. The simplest form of navigational queries is to determine whether there is a path between two vertices, i.e., reachability query. In practice, the result paths of a navigational query is often required to meet certain constraints, among which Regular Path Queries (RPQ) are most commonly used.

Regular Path Query, RPQ. Given a knowledge graph $G = (V, E)$, the set of labels on its edges Σ, a path ρ in G from the vertex v_0 to v_m is a sequence $v_0 a_0 v_1 a_1 v_2 \ldots v_{m-1} a_{m-1} v_m$, where $v_i \in V$, $a_i \in \Sigma$, $(v_i, a_i, v_{i+1}) \in E$. The label of the path ρ is $\lambda(\rho) = a_0 \ldots a_{m-1} \in \Sigma^*$. An RPQ Q on G can be defined as

$$(x, r, y) \tag{2}$$

where (1) x and y are constants or variables; (2) r is a regular expression over Σ, which recursively defined as $r ::= \varepsilon \mid a \mid r/r \mid r|r \mid r^*$, $a \in \Sigma$, $/, |$, and * are concatenation, alternation, and the Kleene closure, respectively.

Given a knowledge graph $G = (V, E)$ and RPQ $Q = (x, r, y)$ on it, the arbitrary path semantics for Q is defined as $Q(G)$ is the set of paths in G whose labels satisfy the regular expression r, i.e., $Q(G) = \{\rho \mid \lambda(\rho) \in L(r)\}$.

Since there can be loops in a knowledge graph G, the set of matching paths in $Q(G)$ may be infinite. In this case, the arbitrary path semantics of RPQ is incomputable. In practice, the semantics need to be restricted to make the RPQ evaluation computable.

The evaluation of RPQ can theoretically be regarded as the multiplication operation of the automaton corresponding to the regular expression r and the automaton corresponding to the knowledge graph G, and its complexity is PTIME [16].

5.3   Analytical Queries

Unlike subgraph Matching and navigational queries, analytical queries do not care about local instances of the graph structure that satisfy a query, but instead focus on measuring the aggregated information of the entire knowledge graph. Simple analytical queries include statistical aggregation of knowledge graphs (such as vertex and edge counts), vertex degrees, maximum/minimum/average degrees in the graph, diameter of the graph, and so on. More complex analytical queries are mainly computationally intensive graph analysis and mining algorithms, including characteristic path length, connected components, community detection, clustering coefficient, PageRank, etc.

6 Reasoning

Reasoning is the feature that is unique to knowledge bases other than general databases. Reasoning on knowledge graphs can obtain new knowledge or even mine hidden knowledge from existing knowledge. Currently, knowledge graph reasoning method can be broadly categorized into rule-based reasoning and learning-based reasoning [11]. The main applications of knowledge graph reasoning include knowledge graph completion, question answering, and recommender systems. From the perspective of knowledge graph data management, there is still a lot of unexplored work to investigate in reasoning, such as reasoning support of knowledge graph storage and query processing.

7 Systems

The existing knowledge graph database management systems can be roughly classified into three categories, i.e., relation-based systems, RDF triple stores, and native graph databases. Table 1 lists the comparison of some common knowledge graph database management systems.

Table 1. The comparison of knowledge graph database management systems

Type	Name	Data model	Storage	Query	Active
Relational	3store	RDF graph	Triple table	SPARQL	No
	Jena	RDF graph	Property table	SPARQL	Yes
	SW-Store	RDF graph	Vertical partitioning	SPARQL	No
	IBM DB2	RDF graph	DB2RDF	SPARQL/SQL	Yes
	Oracle 18c	RDF graph	Relation	SPARQL/PGQL	Yes
RDF triple stores	RDF4J	RDF graph	Native	SPARQL	Yes
	RDF-3X	RDF graph	Sextuple indexing	SPARQL	No
	gStore	RDF graph	VS-tree	SPARQL	Yes
	Virtuoso	RDF graph	Multi-model	SPARQL/SQL	Yes
	AllegroGraph	RDF graph	Native	SPARQL	Yes
	GraphDB	RDF graph	Native	SPARQL	Yes
	BlazeGraph	RDF graph	Native	SPARQL/Gremlin	Yes
	StarDog	RDF graph	Native	SPARQL	Yes
	Apache Rya	RDF graph	Distributed	SPARQL	Yes
Native graph	Neo4j	Property graph	Native	Cypher	Yes
	JanusGraph	Property graph	Distributed	Gremlin	Yes
	OrientDB	Property graph	Native	SQL/Gremlin	Yes
	Cayley	RDF graph	External storage	Gremlin/GraphQL	Yes
	Cypher for Spark	Property graph	Distributed	Cypher	Yes

8 Conclusion

This paper briefly reviews the current models, methods, and systems of knowledge graph data management, which include data models, query languages, storage schemes, query processing, reasoning, and knowledge graph database systems.

Acknowledgments. This work is supported by the National Natural Science Foundation of China (61572353) and the Natural Science Foundation of Tianjin (17JCY-BJC15400).

References

1. Dbpedia. https://wiki.dbpedia.org/. Accessed 29 Nov 2019
2. The linked open data cloud. https://lod-cloud.net/. Accessed 29 Nov 2019
3. Linkedgeodata. http://linkedgeodata.org/. Accessed 29 Nov 2019
4. The neo4j manual v3.5. https://neo4j.com/docs/developer-manual/current/. Accessed 29 Nov 2019
5. Tinkerpop3 documentation v.3.4.4. https://tinkerpop.apache.org/docs/current/reference/. Accessed 29 Nov 2019
6. Uniprot. https://www.uniprot.org/. Accessed 29 Nov 2019
7. Abadi, D.J., Marcus, A., Madden, S.R., Hollenbach, K.: SW-store: a vertically partitioned DBMS for semantic web data management. VLDB J. **18**(2), 385–406 (2009)
8. Angles, R., et al.: G-CORE: a core for future graph query languages. In: Proceedings of the 2018 International Conference on Management of Data, pp. 1421–1432. ACM (2018)
9. Angles, R., Gutierrez, C.: Survey of graph database models. ACM Comput. Surv. (CSUR) **40**(1), 1 (2008)
10. Bornea, M.A., et al.: Building an efficient RDF store over a relational database. In: Proceedings of the 2013 ACM SIGMOD International Conference on Management of Data, pp. 121–132. ACM (2013)
11. Chen, X., Jia, S., Xiang, Y.: A review: knowledge reasoning over knowledge graph. Expert Syst. Appl. **141**, 112948 (2019)
12. Cyganiak, R., Wood, D., Lanthaler, M., Klyne, G., Carroll, J.J., McBride, B.: RDF 1.1 concepts and abstract syntax. W3C Recomm. **25**(02) (2014)
13. Harris, S., Gibbins, N.: 3store: efficient bulk RDF storage (2003)
14. Harris, S., Seaborne, A., Prud'hommeaux, E.: SPARQL 1.1 query language. W3C Recomm. **21**(10), 778 (2013)
15. Kostylev, E.V., Reutter, J.L., Romero, M., Vrgoč, D.: SPARQL with property paths. In: Arenas, M., et al. (eds.) ISWC 2015. LNCS, vol. 9366, pp. 3–18. Springer, Cham (2015). https://doi.org/10.1007/978-3-319-25007-6_1
16. Mendelzon, A.O., Wood, P.T.: Finding regular simple paths in graph databases. SIAM J. Comput. **24**(6), 1235–1258 (1995)
17. Neumann, T., Weikum, G.: RDF-3X: a RISC-style engine for RDF. Proc. VLDB Endow. **1**(1), 647–659 (2008)
18. van Rest, O., Hong, S., Kim, J., Meng, X., Chafi, H.: PGQL: a property graph query language. In: Proceedings of the Fourth International Workshop on Graph Data Management Experiences and Systems, p. 7. ACM (2016)

19. Robinson, I., Webber, J., Eifrem, E.: Graph Databases: New Opportunities for Connected Data. O'Reilly Media, Inc., Sebastopol (2015)
20. Wilkinson, K., Wilkinson, K.: Jena property table implementation (2006)
21. Zou, L., Özsu, M.T., Chen, L., Shen, X., Huang, R., Zhao, D.: gStore: a graph-based sparql query engine. VLDB J.- Int. J. Very Large Data Bases **23**(4), 565–590 (2014)

Local Differential Privacy: Tools, Challenges, and Opportunities

Qingqing Ye[1,2] and Haibo Hu[2,3(✉)]

[1] School of Information, Renmin University of China, Beijing, China
`yeqq@ruc.edu.cn`
[2] Department of Electronic and Information Engineering,
Hong Kong Polytechnic University, Kowloon, Hong Kong, China
`haibo.hu@polyu.edu.hk`
[3] Shenzhen Research Institute, Hong Kong Polytechnic University,
Kowloon, Hong Kong, China

Abstract. Local Differential Privacy (LDP), where each user perturbs her data locally before sending to an untrusted party, is a new and promising privacy-preserving model. Endorsed by both academia and industry, LDP provides strong and rigorous privacy guarantee for data collection and analysis. As such, it has been recently deployed in many real products by several major software and Internet companies, including Google, Apple and Microsoft in their mainstream products such as Chrome, iOS, and Windows 10. Besides industry, it has also attracted a lot of research attention from academia. This tutorial first introduces the rationale of LDP model behind these deployed systems to collect and analyze usage data privately, then surveys the current research landscape in LDP, and finally identifies several open problems and research directions in this community.

Keywords: Data collection · Data analysis · Local differential privacy

1 Motivation

With the prevalence of world wide web and big data, manufacturers and service providers at various layers are increasingly enthusiastic in collecting and analyzing user data to improve their services, lower the operation costs, and provide better personalization. The following are several examples.

1. Social networks and media such as Facebook and Instagram keep track of users' time and frequency spending on various pages in order to profile their favorites and interests. Such profile can be used for better personalized recommendation and advertisement.
2. Insurance company collects policy holders' usage data (for example, health and medical data for medical insurance, driving data for vehicle insurance) to improve actuarial model and personalized pricing.

© Springer Nature Singapore Pte Ltd. 2020
L. H. U et al. (Eds.): WISE 2019, CCIS 1155, pp. 13–23, 2020.
https://doi.org/10.1007/978-981-15-3281-8_2

3. Mobile phone manufacturers collect user' phone usage statistics such as app screen-on time and click frequency in order to design better battery optimization policy.
4. Wearable and IoT devices such as smart watches and smart bulbs collect usage statistics to provide personalized services to users.

However, such data collection comes at the price of privacy risks, not only to users but also to service providers who are vulnerable to internal and external data breaches. With General Data Protection Regulation (GDPR) enforced in EU from May 2018 and California Consumer Privacy Act (CCPA) will be in effect on January 1, 2020, there is a compelling need to provide strong privacy guarantees to users when collecting and analyzing their usage data.

As an answer to privacy-preserving data collection and analysis, Local Differential Privacy (LDP) [11,18,22] is a privacy model where each user perturbs her data locally before sending them to an untrusted party. In that sense, no one else can get access to the original data except the data owners themselves. So far, LDP has been deployed in many real products by several major software and Internet companies, including Google's RAPPOR system [14], Apple's iOS and macOS [33], and Microsoft Windows 10 [9].

The aim of this tutorial is to familiarize the audience with LDP as a popular privacy-preserving technique for data collection and analysis. This talk first introduces the rationale of LDP model and the basic analytical queries built on it, based on which the key technical underpinnings of the above deployed systems are then presented. As for academic research, this tutorial not only surveys the current research landscape in LDP, but also identifies open problem and research directions in this community.

2   Outline of the Tutorial

This tutorial is intended to introduce to WISE participants the new and yet rapidly developing topic of Local Differential Privacy (LDP). Inspired by the real LDP deployments, we structure the core of this tutorial by first describing the rationale of LDP and then introducing the key technical underpinnings of the deployed systems. Finally, we give an overview of the current research landscape and point out some research directions. The detailed outline of this tutorial is given below.

2.1   Preliminaries

Centralized differential privacy [13] assumes a trusted party that does not steal or leak data owner's private information. However, this does not hold in many real-world applications, particularly after the Facebook privacy scandal [31]. To this end, local differential privacy [11,18] is proposed for the setting where each data owner locally perturbs her data using a randomized algorithm, and then sends the perturbed version to a third party. As such, a trusted party is no longer needed for data collection and analysis.

In the LDP setting, the whole database D consists of a set of users, each possessing a private value v in some domain. These users interact with an untrusted aggregator who is allowed to learn some statistics (e.g., mean, frequency, and even the distribution) of the private value in the whole population. LDP ensures the information leakage for each individual is bounded. Specifically, each user perturbs her private value v by a randomized algorithm which takes v as the input and outputs v^*. Upon receiving perturbed values v^* from all users, the aggregator restores the statistics of v in the whole population. ϵ-local differential privacy (or ϵ-LDP) is defined on $\mathcal{A}$ and a privacy budget $\epsilon > 0$ as follows.

Definition 1 (ϵ-local differential privacy). A randomized algorithm $\mathcal{A}$ satisfies ϵ-local differential privacy, if and only if for any two inputs $v, v' \in D$ and for any output v^*, the following inequation always holds.

$$\Pr[\mathcal{A}(v) = v^*] \le e^{\epsilon} \times \Pr[\mathcal{A}(v') = v^*]$$

Intuitively, ϵ-LDP means by observing the output v^*, the aggregator cannot infer whether the input is v or v' with high confidence, which is different from the centralized differential privacy defined on two neighboring databases that only differ in one record.

2.2   Randomized Response and Basic Queries

Randomized Response. Randomized Response (RR) [41] is a technique developed for the interviewees in a survey to give random answer to a sensitive boolean question so that they can achieve plausible deniability. Specifically, each interviewee gives the genuine answer with probability p and gives the opposite answer with probability $1 - p$. To adopt RR to satisfy ϵ-LDP, we set p as $\frac{e^{\epsilon}}{1+e^{\epsilon}}$, so that $\frac{p}{1-p} = e^{\epsilon}$. Note that the percentage of "true" answers (denoted by f) directly obtained from all perturbed answers is biased and thus needs to be calibrated to $\frac{p-1+f}{2p-1}$. Currently, RR and its variants have become the predominant perturbation mechanism for LDP to answer two basic queries—frequency estimation over categorical data and mean estimation over numerical data. We briefly describe the corresponding perturbation mechanism $\mathcal{A}$ for these two queries to achieve ϵ-LDP.

Frequency Estimation over Categorical Data. This is a core problem in LDP, on which many research problems are investigated, including heavy hitter identification [35], frequent itemset mining [38], marginal release [8], spatiotemporal data aggregation [7] and range query [20].

As RR only targets at boolean variables, Generalized Randomized Response (GRR) with a domain size of k is introduced in [17] as follows:

$$\Pr[\mathcal{A}(v) = v^*] = \begin{cases} \frac{e^{\epsilon}}{k-1+e^{\epsilon}}, & \text{if } v = v^* \\ \frac{1}{k-1+e^{\epsilon}}, & \text{if } v \ne v^* \end{cases}$$

GRR is a generalized form of RR, and when $k = 2$ it degenerates to RR. The estimation accuracy of GRR degrades as the domain size k increases, because the probability that a value is correctly reported is approximately inversely proportional to k. Several other perturbation mechanisms have been proposed, including RAPPOR [14], Random Matrix Projection [4] and a mechanism based on the Count sketch with Hadamard transform [3]. Wang *et al.* present a framework to compare different perturbation mechanisms in terms of estimation variance [40]. In the conclusion, they provide guidelines about which mechanism to choose based on the privacy budget the domain size.

Mean Estimation over Numerical Data. There are two state-of-the-art numerical value perturbation mechanisms. The first one is to add Laplace noise [13] to the value and provides the same plausible deniability as with the centralized differential privacy. However, different from the centralized setting where the Laplace noise is added to the query result on a set of users, in the local setting this noise is directly added to the value of each user. This mechanism has been adopted in works of [26,36]. The second one takes RR as the building block, and decompose the mechanism into three major steps—discretization, perturbation and calibration. Specifically, a numerical value is first discretized to a binary one and is then perturbed by RR to satisfy ϵ-LDP. As the perturbation causes the mean estimation to be biased, a calibration of the perturbed value is also needed. This mechanism has been adopted in works of [9,10,12,44].

2.3   State-of-the-Art Deployment

To illustrate the practical use of LDP, we describe three cases of deployment in major software and Internet companies, and introduce the key ideas behind them.

RAPPOR from Google. The first large scale deployment of LDP in industry is RAPPOR. It is deployed in Google Chrome to enable a privacy-preserving collection of statistics in Chrome usage (e.g., about how a malware is hijacking users' settings in Chrome). Such statistics are crucial to improve browser security and user experience. The key idea is to transform a sensitive string into a Bloom Filter and then apply RR method to perturb it. A follow-up work [15] from the same team extends RAPPOR to more complex statistics collection without explicit dictionary knowledge.

Apple's LDP Deployment. This deployment was announced in 2016, and documented in a patent application [33] and a subsequent white paper [1]. The technique exploits several techniques—a Fourier transformation to spread out signal information, and a sketching algorithm to reduce the dimensionality of the domain. The deployed system now runs on hundreds of millions of iOS and macOS devices, performing a variety of data collection tasks, such as identifying popular emojis, popular health data types, and media playback preferences in Safari.

Telemetry Collection from Microsoft. The deployment of LDP in Microsoft collects telemetry data for mean and histogram estimation over time. A rounding technique has been applied to address the problem that privacy guarantee degrades rapidly when telemetry is collected regularly. This deployment has been rolled out since Windows 10 Fall Creator Update in 2017 and is now running on millions of devices to collect application usage statistics in a privacy-preserving manner [9].

2.4 Current Research Landscape

We will briefly describe the current research landscape in LDP for privacy-preserving data collection and analysis.

Heavy Hitter Identification. The goal is to identify the values that are frequent globally. When the size of the domain is small, this problem can be directly solved by frequency estimation. That is, one simply queries the frequency of every value in the range, and then identifies those ones with the highest frequency counts. However, if the domain is very large (e.g., 128 bits or larger), finding the most frequent values in this way is computationally infeasible. The method proposed by Thakurta *et al.* [33] identifies the frequent byte at each location, and uses semantic analysis to filter out meaningless combinations. There are some other works in the pure LDP setting. Hsu *et al.* [16] and Mishra *et al.* [23] propose efficient protocols for heavy hitters, but the error bound is higher than that of the method proposed by Bassily and Smith [4]. A follow-up work by Bassily *et al.* [3] proposes *TreeHish*, which is shown more efficient and accurate than that of the Bassily and Smith method [4]. Bun *et al.* [5] proposes *PrivateExpanderSketch* with state-of-the-art theoretical performance. A concurrent work implements the first real protocol *PEM* [37].

Itemset Mining. This problem considers the setting where each user has a set of items from a domain. For example, when Apple wants to estimate the frequencies of the emojis typed everyday by the users, each user has a set of emojis they have typed [34]. The problem is challenging because the simple method of encoding each itemset as a single value in the domain (power set of the original domain) and applying frequency estimation does not work. A frequency estimation method can only identify items that are very frequent in the population, but it is possible that all items in an infrequent itemset are very frequent. If no itemset in the power set domain is frequent enough, a direct encoding only sends noise to an aggregator. To solve this problem, the *LDPMiner* protocol [25] uses a technique called "padding and sampling". That is, each user first pads her itemset with dummy items to a fixed size l, and then randomly samples one item from the padded set, and finally uses a frequency estimation method to report the item. When estimating the frequency of an item, one multiples the estimated frequency by l. A very recent work [38] further improves the accuracy of *LDPMiner* within the same privacy constraints. The advantage comes from several key observations including privacy amplification under sampling, which is known to hold in the centralized setting [21].

Marginal Release. Marginal statistics, which captures the correlations among a set of attributes, are the building block of many data analysis tasks. A major challenge of marginal release with LDP is that heavy perturbation needs to be introduced in high dimension. Intuitively, marginal statistics can be derived from a space which consists of a noisy frequency of each value in the domain of all attributes. However, this space grows exponentially with the number of attributes, which leads to overwhelming noise in the computed marginals. To address this problem, Cormode et al. [8] apply Fourier Transformation to calculate k-way marginals. It only requires a few coefficients in the Fourier domain. Therefore, each user only needs to submit noisy Fourier coefficients to aggregator to compute the desired k-way marginals, instead of all values in those marginals. Another work [46] proposes to choose sets of attributes to reconstruct all k-way marginals in a local setting, which is inspired by PriView [24], a work for marginal release under a centralized setting.

Graph Data Analysis. Sensitive information among users are embedded in a social graph, e.g., the intimate relationship of two users. As graph data mining has become an important means of knowledge discovery, safeguarding graph data of individuals becomes imperative. Qin et al. proposes LDPGen [26] to build synthetic social networks by a graph generation model named BTER [29]. For each user, a Laplace noise is added to the group-based node degree to satisfy ϵ-LDP. Various mining tasks can then be carried out on the generated synthetic graph. Though this seems to be a general way for graph data analysis, it suffers from low data utility. The most recent work [32] proposes decentralized differential privacy (DDP) on local graph structures to ensure each individual protects not only her own privacy, but also the privacy of her neighbors. Based on DDP, a recursive framework with multi-phase is developed for subgraph counting, including triangles, three-hop paths and k-cliques. Though it is a dedicated solution for a specific graph analysis task, it can achieve better data utility than graph generation method.

Key-Value Data Collection. Key-value pair is a popular data model and pervasive in big data analytics. Intuitively, we could apply existing LDP methods for categorical data to perturb keys, and methods for numerical data to perturb values. However, this solution is not able to retain the key-value correlation that inherently exists between keys and values. A recent work PrivKV [44] proposes an efficient local perturbation protocol and an iterative model to collect key-value data for frequency and mean estimation. The main idea of PrivKV is to perturb the key first, and then apply perturbation on values based on the perturbed results of that key. Therefore, the correlation can be retained. In order to improve the estimation accuracy and reduce the network latency, an optimization strategy called "virtual iteration" is further proposed.

Spatiotemporal Data Aggregation. As location-based service becomes a necessary part in our daily lives, collection spatial data with rigorous privacy guarantee is an urgent need. This problem has been extensively studied in a centralized DP setting. In an LDP setting, Chen et al. [7] are the first to propose a personalized LDP, i.e., each user may individually set her privacy requirements, to learn the user distribution over a spatial domain. It is yet an open problem to evaluate this method on more sophisticated user movement models. With the rapid development of indoor positioning technologies, privacy preserving of users' indoor location information has received increasing attention. To this end, Kim *et al.* [19] propose to apply LDP to the domain of indoor positioning systems to estimate the population density of the specified indoor area. A recent work [6] indicates that existing location privacy-preserving mechanisms may not protect the sensitive information about users' spatiotemporal activities, when a user's locations are released continuously. To address this, a framework called *PriSTE* is proposed to transform an existing location privacy-preserving mechanism into one protecting spatiotemporal privacy.

2.5   Open Problems and New Directions

Finally, based on emerging trends in the literature, we will point to some directions for future work.

Iterative Interactions. Many data analysis tasks need to access the original data multiple times to improve the accuracy of the results. In a local setting, this requires users to perturb their data and then send to the aggregator with multiple rounds of interactions. To exploit such interactions, in each round the aggregator poses new queries in the light of previous responses. This approach has been adopted in several works, including machine learning model [36], heavy hitters estimation [25], synthetic graph modeling [26] and key-value data collection [44]. It is yet an open problem to have a deep understanding of the effectiveness and consequences of multiple rounds of interactions [30].

High-Dimensional Data Analysis. A large amount of potential knowledge and patterns can be extracted through high-dimensional data analysis. To enable privacy-preserving high-dimensional data analysis, some existing works propose to enable LDP for joint distribution estimation [28] or to handle some queries with different types of predicates and aggregation functions (e.g., SUM, AVG and STDEV) [39], with a focus on improving data utility. Besides the effect on data utility, achieving LDP on high-dimensional data analysis raises great challenges in terms of privacy guarantee, computation efficiency and communication overhead. For high-dimensional data, correlations among different dimensions should be taken into account as it may lead to privacy vulnerability [43, 45], thus increasing the success ratio of many reference attacks. In addition, computation efficiency and communication overhead are also concerns, especially for applications that can only afford lightweight operations, such as IoT scenarios and real-time applications.

Privacy-Preserving Data Mining and Machine Learning. Privacy-preserving data mining tasks and machine learning models in a centralized DP setting have been widely investigated, e.g., frequent subgraph mining [42], random forest [27] and deep learning [2]. However, there are very few works in a local setting. To the best of our knowledge, only some of the simple machine learning models [36, 47] (e.g., linear regression, logistic regression and support vector machine) and data mining tasks (e.g., itemset mining on set-valued data [38], and community detection on graph data [26]) have been studied in the context of LDP. The challenges come from two aspects. First, data mining tasks and machine learning models are often based on a global view of the data, and thus need several interactions between users and aggregator, which deviates from the local setting of LDP. Second, comparing with the centralized DP, LDP has stronger privacy model and yet incurs heavier noise, which makes it less practical for complex data mining tasks and machine learning models.

Theoretical Underpinnings. Several works on LDP have addressed questions about the theoretical power and limitation of LDP. For example, what are the lower bounds on the accuracy guarantees (as a function of privacy parameter and population size) [4]? Is there any benefit from adding an additive "relaxation" δ to the privacy definition [5]? And how to minimize the amount of data collected from each user to a single bit [11]?

Acknowledgment. This work was supported by National Natural Science Foundation of China (Grant No: 61572413, U1636205, 91646203, 61532010, 91846204 and 61532016), the Research Grants Council, Hong Kong SAR, China (Grant No: 15238116, 15222118 and C1008-16G).

References

1. Differential Privacy Team, Apple. Learning with privacy at scale (2017)
2. Abadi, M., et al.: Deep learning with differential privacy. In: Proceedings of the 2016 ACM SIGSAC Conference on Computer and Communications Security, pp. 308–318. ACM (2016). https://doi.org/10.1145/2976749.2978318
3. Bassily, R., Nissim, K., Stemmer, U., Thakurta, A.G.: Practical locally private heavy hitters. In: Advances in Neural Information Processing Systems (NIPS), pp. 2288–2296 (2017)
4. Bassily, R., Smith, A.: Local, private, efficient protocols for succinct histograms. In: Proceedings of the 47th Annual ACM on Symposium on Theory of Computing (STOC), pp. 127–135. ACM (2015). https://doi.org/10.1145/2746539.2746632
5. Bun, M., Nelson, J., Stemmer, U.: Heavy hitters and the structure of local privacy. In: Proceedings of the 35th ACM SIGMOD-SIGACT-SIGAI Symposium on Principles of Database Systems (PODS), pp. 435–447. ACM (2018). https://doi.org/10.1145/3196959.3196981
6. Cao, Y., Xiao, Y., Xiong, L., Bai, L.: PriSTE: from location privacy to spatiotemporal event privacy. In: IEEE 35th International Conference on Data Engineering (ICDE), pp. 1606–1609. IEEE (2019). https://doi.org/10.1109/icde.2019.00153
7. Chen, R., Li, H., Qin, A., Kasiviswanathan, S.P., Jin, H.: Private spatial data aggregation in the local setting. In: IEEE 32nd International Conference on Data Engineering (ICDE), pp. 289–300. IEEE (2016). https://doi.org/10.1109/icde.2016.7498248
8. Cormode, G., Kulkarni, T., Srivastava, D.: Marginal release under local differential privacy. In: Proceedings of the 2018 International Conference on Management of Data (SIGMOD), pp. 131–146. ACM (2018). https://doi.org/10.1145/3183713.3196906

9. Ding, B., Kulkarni, J., Yekhanin, S.: Collecting telemetry data privately. In: Advances in Neural Information Processing Systems (NIPS), pp. 3574–3583 (2017)

10. Ding, B., Nori, H., Li, P., Allen, J.: Comparing population means under local differential privacy: with significance and power. In: 32nd AAAI Conference on Artificial Intelligence (2018)

11. Duchi, J.C., Jordan, M.I., Wainwright, M.J.: Local privacy and statistical minimax rates. In: IEEE 54th Annual Symposium on Foundations of Computer Science (FOCS), pp. 429–438. IEEE (2013). https://doi.org/10.1109/focs.2013.53

12. Duchi, J.C., Jordan, M.I., Wainwright, M.J.: Minimax optimal procedures for locally private estimation. J. Am. Stat. Assoc. **113**(521), 182–201 (2018). https://doi.org/10.1080/01621459.2017.1389735

13. Dwork, C., McSherry, F., Nissim, K., Smith, A.: Calibrating noise to sensitivity in private data analysis. In: Halevi, S., Rabin, T. (eds.) TCC 2006. LNCS, vol. 3876, pp. 265–284. Springer, Heidelberg (2006). https://doi.org/10.1007/11681878_14

14. Erlingsson, Ú., Pihur, V., Korolova, A.: RAPPOR: randomized aggregatable privacy-preserving ordinal response. In: Proceedings of the 2014 ACM SIGSAC Conference on Computer and Communications Security (CCS), pp. 1054–1067. ACM (2014). https://doi.org/10.1145/2660267.2660348

15. Fanti, G., Pihur, V., Erlingsson, Ú.: Building a RAPPOR with the unknown: privacy-preserving learning of associations and data dictionaries. Proc. Priv. Enhancing Technol. **2016**(3), 41–61 (2016). https://doi.org/10.1515/popets-2016-0015

16. Hsu, J., Khanna, S., Roth, A.: Distributed private heavy hitters. In: Czumaj, A., Mehlhorn, K., Pitts, A., Wattenhofer, R. (eds.) ICALP 2012. LNCS, vol. 7391, pp. 461–472. Springer, Heidelberg (2012). https://doi.org/10.1007/978-3-642-31594-7_39

17. Kairouz, P., Oh, S., Viswanath, P.: Extremal mechanisms for local differential privacy. In: Advances in Neural Information Processing Systems (NIPS), pp. 2879–2887 (2014)

18. Kasiviswanathan, S.P., Lee, H.K., Nissim, K., Raskhodnikova, S., Smith, A.: What can we learn privately? SIAM J. Comput. **40**(3), 793–826 (2011). https://doi.org/10.1137/090756090

19. Kim, J.W., Kim, D.H., Jang, B.: Application of local differential privacy to collection of indoor positioning data. IEEE Access **6**, 4276–4286 (2018). https://doi.org/10.1109/access.2018.2791588

20. Kulkarni, T.: Answering range queries under local differential privacy. In: Proceedings of the 2019 International Conference on Management of Data, pp. 1832–1834. ACM (2019). https://doi.org/10.1145/3299869.3300102

21. Li, N., Qardaji, W., Su, D.: On sampling, anonymization, and differential privacy or, k-anonymization meets differential privacy. In: Proceedings of the 7th ACM Symposium on Information, Computer and Communications Security (ASIACCS), pp. 32–33. ACM (2012). https://doi.org/10.1145/2414456.2414474

22. Li, N., Ye, Q.: Mobile data collection and analysis with local differential privacy. In: IEEE International Conference on Mobile Data Management (MDM). https://doi.org/10.1109/access.2018.2791588

23. Mishra, N., Sandler, M.: Privacy via pseudorandom sketches. In: Proceedings of the Twenty-Fifth ACM SIGMOD-SIGACT-SIGART Symposium on Principles of Database Systems (PODS), pp. 143–152. ACM (2006). https://doi.org/10.1145/1142351.1142373

24. Qardaji, W., Yang, W., Li, N.: PriView: practical differentially private release of marginal contingency tables. In: Proceedings of the 2014 ACM SIGMOD International Conference on Management of Data (SIGMOD), pp. 1435–1446. ACM (2014). https://doi.org/10.1145/2588555.2588575
25. Qin, Z., Yang, Y., Yu, T., Khalil, I., Xiao, X., Ren, K.: Heavy hitter estimation over set-valued data with local differential privacy. In: Proceedings of the 2016 ACM SIGSAC Conference on Computer and Communications Security (CCS), pp. 192–203. ACM (2016). https://doi.org/10.1145/2976749.2978409
26. Qin, Z., Yu, T., Yang, Y., Khalil, I., Xiao, X., Ren, K.: Generating synthetic decentralized social graphs with local differential privacy. In: Proceedings of the 2017 ACM SIGSAC Conference on Computer and Communications Security (CCS), pp. 425–438 (2017). https://doi.org/10.1145/3133956.3134086
27. Rana, S., Gupta, S.K., Venkatesh, S.: Differentially private random forest with high utility. In: 2015 IEEE International Conference on Data Mining (ICDM), pp. 955–960. IEEE (2015). https://doi.org/10.1109/icdm.2015.76
28. Ren, X., et al.: LoPub: high-dimensional crowdsourced data publication with local differential privacy. IEEE Trans. Inf. Forensics Secur. **13**(9), 2151–2166 (2018). https://doi.org/10.1109/tifs.2018.2812146
29. Seshadhri, C., Kolda, T.G., Pinar, A.: Community structure and scale-free collections of erdős-rényi graphs. Phys. Rev. E **85**(5), 056109 (2012). https://doi.org/10.1103/physreve.85.056109
30. Smith, A., Thakurta, A., Upadhyay, J.: Is interaction necessary for distributed private learning? In: 2017 IEEE Symposium on Security and Privacy (SP), pp. 58–77. IEEE (2017). https://doi.org/10.1109/sp.2017.35
31. Stephanie, B.: Facebook Scandal a 'Game Changer' in Data Privacy Regulation, Bloomberg, 8 April 2018
32. Sun, H., et al.: Analyzing subgraph statistics from extended local views with decentralized differential privacy. In: Proceedings of the 2019 ACM SIGSAC Conference on Computer and Communications Security (CCS), pp. 703–717. ACM (2019). https://doi.org/10.1145/3319535.3354253
33. Thakurta, A.G., et al.: Learning new words. US Patent 9,594,741, 14 March 2017
34. Thakurta, A.G., et al.: Emoji frequency detection and deep link frequency. US Patent 9,705,908, 11 July 2017
35. Wang, N., et al.: PrivTrie: effective frequent term discovery under local differential privacy. In: IEEE 34th International Conference on Data Engineering (ICDE), pp. 821–832. IEEE (2018). https://doi.org/10.1109/icde.2018.00079
36. Wang, N., et al.: Collecting and analyzing multidimensional data with local differential privacy. In: IEEE 35th International Conference on Data Engineering (ICDE) (2019). https://doi.org/10.1109/icde.2019.00063
37. Wang, T., Blocki, J., Li, N., Jha, S.: Locally differentially private protocols for frequency estimation. In: USENIX Security Symposium, pp. 729–745 (2017)
38. Wang, T., Li, N., Jha, S.: Locally differentially private frequent itemset mining. In: IEEE Symposium on Security and Privacy (SP), pp. 127–143. IEEE (2018). https://doi.org/10.1109/sp.2018.00035
39. Wang, T., et al.: Answering multi-dimensional analytical queries under local differential privacy. In: Proceedings of the 2019 International Conference on Management of Data (SIGMOD), pp. 159–176. ACM (2019). https://doi.org/10.1145/3299869.3319891
40. Wang, T., Li, N., Jha, S.: Locally differentially private heavy hitter identification. IEEE Trans. Dependable Secur. Comput. (TDSC) (2019). https://doi.org/10.1109/tdsc.2019.2927695

41. Warner, S.L.: Randomized response: a survey technique for eliminating evasive answer bias. J. Am. Stat. Assoc. **60**(309), 63–69 (1965). https://doi.org/10.2307/2283137
42. Xu, S., Su, S., Xiong, L., Cheng, X., Xiao, K.: Differentially private frequent subgraph mining. In: IEEE 32nd International Conference on Data Engineering (ICDE), pp. 229–240. IEEE (2016). https://doi.org/10.1109/icde.2016.7498243
43. Yang, B., Sato, I., Nakagawa, H.: Bayesian differential privacy on correlated data. In: Proceedings of the 2015 ACM SIGMOD International Conference on Management of Data (SIGMOD), pp. 747–762. ACM (2015). https://doi.org/10.1145/2723372.2747643
44. Ye, Q., Hu, H., Meng, X., Zheng, H.: PrivKV: key-value data collection with local differential privacy. In: IEEE Symposium on Security and Privacy (SP), pp. 317–331. IEEE (2019). https://doi.org/10.1109/sp.2019.00018
45. Zhang, J., Cormode, G., Procopiuc, C.M., Srivastava, D., Xiao, X.: PrivBayes: private data release via Bayesian networks. In: Proceedings of the 2014 ACM SIGMOD International Conference on Management of Data (SIGMOD), pp. 1423–1434. ACM (2014). https://doi.org/10.1145/2588555.2588573
46. Zhang, Z., Wang, T., Li, N., He, S., Chen, J.: CALM: consistent adaptive local marginal for marginal release under local differential privacy. In: Proceedings of the 2018 ACM SIGSAC Conference on Computer and Communications Security (CCS), pp. 212–229. ACM (2018). https://doi.org/10.1145/3243734.3243742
47. Zheng, H., Ye, Q., Hu, H., Fang, C., Shi, J.: BDPL: a boundary differentially private layer against machine learning model extraction attacks. In: Sako, K., Schneider, S., Ryan, P.Y.A. (eds.) ESORICS 2019. LNCS, vol. 11735, pp. 66–83. Springer, Cham (2019). https://doi.org/10.1007/978-3-030-29959-0_4

Intelligent Knowledge Lakes: The Age of Artificial Intelligence and Big Data

Amin Beheshti[1]([✉]), Boualem Benatallah[2], Quan Z. Sheng[1], and Francesco Schiliro[1,3]

[1] Macquarie University, Sydney, Australia
{amin.beheshti,michael.sheng}@mq.edu.au
[2] University of New South Wales, Sydney, Australia
boualem@cse.unsw.edu.au
[3] Australian Federal Police, Canberra, Australia
francesco.schiliro@hdr.mq.edu.au

Abstract. The continuous improvement in connectivity, storage and data processing capabilities allow access to a data deluge from the big data generated on open, private, social and IoT (Internet of Things) data islands. Data Lakes introduced as a storage repository to organize this raw data in its native format until it is needed. The rationale behind a Data Lake is to store raw data and let the data analyst decide how to curate them later. Previously, we introduced the novel notion of Knowledge Lake, i.e., a contextualized Data Lake, and proposed algorithms to turn the raw data (stored in Data Lakes) into contextualized data and knowledge using extraction, enrichment, annotation, linking and summarization techniques. In this tutorial, we introduce Intelligent Knowledge Lakes to facilitate linking Artificial Intelligence (AI) and Data Analytics. This will enable AI applications to learn from contextualized data and use them to automate business processes and develop cognitive assistance for facilitating the knowledge intensive processes or generating new rules for future business analytics.

Keywords: Knowledge Lake · Data Lake · Data analytics · Data curation · Artificial Intelligence · Big data

1 Introduction

Today, the advancement in Artificial Intelligence (AI) and Data Science has the potential to transform business processes in fundamental ways, by assisting knowledge workers in communicating analysis findings, supporting evidences and to make decisions. Almost every organization is now focused on understanding their business and transform data into actionable insights. For example, governments derive insights from vastly growing private, open and social data for improving government services, such as to personalize the advertisements in elections, improve government services, predict intelligence activities and to improve

© Springer Nature Singapore Pte Ltd. 2020
L. H. U et al. (Eds.): WISE 2019, CCIS 1155, pp. 24–34, 2020.
https://doi.org/10.1007/978-981-15-3281-8_3

national security and public health [6,12,16,28,32]. In this context, organizing vast amount of data gathered from various private/open data islands will facilitate dealing with a collection of independently-managed datasets (from relational to NoSQL), diversity of formats and non-standard data models.

The notion of a Data Lake [1,4,20,24,33] has been coined to address this challenge and to convey the concept of a centralized repository containing limitless amounts of raw (or minimally curated) data stored in various data islands. The rationale behind a Data Lake is to store raw data [18] and let the data analyst decide how to cook/curate them later. While Data Lakes, do a great job in organizing big data and providing answers on known questions, the main challenges are to understand the potentially interconnected data stored in various data islands and to prepare them for analytics. In our previous work [5,6], we introduced the novel notion of Knowledge Lake, i.e., a contextualized Data Lake, and proposed algorithms to turn the raw data (stored in Data Lakes) into contextualized data and knowledge using extraction, enrichment, annotation, linking and summarization techniques [11,13,15]. In particular, a Knowledge Lake is a centralized repository containing virtually inexhaustible amounts of both data and contextualized data that is readily made available anytime to anyone authorized to perform analytical activities. The Knowledge Lake will provide the foundation for big data analytics by automatically curating [8,9] the raw data in the Data Lake and to prepare them for deriving insights.

In this tutorial, we introduce Intelligent Knowledge Lakes to facilitate linking Artificial Intelligence (AI) and Data Analytics. This will enable AI applications to learn from contextualized data and use them to automate business processes and develop cognitive assistance for facilitating the knowledge intensive processes or generating new rules for future business analytics [3,12]. We focus on motivating scenarios in policing [27], budget [6] and health [7]; and present how Intelligent Knowledge Lakes can assist knowledge workers in knowledge intensive processes to deal with big data and dig for facts in an easy way.

2   From Data to Big Data

Data. In computing, data is information that has been translated into a form that is efficient for *storage* and *processing*. Data can be generated on various islands of data, from social (e.g., on Twitter [26] and Facebook [23]) and Internet of Things [34] (IoT, e.g., CCTVs and smart cars) to private (e.g., personal and business data) and open (e.g., news and Websites) data islands. For example, when we take a photo using our cell phone, open a banking account, or post a news on a social media (e.g., on Twitter [26] or LinkedIn [31]), we are generating data. Even - when we walk, exercise in gym or watching TV - smart devices such as smart phones, watches and TVs can trace our location, health signs and interests to generate large amount of data. From the storage point of view, data can be structured (e.g., a customer record in a banking system), semi-structured (e.g., a Tweet in Twitter) or unstructured (e.g., a document, audio or video file). Common data processing operations include organizing, curating, analyzing and visualizing.

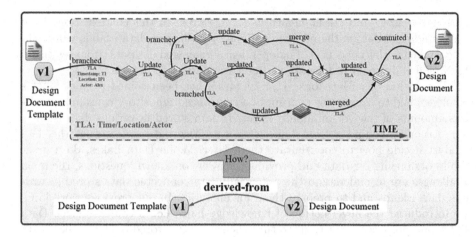

Fig. 1. Provenance, a kind of metadata, refers to the documentation of an object's lifecycle. This documentation (often represented as a graph) should include all the information necessary to reproduce a certain piece of data or the process that led to it [14,25].

Metadata. Metadata is the data that provides information about other data. The goal is to help users properly understand the data. Metadata (e.g., descriptive, structural and administrative metadata) can be generated manually and/or automatically. Tracing is a mechanism to generate metadata. For example, when we use our cell phone, a set of algorithms can trace our movement (location services), what Apps we are using and how frequently. Or, a social network App can trace the activities of a user, including: which days of week and what time of the days the user is more active, what sort of content the user liked or reshared, and what type of people (e.g., from personality, behavior and attitude view points) the user is following. Metadata can also help in generating the story of a digital object from now back to its derivation, i.e., provenance [14,25] (the documentation of an object's lifecycle), including: who created the file, on which system (e.g., IP address) and when, how the digital object evolved over time and more. Figure 1 illustrates an example where provenance can help understanding how a document evolve over time [14].

Big Data. Big data [22,35] is different from a large dataset. For example, we have had super computers to deal with processing and analyzing a large data set. However, big data can be seen as a massive number of small data islands from Private (Personal/Business), Open, Social and IoT Data [3,11]. Typical properties of the big data include: wide physical distribution, diversity of formats, non-standard data models, independently-managed and heterogeneous semantics. Organizing, curating, analyzing and presenting this data is challenging and of high interest. For examples, consider a motivating scenario in policing, in investigation processes such as Boston Marathon bombing[1], the police investi-

---

[1] https://en.wikipedia.org/wiki/Boston_Marathon_bombing.

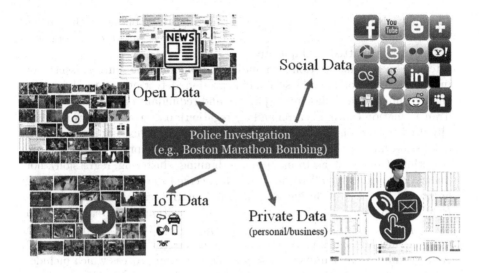

Fig. 2. An example of the big data problem in police investigation [27]. Big data can be seen as a massive number of small data islands from Private (Personal/Business), Open, Social and data islands [3,11].

gator needs to understand the big data generated on various private, social, open and IoT data islands; analyze them and link them to police historical data. This is quite important, as modern police investigation processes are often extremely complex, data-driven and knowledge-intensive. Linking big data to process execution, will facilitate communicating analysis findings, supporting evidences and to make decisions. Figure 2 illustrates a big data problem scenario in policing [27].

3   Data Curation: From Ingestion and Cleaning to Extraction an Enrichment

One of the main challenges in understanding big data is to transform raw data into actionable insights. To achieve this goal it will be vital to prepare and curate the raw data for analytics. Data curation has been defined as the active and on-going management of data through its lifecycle of interest and usefulness [17,29]. Data curation includes all the processes needed for principled and controlled data creation, maintenance, and management, together with the capacity to add value to data. Big data curation should involve [6,21,22,29]:

- Identifying Relevant Data Islands: with more data repositories constantly being published every day, choosing appropriate data sources for a specific analyst goal becomes very important.
- Ingesting Data and Knowledge: data ingestion is the process of obtaining and importing data for immediate use or storage in a database. Data can be streamed in real time or ingested in batches.

- Cleaning: also known as data cleansing and data scrubbing, is the process of amending or removing data in a database that is incorrect, incomplete, improperly formatted or duplicated.
- Integration: data integration combines data from multiple sources. Issues during data integration include: schema integration, detecting and resolving data value conflicts, and removing duplicates and redundant data.
- Transformation (normalization and aggregation): data transformation is usually used to smooth the noisy data, summarize, generalize, or normalize the data scale falls within a small, specified range. The process may include: smoothing (remove noise from data, e.g., binning, clustering, regression), normalization (scaled to fall within a small, specified range such as -1.0 to 1.0 or 0.0 to 1.0), feature construction (e.g., new attributes constructed or added from the given ones), aggregation (e.g., summarization or aggregation operations apply to data) and generalization (e.g, concept hierarchy climbing. For example, low level/ primitive/raw data are replace by higher level concepts).
- Adding Value: a very important step in the curation process which includes: extraction, enrichment, annotation, linking (to external knowledge sources and services) and summarization tasks. Figure 3 illustrates an example of adding value to a raw tweet [9].

4   From Data Lakes to Knowledge Lakes

Organizing vast amount of raw data gathered from various data islands, i.e., *Data Lake* [1,4,33], will facilitate dealing with a collection of independently-managed datasets in private (personal and business data), open (news and Websites), social (such as Twitter, Facebook and LinkedIn) and IoT (smart entities such as CCTVs and smart cars) data islands. The notion of a Data Lake has been coined to address this challenge and to convey the concept of a centralized repository containing limitless amounts of raw (or minimally curated) data stored in various data islands. The rationale behind the Data Lake is to store raw data and let the data analyst decide how to cook/curate them later.

In our previous work [5,6], we introduced the notion of *Knowledge Lake*, i.e. a contextualized Data Lake, as a centralized repository containing virtually inexhaustible amounts of both data and *contextualized data* that is readily made available anytime to anyone authorized to perform analytical activities. The term *Knowledge* here refers to a set of facts, information, and insights extracted from the raw data using data curation techniques used to transfer an Information-Item into a Featurized-, Semantic- and Contextualized-Items [6]. The Knowledge Lake will provide the foundation for big data analytics by automatically curating the raw data in the Data Lake and to prepare them for deriving insights. For the raw information items stored in the Lake, we provide services to automatically [15]: extract features, enrich them, link them to external knowledge sources, and annotate them. On top of the Knowledge Lake, we provide a single federated search service which enables the analyst querying the raw data (in the Data

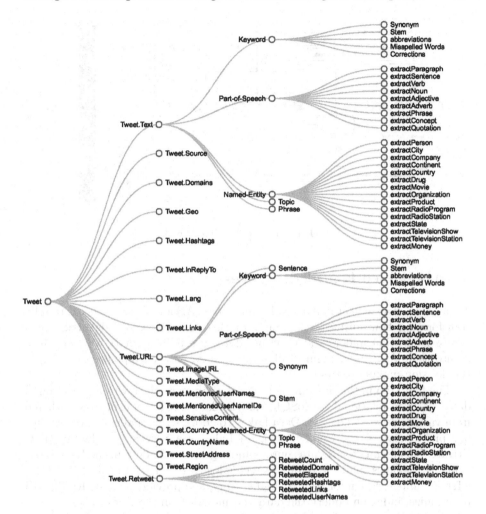

Fig. 3. An example of an automatically curated tweet [9]. Data Curation is the process of transforming raw data into contextualized data and knowledge. The first step is to extract features from raw data, e.g., extract keywords or name entities from the text of the tweet or extract objects from an image mentioned in the tweet [13,15]. The next step is to enrich the extracted features, annotate them and link them to external knowledge sources and services [6]. For example, to enrich an extracted keyword with synonyms (e.g., using wordnet [30]) and similar keywords (e.g., using word2vec [19]) or link an extracted named entity to Wikidata (wikidata.org/).

Lake) as well as the contextalized items in the Knowledge Lake using Full-text Search, SQL and SPARQL. Figures 4 and 5 illustrate the architecture and the main components of the Data Lake and Knowledge Lake respectively.

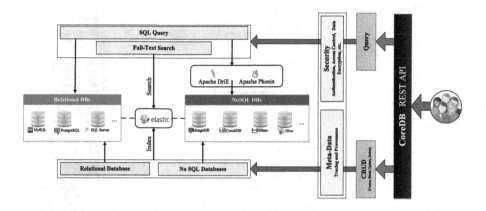

Fig. 4. Data Lake Architecture [4].

5   AI-enabled Knowledge Lakes

Today, the advancement in Artificial Intelligence (AI) and Data Science is rapidly transforming how businesses operate. In this context, Knowledge Lakes can help organization understand their big data, use it in a smart way, and feed it into their AI engine. Figure 6 illustrates an AI-enabled pipeline to facilitate the decision-making process.

The first step in the pipe line is to assist analysts to deal with a collection of datasets, from relational to NoSQL, that holds a vast amount of data gathered from various data islands, i.e., Data Lake. To address this challenge, we leverage our previous work [4], CoreDB: a Data Lake as a Service, to identify (IoT, Private, Social and Open) data sources and ingest the big data in the Data Lake. CoreDB manages multiple database technologies (from relational to NoSQL), offers a built-in design for security and tracing, and provides a single REST API to organize, index and query the data and metadata in the Data Lake.

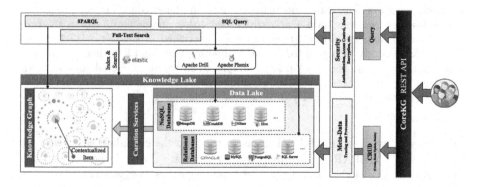

Fig. 5. Knowledge Lake Architecture [5].

Next, we provide services [15] to automatically curating the raw data in the Data Lake and to prepare them for deriving insights. To address this challenge, we leverage our previous work [5], CoreKG: a contextualized Data Lake, to provide the foundation for big data analytics. The data curation APIs [15] in the Knowledge Lake provide curation tasks such as extraction, linking, summarization, annotation, enrichment, classification and more. This will enable us to add features - such as extracting keyword, part of speech, and named entities such as Persons, Locations and Organizations; providing synonyms and stems for extracted information items leveraging lexical knowledge bases for the English language such as WordNet [30]; linking extracted entities to external knowledge bases such as Google Knowledge Graph[2] and Wikidata[3]; discovering similarity among the extracted information items; classifying, indexing, sorting and categorizing data - into the data and knowledge persisted in the Knowledge Lake.

The data and knowledge in the knowledge lake will form a large graph, i.e. Knowledge Graph, of entities[4] and relationships among them. Entities can be simple such as a raw data (e.g. a document). Entities can be atomic such as a keyword and topic extracted from a document. The major challenges here are: (i) how to extend decision support on multidimensional networks, considering both data objects and the relationships among them; and (ii) providing multiple views at different granularities is subjective: depends on the perspective of analysts how to partition graphs and apply further operations on top of them.

To achieve this goal, we present novel techniques (including our work on graph OLAP [11]) for intelligent narrative discovery to summarize the large amount of curated data in the Knowledge Lake and to transform a Knowledge Lake into a smart and intelligent lake. Figure 6 illustrates a pipeline to leverage Domain Experts and Crowd Knowledge (e.g., using feedback, surveys, interviews etc. to build a domain specific knowledge base) and use that knowledge to summarize the large knowledge graph (in a Knowledge Lake) and enable intelligent narrative discovery. This will enable AI applications to learn from contextualized data, link them to domain knowledge and use them to automate business processes and develop cognitive assistance for facilitating the knowledge intensive processes or generating new rules for future business analytics [3,12].

In this tutorial, we present three motivating scenarios from our recent work:

- DataSynapse [6,10]: we present a scenario for analyzing Urban Social Issues from Twitter as it relates to the Government Budget: it is paramount to stabilize the economy through timely and dynamic adjustment in expenditure plans by considering related social issues such as a problem or conflict raised by society ranging from local to national issues such as Health, Social Security, Public Safety, Welfare Support and Domestic Violence.
- personality2vec [7]: we discuss how we design intelligent Knowledge Lakes extended with deep learning techniques to analyze and summarize social data

---

[2] https://developers.google.com/knowledge-graph.
[3] https://www.wikidata.org/.
[4] An entity E is represented as a data object that exists separately and has a unique identity. Entities are described by a set of attributes.

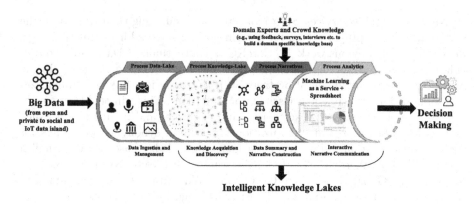

Fig. 6. Intelligent Knowledge Lakes.

to predict patterns of behavioral disorders (e.g., criminal and extremist behaviors) on social networks.

– iCOP [8,27]: we present a cognitive assistant, namely iCOP, that we developed to help police investigators identify evidences from the Knowledge Lake in an easy way. In iCOP, we proposed novel techniques to summarize the Knowledge Lake to construct process narratives and enable the analysis of narratives and dig for facts in an easy way, using smart sheets [2].

Acknowledgements. We Acknowledge the AI-enabled Processes (AIP) (https://aip-research-center.github.io/) Research Centre for funding part of this research.

References

1. Alsubaiee, S., et al.: Storage management in AsterixDB. Proc. VLDB Endow. **7**(10), 841–852 (2014)
2. Amouzgar, F., Beheshti, A., Ghodratnama, S., Benatallah, B., Yang, J., Sheng, Q.Z.: iSheets: a spreadsheet-based machine learning development platform for data-driven process analytics. In: Liu, X., et al. (eds.) ICSOC 2018. LNCS, vol. 11434, pp. 453–457. Springer, Cham (2019). https://doi.org/10.1007/978-3-030-17642-6_43
3. Beheshti, A., Benatallah, B., Motahari-Nezhad, H.R.: ProcessAtlas: a scalable and extensible platform for business process analytics. Softw.: Pract. Exp. **48**(4), 842–866 (2018)
4. Beheshti, A., Benatallah, B., Nouri, R., Chhieng, V.M., Xiong, H., Zhao, X.: CoreDB: a data lake service. In: Proceedings of the 2017 ACM on Conference on Information and Knowledge Management, CIKM 2017, Singapore, 06–10 November 2017, pp. 2451–2454 (2017)
5. Beheshti, A., Benatallah, B., Nouri, R., Tabebordbar, A.: CoreKG: a knowledge lake service. PVLDB **11**(12), 1942–1945 (2018)
6. Beheshti, A., Benatallah, B., Tabebordbar, A., Motahari-Nezhad, H.R., Barukh, M.C., Nouri, R.: DataSynapse: a social data curation foundry. Distrib. Parallel Databases **37**(3), 351–384 (2019)

7. Beheshti, A., Moraveji-Hashemi, V., Yakhchi, S., Motahari-Nezhad, H.R., Ghafari, S.M., Yang, J.: personality2vec: enabling the analysis of behavioral disorders in social networks. In: Proceedings of the 13th ACM International Conference on Web Search and Data Mining, WSDM 2020, Houston, Texas, USA (2020)
8. Beheshti, A., et al.: iProcess: enabling IoT platforms in data-driven knowledge-intensive processes. In: Weske, M., Montali, M., Weber, I., vom Brocke, J. (eds.) BPM 2018. LNBIP, vol. 329, pp. 108–126. Springer, Cham (2018). https://doi.org/10.1007/978-3-319-98651-7_7
9. Beheshti, A., Vaghani, K., Benatallah, B., Tabebordbar, A.: CrowdCorrect: a curation pipeline for social data cleansing and curation. In: Mendling, J., Mouratidis, H. (eds.) CAiSE 2018. LNBIP, vol. 317, pp. 24–38. Springer, Cham (2018). https://doi.org/10.1007/978-3-319-92901-9_3
10. Beheshti, S., Benatallah, B., Motahari-Nezhad, H.R.: Galaxy: a platform for explorative analysis of open data sources. In: Proceedings of the 19th International Conference on Extending Database Technology, EDBT 2016, Bordeaux, France, 15–16 March 2016, pp. 640–643 (2016)
11. Beheshti, S., Benatallah, B., Motahari-Nezhad, H.R.: Scalable graph-based OLAP analytics over process execution data. Distrib. Parallel Databases **34**(3), 379–423 (2016)
12. Beheshti, S., et al.: Process Analytics - Concepts and Techniques for Querying and Analyzing Process Data. Springer, Cham (2016). https://doi.org/10.1007/978-3-319-25037-3
13. Beheshti, S., Benatallah, B., Venugopal, S., Ryu, S.H., Motahari-Nezhad, H.R., Wang, W.: A systematic review and comparative analysis of cross-document coreference resolution methods and tools. Computing **99**(4), 313–349 (2017)
14. Beheshti, S., Motahari Nezhad, H.R., Benatallah, B.: Temporal provenance model (TPM): model and query language. CoRR, abs/1211.5009 (2012)
15. Beheshti, S., Tabebordbar, A., Benatallah, B., Nouri, R.: On automating basic data curation tasks. In: Proceedings of the 26th International Conference on World Wide Web Companion, Perth, Australia, 3–7 April 2017, pp. 165–169 (2017)
16. Berners-Lee, T.: Designing the web for an open society. In: Proceedings of the 20th International Conference on World Wide Web, WWW 2011, Hyderabad, India, 28 March–1 April 2011, pp. 3–4 (2011)
17. Freitas, A., Curry, E.: Big Data Curation. In: Cavanillas, J.M., Curry, E., Wahlster, W. (eds.) New Horizons for a Data-Driven Economy, pp. 87–118. Springer, Cham (2016). https://doi.org/10.1007/978-3-319-21569-3_6
18. Gitelman, L.: Raw Data Is an Oxymoron. MIT Press, Cambridge (2013)
19. Goldberg, Y., Levy, O.: word2vec explained: deriving Mikolov et al'.s negative-sampling word-embedding method. arXiv preprint arXiv:1402.3722 (2014)
20. Hai, R., Geisler, S., Quix, C.: Constance: an intelligent data lake system. In: Proceedings of the 2016 International Conference on Management of Data, pp. 2097–2100. ACM (2016)
21. Lord, P., Macdonald, A., Lyon, L., Giaretta, D.: From data deluge to data curation. In: Proceedings of the UK e-science All Hands meeting, pp. 371–375. Citeseer (2004)
22. McAfee, A., Brynjolfsson, E., Davenport, T.H., Patil, D., Barton, D.: Big data: the management revolution. Harv. Bus. Rev. **90**(10), 60–68 (2012)
23. Miller, D.: Tales from Facebook. Polity, Cambridge (2011)
24. Miloslavskaya, N., Tolstoy, A.: Big data, fast data and data lake concepts. Procedia Comput. Sci. **88**, 300–305 (2016)

25. Moreau, L., et al.: The open provenance model core specification (v1.1). Future Gener. Comput. Syst. **27**(6), 743–756 (2011)
26. Murthy, D.: Twitter. Polity Press, Cambridge (2018)
27. Schiliro, F., et al.: iCOP: IoT-enabled policing processes. In: Liu, X., et al. (eds.) ICSOC 2018. LNCS, vol. 11434, pp. 447–452. Springer, Cham (2019). https://doi. org/10.1007/978-3-030-17642-6_42
28. Shadbolt, N., et al.: Linked open government data: Lessons from data.gov.uk. IEEE Intell. Syst. **27**(3), 16–24 (2012)
29. Stonebraker, M., et al.: Data curation at scale: the data tamer system. In: CIDR (2013)
30. Strapparava, C., Valitutti, A., et al.: Wordnet affect: an affective extension of wordnet. In: Lrec, vol. 4, pp. 40. Citeseer (2004)
31. Sumbaly, R., Kreps, J., Shah, S.: The big data ecosystem at linkedin. In: Proceedings of the 2013 ACM SIGMOD International Conference on Management of Data, pp. 1125–1134. ACM (2013)
32. Tene, O., Polonetsky, J.: Big data for all: privacy and user control in the age of analytics. Nw. J. Tech. Intell. Prop. **11**, xxvii (2012)
33. Terrizzano, I.G., Schwarz, P.M., Roth, M., Colino, J.E.: Data wrangling: the challenging journey from the wild to the lake. In: CIDR (2015)
34. Xia, F., Yang, L.T., Wang, L., Vinel, A.: Internet of things. Int. J. Commun. Syst. **25**(9), 1101 (2012)
35. Zomaya, A.Y., Sakr, S.: Handbook of Big Data Technologies. Springer, Cham (2017). https://doi.org/10.1007/978-3-319-49340-4

Demos

Tourism Analysis on Graphs
with Neo4Tourism

Gaël Chareyron, Ugo Quelhas, and Nicolas Travers[✉]

Léonard de Vinci Pôle Universitaire, Research Center, Paris La Défense, France
{gael.chareyron,ugo.quelhas,nicolas.travers}@devinci.fr

Abstract. Tourists' behavior analysis has become a popular mean with Digital Tourism. Traditional ground studies has been extended with massive data analysis to confront models. Tourism actors are faced with the need to deeply understand tourists' circulation both quantitatively and qualitatively. Thus, the challenge is to deal with data from tourist oriented social networks by integrating huge volumes of data. We propose in this paper the Neo4Tourism framework based on a graph data model specialized in digital tourism analysis. Our model is dedicated to tourists' circulation and aims at simulating tourists' behavior. In this demonstration we discuss how our system (1) integrates data from TripAdvisor in a *Neo4j* graph database, (2) produces circulation graphs, (3) enhances graphs manipulations and deep tourists' analysis with centrality.

Keywords: Graph databases · Digital Tourism · Neo4j · Geodesy

1 Introduction

Social Networks dedicated to tourism experience have witnessed an enormous growth since the last decade such as *TripAdvisor, Instagram, Flickr, Booking*, etc. Consequently actors of tourism are faced with the problem of analyzing a huge volume of data in order to understand the evolution of tourists' behavior [6]. One issue is to analyze tourists circulation and centrality of some locations in Geo-Spatial context [4]. With millions of comments on locations it becomes a real challenge to understand how trips evolve over time. It needs to take into account both space, time and tourists' profile like nationality or age.

Some studies tried to model trips with graphs over a map [4,7,8]. It focuses on various centrality algorithms on networks that are combined with maps. Few studies target the problematic of geodesic theory for tourism [3,5,9] which combines space and time on maps. In this context, it becomes a real challenge to identify key points in the graph that evoluate over time. [5] proposes graph similarities between nodes and locations based on different centrality measures.

However, those solutions lacks of flexibility in the way to manipulate the graph content for wide analyzes and they rely only on small areas which do not scale up. Moreover, they hardly deal with evolution of maps or user profiles. We need to provide a way to compute and compare graphs in a dedicated setting like in graph databases [1,2] while preserving geographic and user characteristics.

© Springer Nature Singapore Pte Ltd. 2020
L. H. U et al. (Eds.): WISE 2019, CCIS 1155, pp. 37–44, 2020.
https://doi.org/10.1007/978-981-15-3281-8_4

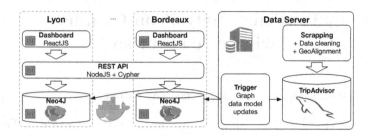

Fig. 1. Neo4Tourism architecture

Moreover, it is necessary to cope with various levels of granularities (local vs global) which is barely compared in literature.

We propose the Neo4Tourism framework to model with various levels of granularity the circulation of tourists over a social network like *TripAdvisor*. Tourists' comments can be considered as time series of events which links users to locations over time. We model those series into a graph data model that integrates either links between locations, time evolution, and tourist characteristics. The goal is to ease the way to manipulate graphs and to propose ways to aggregate nodes based on geographic correlations in order to produce new graphs and consequently more global tendancies on cities, departments, regions or countries.

We have implemented the graph data model in *Neo4j* in which we apply manipulations on aggregated graphs to extract communities or circulations. Those manipulating features on geodesy are for the first time introduced in this context.

2 Neo4Tourism Architecture

Neo4Tourism relies on several computation layers as shown in Fig. 1.

The **Data Server** stores all data gathered from Social Networks dedicated to tourism (*i.e., TripAdvisor*). The *scrapping* step checks, anonymizes and cleans every new piece of information from the website, then it aligns locations with a geolocalization database containing shapes like GADM 3.6[1]. The latter will be used to geolocalize information like cities, departments, regions and countries. The *Trigger* detects any new relevant data from the database and pushes them to the *Neo4j* servers to update graphs on the corresponding destination (study).

Each **Neo4j** server contains the whole graph dedicated to the study. Extracted data are defined by the location of the study such as Lyon or Bordeaux which will be detailed in the following. The graph relies on links between users and locations through their reviews. A circulation graph is thus modeled.

The **REST API** layer links dashboards to *Neo4j* servers by routing queries to the corresponding database. It contains all template queries that will manipulate underlying graphs: filters, aggregations or centrality. The hierarchy of the

---

[1] GADM maps and data: https://gadm.org/index.html (386,735 administrative areas).

REST API handles implicitly query parameters in order to define the required study (target database), the granularity of the query (cities, regions...) and settings for studies (circulation, centrality...). It also allows to manage database security and queries consistency according to the corresponding studies.

The **Dashboard** layer interacts with the REST API with the study identifier. A default web template is given in ReactJS and allows to defined a dedicated visualisation according to tourist actors needs.

3 A Tourism Circulation Model

Modeling tourism data requires to take into account locations information, users properties and their interactions. In the *Neo4Tourism* database, we propose two graph data models in order to deal with interactions on locations.

3.1 Data Types

Our database is composed of geolocalized locations, reviews and users. A location is composed of a type (hotel, restaurant, attraction), a localization (lat, long) and a rating ($r \in \mathbb{R} \wedge r \in [1.0, 5.0]$). Each location l is linked to an area a if its geolocalization (*i.e.,* lat, long) is contained into an administrative area's shape (GADM), such that the $SP(l.lat, l.long) = a$ (*SpatialPolygon* function SP). This area is defined by: $area(country, region, department, city)$. Thus, each location l is identified by: $l \in \mathcal{L}(type, r, a)$.

A user u is identified by his nationality and age, $u \in \mathcal{U}(nat, age)$.

A review is a note ($n \in \mathbb{N} \wedge n \in [1, 5]$) given by a user u on a location l at time t (t is in the discrete time domain $\mathcal{T}$). Each review is then defined by an event r_t such that: $r_t = (l, u, n)$.

The stream of reviews $\mathcal{S}$ is a time series of r_{t_i} events: $\mathcal{S} = \{r_{t_1}, r_{t_2}, r_{t_3}, r_{t_4}...\}$.

3.2 Study on a Destination

In order to understand tourists behavior in the study of a given destination, we need to target tourists. For this, we focus only on users u who visit a location at that destination at least once. Then we get all the reviews they made, even elsewhere, in order to gather their circulations all over the world. This filter on stream $\mathcal{S}$ will help to scale up the database by focusing only on interesting users to provide relative analysis. $\mathcal{S}_{dest}$ denotes a study on a given area, it contains both the visited locations of $dest$ and elsewhere.

$$r_{t_i} \in \mathcal{S}_{dest} \Rightarrow \exists r_{t_j} \in \mathcal{S} | r_{t_j}.l.a = dest \wedge r_{t_j}.u = r_{t_i}.u$$

3.3 Graph Data Models

The first graph data model T is a natural bipartite graph which links users to locations for each events from $\mathcal{S}_{dest}$, as illustrated in Fig. 2. User nodes are typed as $\mathcal{U}(nat, age)$ and location nodes as $\mathcal{L}(type, r, a)$. Oriented edges link users to locations and are labelled with review's timestamp t_i and user note n.

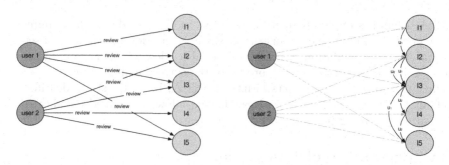

Fig. 2. *TripAdvisor* bipartite graph   **Fig. 3.** Circulation graph

Definition 1. *Consider the TripAdvisor bipartite graph $T(V, E)$ where $V \in \mathcal{L} \cup \mathcal{U}$ denotes the set of vertices and E the set of edges, such that:*

$$e_{u \to l}(t_i, n) \in E \Rightarrow \exists r_{t_i}(l, u, n) \in \mathcal{S}_{dest}$$

3.4 Circulation Graph Data Model

The graph data model T will not ease the way to manipulate information or extract circulation of tourists. Since our analyzes require several levels of studies (*i.e.*, international to local), we propose to build a new graph data model based on T by focusing on circulations between locations.

The circulation graph model $C(V', E')$ relies on the fact that tourists can review several locations during their journey. Consequently, the sequence of reviews $\mathcal{S}_{dest}^u$ of user u generates new edges between locations. However, we consider that a journey is composed of reviews written at most at 7 days apart. Two consecutive events from user u that occur within 7 days generate an edge e (Definition 2). Figure 3 illustrates the transformation of graph T.

Definition 2. *Consider the Circulation Graph $C(V', E')$ where $V' \in \mathcal{L} \subset V$ denotes the set of vertices and E' the set of edges, such that for each user $u \in \mathcal{U}$:*

$$e_{l_j \to l_k}(t_i, u) \in E' \Rightarrow \exists r_{t_i}(l_j, u, n_j), r_{t_{i+1}}(l_k, u, n_k) \in \mathcal{S}_{dest}^u | days(t_{i+1} - t_i) <= 7$$

3.5 Aggregated Graphs

Tourism actors need to focus their studies in a geodesic point of view (time and space). Thus, we need to provide studies on both graphs T and C by aggregating vertices and edges, while filtering on properties (*i.e.*, users, locations, time).

Graphs AT aggregate nodes according to a property P (*e.g.*, city) and produced edges gives the number of edges in E' between aggregated nodes.

Definition 3. *The Aggregated Graph AT is a derived graph from T, such that $AT(V'', E'')$ is a graph where $V'' \in P(V)$ denotes the set of vertices av merged from V on values of property P:*

$$av(P) \in V'' \Rightarrow \exists v \in V | P(av) = P(v), \nexists av' \in V'' | P(av') = P(av)$$

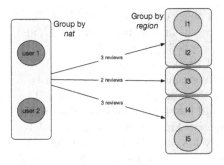 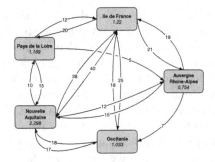

Fig. 4. Graph aggregation   **Fig. 5.** Filtered Circulation graph

and E'' the set of aggregated edges:

$ae_{av_i \to av_j}(year, month, nat, age, nb) \in E'' \Rightarrow$

$\quad \exists av_i, av_j \in V'', e_{u \to l}(t, n) \in E | P(u) \neq P(l) \land P(u) = P(av_i) \land P(l) = P(av_i)$

$\quad \land\ year = year(e.t) \land month = month(e.t) \land nat = u.nat \land age = u.age \land nb = |e|$

$\quad \nexists ae'_{av_i \to av_j} \in E'' | ae.year = ae'.year \land ae.month = ae'.month \land ae.nat = ae'.nat$

$\quad \land\ ae.age = ae'.age$

The AT graph (Definition 3) verifies that each new node has a unique value from property P on which it is aggregated (*e.g.*, city, country). Then, for each corresponding two nodes from V that do not belong to the same aggregated nodes in V'', an edge ae is created that aggregates all the edges e between this two aggregated nodes (same properties). We can notice that time is discretized on both years and months to exploit evolution of tourists behavior.

Also, the aggregated properties can be different between users u and locations l. Definition 3 can be adapted to separate those properties. This is illustrated in Fig. 4 where an aggregated graph AT merges users from T on nationality and locations on regions.

Moreover, this transformation is applicable similarly on the circulation graph C to obtain an aggregated graph in the same way (between V' nodes). This aggregated circulation graph is denoted by AC and focuses on circulation between groups of locations (*e.g.*, regions in Fig. 5).

4   Implementation with *Neo4j*

In our study on tourists behavior, we will focus especially on aggregated graphs AT and AC. To manipulate them, we chose the *Neo4j* database which will ease the definition of templates with its query language *Cypher*.

4.1   Aggregated Graph Materialization

The circulation graph C is generated by a Java program that produces a time serie for each user by extracting data from graph T. For efficiency purpose, only aggregated graphs AT and AC are stored in the *Neo4Tourism* database. This strategy benefits from two folds: aggregated graphs are smaller than T or C, and the time constraint implies that updates are applied incrementally.

Our study requires several granularities of studies (*e.g.*, regions, cities), it is then necessary to compute queries on various aggregate graphs. However, instead of materializing every graphs, we will produce the more precise one on cities. This graph contains at most 35,000 cities/nodes and hundred thousands edges which will be merged according to the required query. This setting is easily scalable by merging and filtering most of edges (*i.e.*, years, months, nationalities, ages). To produce other aggregated graphs, we merge city nodes that share a same property (department, region) by using the WITH clause in Cypher.

4.2 Templated Cypher with REST

In order to provide analysis features on aggregated graphs, we rely on the geodesic properties of the graphs. In fact, destinations and time are strong constraints that must be applied in every queries. Consequently, we have designed a REST API that integrates templated geodesic queries in *Cypher*.

The following templated query gives per nationality the monthly evolution of reviews during a given year and age range. We rely on the AT aggregated graph where tourists circulate from any u node to l (city of *Bordeaux*). The RETURN clause aggregates all edges r on nationalities and months.

```
MATCH (u:av) -[r:ae]-> (l:av{city:"Bordeaux"}) WHERE r.year={YEAR_PARAM} AND r.age={AGE_PARAM}
RETURN u.nat, r.month, SUM(r.nb) as nb_reviews
```

The *Neo4tourism* REST API integrates various templated queries. The REST URL targets the template used on the required **destination**. Then, on the aggregated **graph**, we apply the **template** query with parameters. This REST API helps to define combination of analysis on graphs with different settings and new templated queries: aggregation on age ranges, regions, etc.

```
/{destination}/{graph}/{template}?year={YEAR_PARAM}&age={AGE_PARAM}
```

4.3 Advanced Manipulations

Now we have circulation graphs at different levels of granularity (cities, etc.), we can identify central nodes and compare the evolution of this centrality over time. This will help to identify effects of events or tendancies in an area especially by filtering nationalities or age ranges. To achieve this, we apply standard graph algorithms like *PageRank* or *Betweeness Centrality* within templated queries.

The following query integrates a callable function from the *graph-algorithm* package[2] to produce PageRank scores for each city within the "*Gironde*" department. We can see that the AC graph is filtered on a given year and nationality. Each edge of the new graph (second parameter of the "*stream*" function) is weighted by the sum of the number of reviews, the PageRank will use this value

---

[2] https://github.com/neo4j-contrib/neo4j-graph-algorithms/releases.

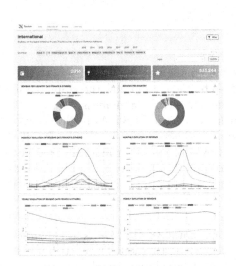

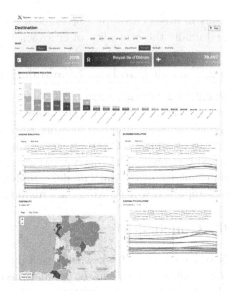

Fig. 6. International Neo4Tourism's UI   **Fig. 7.** Destination Neo4Tourism's UI

to compute scores (*"weightProperty"* in the 3rd parameter). Figure 5 gives an example of this result on regions' PageRank score.

```
CALL algo.pageRank.stream(
  "MATCH (a:av{department:'Gironde'}) RETURN id(a) as id",
  "MATCH (a0:av)-[r:ae{year:{YEAR}}]->(a2:av) WHERE r.nat = {NAT}
  RETURN id(a0) as from, id(a2) as to, sum(toFloat(a1.nb)) as weight",
  {dampingFactor:0.85, iterations:50, weightProperty:"weight"} )  YIELD node, score
RETURN node.city, sum(score) as score;
```

5   Demonstration

In this demonstration we wish to showcase how our framework eases the analysis of tourists' behavior and the interaction with the aggregated graphs. The scenario of this demonstration based on the city of *Bordeaux*.

5.1   Neo4Tourism UI

The Neo4Tourism UI shows tourists' circulation evolution at different levels of granularity: international, national, region and department. The demonstration will showcase each of those levels in order to understand the interaction on the REST API with the underlying graphs, the impact of circulation and centrality.

Figure 6 gives a screenshot of one interactive webpage at the international level. We can filter on users' profile and settings of the study. It shows the global characterics of reviews, their evolution over time. This level of study helps to understand which population of tourists interacts with a given destination.

Figure 7 shows a second screenshot of the web interface that shows a local view on the study. It focuses on the region area and showcase the circulation of users between cities: proportion and evolution of ingoing and outgoing tourists, and finally the centrality of cities within the area.

5.2   Graph Database Manipulation

Finally, the demonstration will show the underlying graph in *Neo4j*. The extraction of nodes and edges on the study will help to understand how the graph data model has been designed in order to produce this setting of analysis.

The templated *Cypher* queries implemented into the REST API will be executed directly on the *Neo4j* UI in order to display corresponding graphs. It will especially show the data model complexity through edges that are generated by our approach which favors data manipulation.

6   Conclusion

Neo4Tourism is a framework based on a graph database that helps to enhance impact of events, seasons or populations on a given destination. The contribution of this approach is a dynamic manipulation of circulation graphs at various scales in a geodesic context. It will open discussions on identicators definition for tourist actors (tourist offices, metropoles, marketing, etc.) like circulation density, practices evolution or communities.

References

1. Aggarwal, C.C., Wang, H.: Graph data management and mining: a survey of algorithms and applications. In: Aggarwal, C., Wang, H. (eds.) Managing and Mining Graph Data. ADBS, vol. 40, pp. 13–68. Springer, Boston (2010). https://doi.org/10.1007/978-1-4419-6045-0_2
2. Bonifati, A., Fletcher, G., Voigt, H., Yakovets, N.: Querying graphs. Synth. Lect. Data Manag. **10**(3), 1–184 (2018)
3. Borgatti, S.P.: Centrality and network flow. Soc. Netw. **27**(1), 55–71 (2005)
4. Brandes, U.: A faster algorithm for betweenness centrality. J. Math. Sociol. **25**(2), 163–177 (2001)
5. Cervantes, O., Gutiérrez, E., Gutiérrez, F., Sánchez, J.A.: Social metrics applied to smart tourism. ISPRS Ann. Photogramm. Remote. Sens. Spat. Inf. Sci. **4**, 117 (2016)
6. Keng, S.S., Su, C.H., Yu, G.L., Fang, F.C.: AK tourism: a property graph ontology-based tourism recommender system. In: KMICe, pp. 83–88. UUM, Miri Sarawak, Malaysia, July 2018
7. Lee, S.H., Choi, J.Y., Yoo, S.H., Oh, Y.G.: Evaluating spatial centrality for integrated tourism management in rural areas using gis and network analysis. Tour. Manag. **34**, 14–24 (2013)
8. Shih, H.Y.: Network characteristics of drive tourism destinations: an application of network analysis in tourism. Tour. Manag. **27**(5), 1029–1039 (2006)
9. Yochum, P., Chang, L., Gu, T., Zhu, M., Zhang, W.: Tourist attraction recommendation based on knowledge graph. In: Shi, Z., Mercier-Laurent, E., Li, J. (eds.) IIP 2018. IAICT, vol. 538, pp. 80–85. Springer, Cham (2018). https://doi.org/10.1007/978-3-030-00828-4_9

Personalised Drug Prescription for Dental Clinics Using Word Embedding

Wee Pheng Goh[1,2(✉)], Xiaohui Tao[1], Ji Zhang[1], Jianming Yong[1],
XueLing Oh[2], and Elizabeth Zhixin Goh[2,3]

[1] University of Southern Queensland, Toowoomba, Australia
{weepheng.goh,xtao,ji.zhang,jianming.yong}@usq.edu.au
[2] Glory Dental Surgery Pte. Ltd., Singapore, Singapore
xueling.oh@glorydental.com
[3] University of Queensland, Brisbane, Australia
elizabeth.goh@uqconnect.edu.au

Abstract. The number of drugs in drug databases is constantly expanding with novel drugs appearing on the market each year. A dentist cannot be expected to recall all the drugs available, let alone potential drug-drug interactions (DDI). This can be problematic when dispensing drugs to patients especially those with multiple medical conditions who often take a multiple medications. Any new medication prescribed must be checked against the patient's medical history, in order to avoid drug allergies and reduce the risk of adverse reactions. Current drug databases allowing the dentist to check for DDI are limited by the lack of integration of the patient's medical profile with the drug to be prescribed. Hence, this paper introduces a software which predicts the possible DDI of a new medication against the patient's medical profile, based on previous findings that associate similarity ratio with DDI. This system is based conceptually on a three-tier framework consisting of a knowledge layer, prediction layer and presentation layer. The novel approach of this system in applying feature vectors for drug prescription will be demonstrated during the conference (http://r.glory.sg/main.php). By engaging with the interactive demonstration, participants will gain first-hand experience in the process from research idea to implementation. Future work includes the extension of use from dental to medical institutions, and it is currently being enhanced to serve as a training tool for medical students.

Keywords: Feature vector · Similarity ratio · Drug interaction

1 Introduction

The increasing number of patients taking multiple drugs for a multitude of medical problems emphasis-es the importance for dentists to take precautions during drug prescription. Remembering all the potential DDI can be a significant burden [6], hence our decision support tool aims to assist the prescription process through integration with the patient's medical profile and DDI prediction at

L. H. U et al. (Eds.): WISE 2019, CCIS 1155, pp. 45–54, 2020.
https://doi.org/10.1007/978-981-15-3281-8_5

point-of-care in order to reduce prescription error and subsequent adverse drug reactions. A common cause of hospital admissions worldwide is adverse drug reactions, with incidence reaching 24% [7]. Many such admissions could have been avoided if more care was taken in drug prescription, such as by considering the patient's drug allergies. The design of the demonstration system which predicts a drug-pair's DDI potential is based on previous findings that the more similar the drug-pair, the higher the similarity ratio. The drug-pair's similarity ratio is obtained from word embedding associated with the neighbouring terms of each drug in the drug-pair. This prediction process within the prediction layer combines with a knowledge layer and presentation layer to form a three-tier conceptual framework.

The rest of the paper is as follows: Sect. 2 outlines the related work in DDI and shows how our model differs in the way the drug-drug relationship is detected and utilised. Section 3 discusses the previous findings in terms of the conceptual framework and how word embedding is used to determine a drug-pair's similarity ratio to determine if it is appropriate for prescription. Section 4 then illustrates use of the demonstration system in the dental setting to assist the dentist in safe drug prescription. The demonstration plan of the system is outlined in Sect. 5 with additional functions to the system being reported in Sect. 6.

1.1 Why Is Such a System Needed

There is increasing use of technology in healthcare to store and retrieve patient records, and other applications such as treatment planning and drug prescription should also be considered. A system is required not just to advise if two drugs adversely react with one another, but whether a drug to be prescribed is safe for a particular patient. In other words, the system should be integrated with the medications the patient is currently taking and their drug allergies. The statutory requirements of having electronic treatment plans, electronic medical records, and the daily reporting of diagnoses and drugs dispensed compound the need for such a decision support system.

1.2 Features of the Demonstration System

Participants during the conference will have first-hand opportunity to experience the novel features of the system. This includes:

- Predicting if a drug is safe for prescription
- Dynamic presentation of safe drugs for prescription in relation to the patient's medications and drug allergies by varying the threshold value
- Security features assigning different levels of privilege to different user categories
- Standardised clinical terminology such as the Systematized Nomenclature of Medicine - Clinical Terms (SNOMED CT) employed for the drug codes to ensure portability with existing systems and adherence to international clinical standards.

2   Related Work

A common technique to extract drug information from bio-medical corpus is to extract feature vectors and build a predictive model [2] to determine the adverse relationship of the drug-pair. By identifying neutral candidates, negation cues and scopes from bio-medical text, a similar work to determine the confidence level of a drug interaction was also carried out by Bokh et al. [1]. A recent approach by Sahu and Anand based on long short-term-memory claimed to outperform traditional methods that explicitly relies on feature engineering [9].

The use of neural networks in extracting information on drug interaction has become a recent trend. By using word embedding technique to build word vectors, neural network is employed to learn the context features for extracting information on drug interaction [11]. In a recent work, contextual features were obtained and used to extract drug information from bio-medical literature. This was made possible from semantic embeddings and position embeddings employed within a neural network [10].

Although these studies use data mining methods to extract relevant information to predict DDI, they do not take into account the drug profile of the patient.

Although there are a wide variety of decision support tools to assist the dentist in drug prescription, these tools only provide information on whether a drug-pair is in an adverse relationship. Even with Micromedex[1], one of the common packages which obtained the highest scores in terms of completeness and consistency in an evaluation of drug resources for drug-ethanol and drug-tobacco interactions, there is no integration with the medical profile of the patient, not to mention the availability of daily reports for the patients which are commonly needed by the clinics for effective patient care and inventory control.

Such tools are only as helpful as they claimed to be provided that the search terms are entered correctly. In addition, most of these systems do not take into account the allergy that the patient has, not to mention that the system is not integrated with the patient's medical profile.

The crucial need to integrate the patient's medical profile with the knowledge obtained from data mining motivated us to embark on this study. Although our system is similar to that proposed by [3] in terms of using information from the patient, the unique approach adopted in this paper goes one step further in using such information to support the decision-making process for the dentist at point-of-care within the clinical work-flow. Moreover, the word embedding method is also adopted which uses features that relate the similarity of a drug-pair in terms of how closely the words are related to each drug of the drug-pair. This approach distinguishes from our earlier work where feature vectors were constructed based on term similarities within the drug corpus [5]. In the application that is demonstrated here, the prescription of the drug will take into account the current drug that the patient is taking and the drug that the patient is allergic to. The framework of the customised system will be explained in the next section.

---

[1] https://www.micromedexsolutions.com.

3   Research Findings

In view of the need for the professional user to dispense the drug efficiently and effectively, an approach is needed to ensure that drugs prescribed are not in an adverse relationship with the drugs that patient is currently taking. At the same time, it must not belong to the same class of drugs which the patient is allergic to.

To solve this problem, we have discovered a novel approach in predicting the probability of an interaction of a drug-pair. Based on this approach, a system has also been built and ready for deployment in a dental clinic, which will be described in the demonstration plan in this paper. This section describes the conceptual framework behind the deployment model and the details of the prediction layer of the conceptual framework.

3.1   Conceptual Framework

The conceptual model behind such a system is based on the innovative 3-tier framework shown in Fig. 1.

Knowledge Layer. The knowledge layer consists of the bio-medical text which described the properties of the drugs. It comprises the domain knowledge in raw data form. Drugbank is used in this study where relevant information is extracted to construct a new taxonomy relating to interactions and side-effects. With this knowledge base, information is enhanced from the raw data available at Drugbank. As this is being constructed and made available in a structured format, different models can be developed and used to determine and predict if the drug is in an adverse relationship with another drug. Features relating to each drug like their potential side-effects can also be easily retrieved.

Prediction layer. From the drug taxonomy, text mining was conducted to extract relevant information, where the text for each drug was extracted, cleaned and stored in order to provide information on the underlying properties of a drug-pair, enabling the similarity of the drug-pair to be computed. The flexibility and robustness of the three-tier framework allowed the calculation of drug-pair similarity to proceed with various approaches. Many approaches can be used

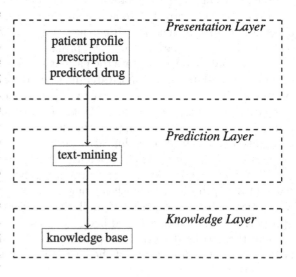

Fig. 1. Three-tier conceptual framework

within this layer but for this paper, the word embedding approach is described and demonstrated.

This word embedding approach uses word vectors to compute the feature vectors which are then used to predict the similarity of a drug-pair. With such information, it can be readily applied to a decision support system to assist dentist in their drug-prescription at point-of-care.

In order to compute feature vectors, a trained model of embedded vectors is needed. One of the tools which has the text corpus trained is the Gensim implementation of word2Vec[2] where similar words can be efficiently obtained. Given a target word, Word2Vec predicts the occurrence of context words neighbouring the target word.

Suppose v_t is a target embedding vector for the target word t and v_c is a context embedding vector for the context word c, then P, the conditional probability in the neural probabilistic language model can be defined as:

$$P(c|t) = \frac{exp(v_c^T v_t)}{\sum\limits_{i=1}^{k} exp(v_c^T v_{t_i})} \tag{1}$$

where k is the size of the vocabulary of the corpus.

The aim in the training of the corpus is then to maximise J, the log function of P. Hence from Eq. (1),

$$J = logP(c|t) = logexp(v_c^T v_t) - log \sum\limits_{i=1}^{k} exp(v_c^T v_{t_i}) \tag{2}$$

Once the text corpus has been trained by word2Vec, the output vector for any name of a drug can be conveniently obtained through built-in Java methods included in word2Vec.

Presentation Layer. This layer is important as it serves as an interface between the prediction layer and the user. A well-designed user-friendly interface will help dentists adopt such a system in their clinical work-flow. As highlighted in Table 1 for the three layers in the framework, user requirements in the user layer need to be efficiently mapped onto the prediction layer to enable useful and relevant information to be extracted for further computing of the similarity ratio.

Table 1. Features of conceptual framework

Presentation layer	Prediction layer	Knowledge layer
• Efficient mapping of user requirements	• Efficient choice of programming approach	• Bio medical data sources, drug taxonomy
• User friendly interface	• Implementation of data mining	• Drug properties
	• Algorithm design	

[2] https://radimrehurek.com/gensim/models/word2vec.html.

The user layer also distinguish our system from many other systems as it contains personalized information of the patient.

Besides, the presentation layer also presents the results from the prediction layer. Hence this layer is important as a supporting tool to the dentist in deciding whether the drug to be prescribed is safe for the patient.

The drug which the dentist is going to prescribe is also stored in this layer. Such information is needed in the predictive layer for extraction of feature vectors. In order to maintain user-friendliness, which is crucial for clinical adoption of the system, it is important for this layer to present the results such that the user can easily understand.

Based on the result transmitted from the predictive layer, the service at this layer will then advise the user if the drug to be prescribed is safe for prescription. This approach allows the presentation layer to crystallize the results in a meaningful and friendly manner. More details on this layer is described in demonstration plan.

The drug taxonomy used in this research is taken from DrugBank, an open source bio-medical corpus. DrugBank is used just for convenience, though any other sources of corpus can be used. In order to build the model for subsequent knowledge discovery and decision making pertaining to drug prescription, a knowledge base has to be built.

Many methods exists to predict the interaction of a drug pair. To make use of the plethora of drug information within the bio-medical domain, textual data related to drug interactions are used in this demonstration. It has been found that the more similar the text between the pair of drugs, the higher the probability that the drug pair is similar. The novel approach in using textual data for computing similarity ratio is explained in this section. A survey of existing packages in drug interaction is also described.

3.2 Evolution of Discovered Drug Interactions

Along with the conceptual framework, the research findings on the approach that is used in predicting the similarity is proposed and developed in this section.

Based on research findings that similar drugs has similar patterns from word embeddings associated with the textual description of the drugs [4], a prototype can be constructed which aligns with the presentation layer of the conceptual framework.

Once the data is transformed from the unstructured textual data to structured patterns, data mining is performed to extract appropriate information. The remaining stages are evaluation, visualisation and decision making based on the knowledge obtained. These stages can be iterative where the output of one stage may indicate the need for the previous stage to be refined. For example in the evaluation stage, if the results are not satisfactory, the process of transforming the data or data mining methods can be amended.

This is achieved from data mining and evaluation which aims to discover patterns and meanings from the knowledge base. These two stages leads to the knowledge needed for the user to decide if a drug is safe to be prescribed to the patient.

Research work has been done to observe the relationship between drug inter-actions and word embeddings from the textual data that describe the drugs [4,5]. As cited by Nguyen from linguist JR Firth that "you shall know a word by the company it keeps" [8], related words and hence similar drugs can be known by finding similar words that describe the drugs. From word embeddings which is a vector representation of the words, similarity ratio of each drug can be obtained for comparison.

Within the predictive layer, a model is developed to compute the feature vectors from the textual description of the drug. These feature vectors are an indication of the probability of an adverse interaction of a drug-pair. With such information, it can be readily applied to various applications like the deployment of the drug prescription system proposed in this paper.

With the use of word2Vec, vectors related to a given drug can be obtained. Given the word embedding obtained for each neighbouring terms of the drugs d_i and d_j, feature vectors $\vec{f_i}$ and $\vec{f_j}$ can be obtained as follows:

$$\vec{f_i} = \left[w_{i1}, w_{i2} \ldots w_{ik} \right] \tag{3}$$

$$\vec{f_j} = \left[w_{j1}, w_{j2} \ldots w_{jk} \right] \tag{4}$$

Where w_{ik} and w_{jk} are the respective word embeddings of the neighboring words of drugs d_i and d_j and k is the number of neighboring words for each drug in the drug pair. It also follows that $|\vec{f_i}|$ and $|\vec{f_j}|$ is k.

The similarity ratios $sim(d_i, d_j)$ for the drug pair d_i and d_j can then be computed as:

$$sim(d_i, d_j) = \frac{\sum\limits_{p=1}^{k} w_{ip} \times w_{jp}}{\sqrt{\sum\limits_{p=1}^{k} w_{ip}^2} \times \sqrt{\sum\limits_{p=1}^{k} w_{jp}^2}} \tag{5}$$

Word2vec is used to obtain the vectors as it is versatile in predicting related words.

As an illustration, Fig. 2 shows a plot where related words like *painkillers* and *Tylenol* are clustered together. Similar entities like *Android* and *Note 5* are displayed towards the right.

While word2Vec is not strictly a deep neural network, the output vector that it produces in numerical format within the deep

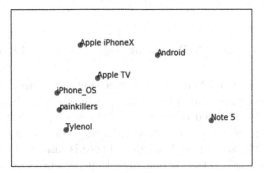

Fig. 2. Grouping of similar words

learning models can be easily understood by other deep networks making it very suitable for use in such works.

4   Use Case Scenario

This section illustrates how the prototype can be used at point-of-care to advise if the drug prescribed by the dentist is safe for the patient, and if not, to suggest alternatives, taking into account the drug profile of the patients.

4.1   Patient Registration

Once the user is signed into the system, the user can either register a new patient into the system or search for the record of an existing patient. The drug profile of the patient is shown beneath the patient's demographic record. The user can either edit them or click on the **Prescribe Drug** button to begin prescribing a drug for the patient.

4.2   Drug Prescription

At the screen on prescribing drug (Fig. 3), the user may enter any part of the name of the drug and the system will display all the drugs with names that contains the pattern of the string of words entered by the user. For example, if user enter *rfar*, the drug *warfarin* will appear.

Fig. 3. Prescribing drug

Fig. 4. Alternative drugs for selection

Figure 4 shows the list of alternative drugs for the user's consideration since the prescribed drug *Ibuprofen* interacts with the existing drug *Warfarin* which patient is currently taking. The size of the list of drugs varies depending on the threshold set by the user. In this case, the suggested candidate drug is at least 70% similar to *Ibuprofen*. There is also at least a 50% chance that the drug is similar to the current drug that patient is taking.

5   Demonstration Plan

The use case scenario described in Sect. 4 will be demonstrated interactively on the desktop with the aim of illustrating how the prototype can be used at point-of-care to advise if the drug prescribed by the dentist is safe for the patient, and if not, to suggest alternatives, taking into account the drug profile of the patients. The audience will be able to get first hand experience on the way the system is designed and implemented based on the research findings that similar drugs have similar feature vectors.

The demonstration plan is outlined below:

- Illustrate the versatility of word2Vec in relation to the ability to find similar words.
- Introduce the research problem and explain the main motivation behind this study and the creation of the system. The framework of the system is also presented to the conference participants.
- Demonstrate on the use of the system with a scenario of how a dentist can utilise this to prescribe a painkiller to a patient using the patient's medical profile. Next, a search on a typical painkiller will be conducted with the system displaying a list of recommended drugs.
- Show the various features of the system, including the daily reporting system as well as the security features of the system. The daily reporting system allows the user to generate a daily report on drugs that are dispensed for the day, for good clinical record keeping.

From the demonstration and participation in the interactive sessions, conference attendees will be engaged with first hand experience and appreciate the way research findings related to word embedding can be deployed for practical purposes.

6   Conclusions

This paper presents a novel approach in advising the suitability of a drug for prescription by predicting the similarity of a drug-pair and in practical terms, integrating this with the patient's medical status by considering their drug allergies to avoid allergic reactions, and the drugs they are currently taking to avoid adverse DDI. The demonstration system's algorithm is based on our previous findings that the similarity ratio of a drug-pair is an indicator of the probability of an adverse DDI within the drug-pair. The use of such a prototype can be extended from the dental clinic to medical institutions. The system is currently being enhanced so that it can be used on mobile devices, not only as a decision support tool, but also as a training tool for medical students.

Acknowledgment. This paper is undertaken collaboratively with the panel of dentists from Glory Dental Surgery Pte Ltd. The authors would like to thank the panel of dentists for their technical contribution and enriching the author's understanding of the requirements in drug dispensing. Feedback from the dental clinic is taken into consideration so that the deployment of the system aligns with the clinical work flow of a typical dental clinic.

References

1. Bokharaeian, B., Diaz, A., Chitsaz, H.: Enhancing extraction of drug-drug interaction from literature using neutral candidates, negation, and clause dependency. PLoS One **11**(10), 1–20 (2016)
2. Bui, Q., Sloot, P., vanMulligen, E., Kors, J.: A novel feature-based approach to extract drug-drug interactions from biomedical text. Bioinformatics **30**(23), 3365–3371 (2014)
3. Casillas, A., Perez, A., Oronoz, M., Gojenola, K., Santiso, S.: Learning to extract adverse drug reaction events from electronic health records in spanish. Expert Syst. Appl. **61**, 235–245 (2016)
4. Goh, W.P., et al.: Exploring the use of a network model in drug prescription support for dental clinics. In: 2018 5th International Conference on Behavioral, Economic, and Socio-Cultural Computing, pp. 168–172 (2018)
5. Goh, W.P., Tao, X., Zhang, J., Yong, J.: Mining drug properties for decision support in dental clinics. In: Kim, J., Shim, K., Cao, L., Lee, J.-G., Lin, X., Moon, Y.-S. (eds.) PAKDD 2017. LNCS (LNAI), vol. 10235, pp. 375–387. Springer, Cham (2017). https://doi.org/10.1007/978-3-319-57529-2_30
6. Kheshti, R., Aalipour, M., Namazi, S.: A comparison of five common drug-drug interaction software programs regarding accuracy and comprehensiveness. J. Res. Pharm. Pract. **5**, 257–263 (2016)
7. Lieber, N.S.R., Ribeiro, E.: Adverse drug reactions leading children to the emergency department. Rev. Bras. Epidemiol. **15**, 265–274 (2012)
8. Nguyen, T., Le, N., Ho, Q., Phan, D., Ou, Y.: Using word embedding technique to efficiently represent protein sequences for identifying substrate specificities of transporters. Anal. Biochem. **577**, 73–81 (2019)
9. Sahu, S.K., Anand, A.: Drug-drug interaction extraction from biomedical texts using long short-term memory network. J. Biomed. Inform. **86**, 15–24 (2018)
10. Sun, X., Dong, K., Ma, L.: Drug-drug interaction extraction via recurrent hybrid convolutional neural networks with an improved focal loss. J. Biomed. Inform. **21**, 37 (2019)
11. Sudrez-Paniagua, V., Segura-Bedmar, I., Martínez, P.: Exploring convolutional neural networks for drug-drug interaction extraction. Database **2017**, bax019 (2017)

NRGQP: A Graph-Based Query Platform for Network Reachability

Wenjie Li[1], Peng Peng[1(✉)], Zheng Qin[1], and Lei Zou[2]

[1] Hunan University, Changsha, China
{liwenjie,hnu16pp,zqin}@hnu.edu.cn
[2] Peking University, Beijing, China
zoulei@pku.edu.cn

Abstract. This demo designs and implements a system called $NRGQP$ that can efficiently support a variety of network reachability query services while considering the network security policies. $NRGQP$ constructs a knowledge graph based on the network security policies and designs an algorithm over the graph for the network reachability. Furthermore, for supporting a user-friendly interface, a structural query language named $NRQL$ is proposed in $NRGQP$ for the network reachability query.

1 Introduction

Network reachability is an important basis for network security services, which has attracted more and more attentions of the experts and scholars. Network reachability is a functional characteristic of the network, which ensuring smooth communication between nodes in order to users conveniently access the resources of network.

Recently, there are some effective works on the network reachability. Xie *et al.* propose a pioneering work. They define the network and propose a method to model the static network reachability [1]. The key idea is to extract the configuration information of routers in the network and reconstruct the network into a graph in a formal language. Thus, the network reachability can be computed out through classical problems such as closure and shortest path. Zhang *et al.* propose a method to merge the IP addresses with the same reachability into the IP address sets [2]. When the network reachability is changed, the affected IP address sets can be reconstructed quickly by splitting or merging to update the network reachability in real time. However, they do not provide an algorithm to answer whether an IP is reachable along a certain path to another IP. Benson *et al.* introduce the concept of the policies unit [3]. The policies unit is a set of IP addresses affected by the same security policies. A policies unit may be distributed in many subnets, or there may be many different policies units in a subnet. They also do not provide a algorithm for the network reachability query.

In this demo, we design and implement a novel query platform for the network reachability called $NRGQP$. In $NRGQP$, a knowledge graph of network reachability based on the network security policies is constructed, and a novel

L. H. U et al. (Eds.): WISE 2019, CCIS 1155, pp. 55–63, 2020.
https://doi.org/10.1007/978-981-15-3281-8_6

structured query language called $NRQL$ for network reachability is introduced for supporting an user-friendly interface. Users can send the query requests to $NRGQP$ using the natural language. $NRGQP$ can parse the user query requests to the $NRQL$ statements and evaluate the statements efficiently.

2   Problem Definitions

The essence of network reachability query is to determine whether a certain type of network packet can reach another node from one node or from one subnet to another. Given two subnets N_1 and N_2, and two host nodes v_1 and v_2, where v_1 is a node of N_1, so $v_1 \in N_1$ holds, and v_2 is a node of N_2, so $v_2 \in N_2$ holds. The network reachability query in this paper can be divided into three categories as follows according to the query targets.

1. **Node to Node.** This category of query is mainly used to check the network reachability between nodes. We use $v_1 \rightarrow v_2$ to denote that v_1 to v_2 is reachable, and use $v_1 \nrightarrow v_2$ to denote that v_1 to v_2 is unreachable.
2. **Node to Subset.** This category of query is mainly used to check the network reachability between nodes and subsets. We use $v_1 \rightarrow N_2$ to denote that v_1 to N_2 is reachable, and use $v_1 \nrightarrow N_2$ to denote that v_1 to N_2 is unreachable. Obviously, the following formula holds.

$$v_1 \rightarrow N_2 \Leftrightarrow \exists v_j, \ v_j \in N_2 \wedge v_1 \rightarrow v_j$$

3. **Subset to Subset.** This category of query is mainly used to check the network reachability between subnets. We use $N_1 \rightarrow N_2$ to denote that N_1 to N_2 is reachable, and use $N_1 \nrightarrow N_2$ to denote that N_1 to N_2 is unreachable. Obviously, the following formula holds.

$$N_1 \rightarrow N_2 \Leftrightarrow \exists v_i \exists v_j, \ v_i \in N_1 \wedge v_j \in N_2 \wedge v_i \rightarrow v_j$$

We also can divide the network reachability query into two categories as follows according to the result of query.

1. **Boolean query.** The result of the query is a boolean value (such as yes or no). For example, "SMTP server 192.168.0.32 to host 192.168.0.54 is reachable?", and the result is "yes" or "no".
2. **Node query.** The result of the query is a set of nodes that satisfy the query condition. For example, "Which hosts in subset 192.168.0.0/24 can receive the email from the SMTP server 192.168.0.32?". The result is a set of nodes.

3   System Architecture

In this paper, we propose a query platform for network reachability based on network security policies, $NRGQP$. Figure 1 shows the system architecture of NRGQP. NRGQP consists of two parts as follows.

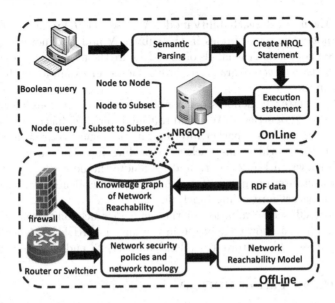

Fig. 1. The system architecture of NRGQP

3.1 The Offline Part of NRGQP

In the offline part of NRGQP, we collect and organize the network security policies (including ACL and routing table). First, we remove the network security
policies which the action field value is *deny* and extend OPTree [4] for maintaining the network security policies. OPTree is a homomorphic structure of
network security policies, and the redundancy policies and the conflict policies
can be removed when constructing OPTree. Then, we propose a network reachability model based on the network topology and the network security policies,
and construct a knowledge graph based on the network reachability model.

The network reachability model in our demo is defined as follows. Given a
subnet N and there are n devices $(D_1, D_2, \ldots, D_n)$ in N. Because the topological
structure of the network is a graph model, we use the graph as the basic data

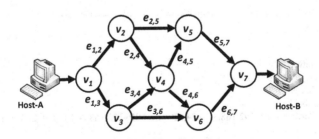

Fig. 2. An example of the network reachability model

structure of the network reachability model. We use $G(V, E)$ to denote the graph, which V denotes the set of nodes in the subnet N and E denotes a set of the edges between nodes, and the labels of the edges are the network security policies. Obviously, G is a directed graph. Figure 2 shows an example of the network reachability model.

In Fig. 2, a vertex v_i denotes a device, such as firewall, router or switcher. According to the properties of ACL and routing table, if v_i has only one edge, v_i denotes a device which has packet filtering function, such as firewall; otherwise, v_i denotes a device which has packet forwarding function, such as router or switcher. As shown in Fig. 2, v_5, v_6 and v_7 denote the network security devices which has packet filtering function, and v_1, v_2, v_3 and v_4 denote network security devices which packet forwarding function.

To support efficient evaluation of the network reachability query, we treat the above graph as a knowledge graph in the model of RDF [5] and maintain it in graph databases, like gStore [6,7], Jena [8], rdf4j [9] and Virtuoso [10].

3.2   The Online Part of NRGQP

The online part of NRGQP is mainly responsible for processing user query requests. In this part, we propose a structured query language, called $NRQL$ (Network Reachability Query Language) for network reachability query.

As we treat the graph of network reachability based on the network security policies as a knowledge graph in the model of RDF, the straightforward method to represent the user query request is to use the standard structured query language, SPARQL [11], for accessing the knowledge graph. However, SPARQL does not support matching operations related to the *policy matching condition*. A SPARQL statement only supports queries with limited steps, while we often do not know how many edges are there between the starting node and the target node in the query of the network reachablility. Therefore, we propose a query language $NRQL$ to extend the SPARQL language to support the query request.

A NRQL statement consists of two parts: a query target clause beginning with keyword *select* and a ? to denote a query variable. Therefore, a query target clause contains several query targets by several query variables. Figure 3 shows an example of NRQL statement, and there are two query targets in Fig. 3.

```
Select ?x,?y
Where
{
    ?x  Network ?y.
    ?x  DeviceType "Host".
    ?z  NextNode ?x.
    ?z  Label ?k.
    ?k  <nr:in> <SIP=192.168.32.0/24,SP=any, DIP=192.168.24.212,DP=23,P=tcp>.
}
```

Fig. 3. Example node query

```
Select exist(?x)
Where
{
    ?x  Network ?y.
    ?x  DeviceType "Host".
    ?z  NextNode ?x.
    ?z  Label ?k.
    ?k  <nr:in> <SIP=192.168.32.0/24,SP=any, DIP=192.168.24.212,DP=23,P=tcp>.
}
```

Fig. 4. Example Boolean query

Figure 3 shows a node query. We use the keyword *exist* to describe the boolean query, and we only add *exist* for the query variables of the query statement for boolean query is shown in Fig. 4.

The other part of the NRQL statement is a query condition clause beginning with keyword *where*, which is wrapped with braces and contains several triple patterns. Each triple pattern is a query condition for edges in knowledge graph.

Here, to support matching the data package with network security policies in the network reachability query, we define a new predicate "<nr: in >" in NRQL. This predicate means that the content of the object is regarded as a data packet, and then the process is transformed into the problem of checking whether a data packet is matched with a set of network security policies. We define this query condition clause as a *policy matching condition*. In a query condition clause, there is only one *policy matching condition*. Here, as discussed before, we extend OPTree [4] to maintain the network security policies, which solve the problem of evaluating the policy matching condition efficiently. This is because the problem of evaluating the policy matching condition can be transformed into finding a predicate path in OPTree, which can be solved efficiently by using the search algorithm of OPTree.

Users send the query requests to NRGQP using the natural language. NRGQP parses the user query requests and generates the NRQL statements. The key of NRGQP query is to match the query conditions by using OPTree in the network reachability model. In order to adapt to *OPTree*, we propose a NRQL query parsing algorithm based on OPTree query algorithm. NRGQP can provide three categories of queries: "node to node", "node to subnet" and "subnet to subnet". The results of those queries can be either "Yes" or "NO", or a set of nodes satisfying the query conditions.

Considering the high real-time requirement of network reachability query, the relatively low frequency of network security policies change, and the long time-consuming construction of the network reachability model based on OPTree, we construct or update the network reachability model through timing scheduling in the offline part. In the online part, NRGQP provides a real-time network reachability query service based on the high query efficiency of graph databases. In terms of system deployment, the online part and the offline part can be deployed independently, in which the offline part can be deployed in the intranet environment to isolate ordinary users, and the online part can be deployed in the extranet environment to provide network reachability query services to ordinary users by the GUI of NRGQP.

4   Demonstration

4.1   Setting

We implement our prototype system of NRGQP using Java. The demo system is conducted on a Linux machine with 16 GB memory and 4 cores of Intel(R) Xeon(R) processor (3.3 GHz). The graph database of the network reachability model are maintained in gStore. To store the data for system login, system log and system parameters, we also use the relation database MySQL 5.6 in our prototype system.

We use a random function to generate the topology of network and use the network security policies generation tool *ClassBench* proposed in [12], which is widely used in policies generation to generate the network security policy sets of the devices in the network.

4.2   System Functions

Our demo is a web application, Fig. 5 shows the index page of NRGQP, and NRGQP provides the following functions.

Fig. 5. The index page of NRGQP

(1) Parsing the users' query requests.

The function provides an input window. The users can input the network reachability query requests with the natural language in the window. The system can automatically parse the network reachability query request and generate NRQL query statements. Figure 6(a) shows the input page of the user's query request. Figure 6(b) shows the result for the user's query request: "Can the host of 192.168.12.3 receive mail from SMTP mail server 192.168.4.2?".

(2) Evaluating Boolean query of network reachability.

The function is to execute a boolean query of network reachability and show the results to users. Because of the result of boolean query is *true* or *false*, the system uses a bullet-box to inform users of the result. The result is shown in Fig. 7.

(3) Evaluating node query of network reachability.

The function is to execute a NRQL node query statement and feedback the results to users. When NRQL node query is executed, the system records the query nodes and paths, so this function can not only query the node information that satisfied with the query conditions, but also return the query path, as shown in Fig. 8.

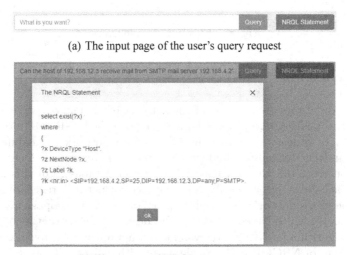

(a) The input page of the user's query request

(b) The generated NRQL query statement

Fig. 6. The page of the network reachability query

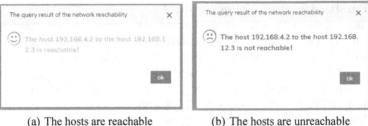

(a) The hosts are reachable   (b) The hosts are unreachable

Fig. 7. The result of the boolean query

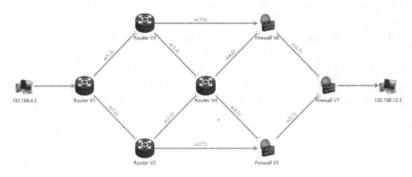

Fig. 8. The result of node query

5   Conclusions

In this demo, we propose a model of the network reachability based on the network security policies, and propose a query engine called "NRGQP" for network reachablity. In order to improve the efficiency of network reachability query, the popular RDF technology and graph database management technology are used to construct the network reachability graph database. On this basis, the network reachability graph database is proposed for network reachability query. To describe user's network reachability query requests, we propose a structured query language, which called "NRQL", and design the construct algorithm and the query algorithm for NRQL. To evaluate our approach, we implement the prototype system of NRGQP and provide users with convenient and fast network accessibility query service.

Acknowledgment. This work was supported by The National Key Research and Development Program of China under grant 2017YFB0902900, 2018YFB1003504, National Natural Science Foundation of China (61872130, 61772191, 61300217, 61472131, 61272546, 61702171, 61622201, 61532010), Hunan Provincial Natural Science Foundation of China under grant 2018JJ3065, Science and Technology Key Projects of Hunan Province (2015TP1004, 2016JC2012, 2018TP1009), Science and Technology Key Projects of ChangSha City (kq1801008, kq1804008), and the Fundamental Research Funds for the Central Universities.

References

1. Xie, G.G., Zhan, J., Maltz, D.A., Zhang, H., Greenberg, A.G.: On static reachability analysis of IP networks. In: IEEE INFOCOM, pp. 2170–2183 (2005)
2. Zhang, B., Eugene, T.S., Wang, N.G.: Reachability monitoring and verification in enterprise networks. In: ACM SIGCOMM, pp. 459–460 (2008)
3. Benson, T., Akella, A., Maltz, D.A.: Mining policies from enterprise network configuration. In: The 9th ACM SIGCOMM Conference on Internet Measurement Conference, pp. 136–142 (2009)
4. Li, W., Qin, Z., Li, K., Yin, H., Lu, O.: A novel approach to rule placement in software-defined networks based on OPTree. IEEE Access **7**(1), 8689–8700 (2019)
5. RDF - Semantic Web Standards. https://www.w3.org/RDF/
6. Zou, L., Mo, J., Chen, L.: gStore: answering SPARQL queries via subgraph matching. VLDB Endow. **4**(8), 482–493 (2011)
7. Zou, L., Özsu, M.T., Chen, L., Shen, X., Huang, R., Zhao, D.: gStore: a graph-based SPARQL query engine. VLDB J. **23**(4), 565–590 (2014)
8. Apache Jena. http://jena.apache.org/
9. Eclipse RDF4J—The Eclipse Foundation. http://www.rdf4j.org/
10. OpenLink Virtuoso Universal Server. https://virtuoso.openlinksw.com/
11. SPARQL Query Language for RDF. https://www.w3.org/TR/rdf-sparql-query/
12. Taylor, D.E., Turner, J.S.: ClassBench: a packet classification benchmark. IEEE/ACM Trans. Netw. **15**(3), 499–511 (2007)

ReInCre: Enhancing Collaborative Filtering Recommendations by Incorporating User Rating Credibility

Naime Ranjbar Kermany[1]([envelope]) [iD], Weiliang Zhao[1] [iD], Jian Yang[1,2] [iD], and Jia Wu[1] [iD]

[1] Macquarie University, Sydney, NSW 2109, Australia
naime.ranjbar-kermany@hdr.mq.edu.au,
{weiliang.zhao,jian.yang,jia.wu}@mq.edu.au
[2] Donghua University, Shanghai, China

Abstract. We present ReInCre (Demo video available at https://youtu.be/MyFczz7Vefo) as a solution demo for incorporating user rating credibility in Collaborative Filtering (CF) approach to enhance the recommendation performance. The credibility values of users are calculated according to their rating behavior and they are utilized in discovering the neighbors (Code available at https://github.com/NaimeRanjbarKermany/Cred). To the best of our knowledge, it is the first work to incorporate the rating credibility of users in a CF recommendation. Our approach works as a powerful add-on to existing CF-based recommender systems in order to optimize the neighborhood. Experiments are conducted on the real-world dataset from Yahoo! Movies. Comparing with the baselines, the experimental results show that our proposed method significantly improves the quality of recommendation in terms of *precision* and F_1-*measure*. In particular, the standard deviation of the errors between the prediction values and the real ratings becomes much smaller by incorporating credibility measurements of the users.

Keywords: User credibility · Neighbor optimization · Collaborative filtering · User rating behavior

1 Introduction and Motivation

Recommender systems are developed for people to find the desired items among the large number of available candidates on the Internet [1]. Recommender systems have been used in various domain areas, e.g., movies [2], music [3], news [4], and social network [5].

A widely-used approach adopted in recommendation systems is neighbor-based collaborative filtering (CF) [1]. In this method, recommendations are based on the ratings of neighboring users [1]. CF has been widely adopted due to its good performance, flexible implementation, and the capability to cover the

© Springer Nature Singapore Pte Ltd. 2020
L. H. U et al. (Eds.): WISE 2019, CCIS 1155, pp. 64–72, 2020.
https://doi.org/10.1007/978-981-15-3281-8_7

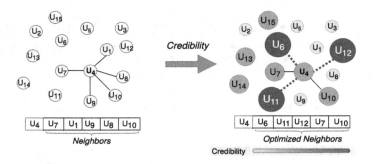

Fig. 1. An example of neighbor optimization using credibility of users; each node is a user, and the size and color of nodes show the degree of credibility. It can be observed that the top-5 neighbors of $u4$ are optimized to {u6, u11, u12, u7, u10} from {u7, u1, u9, u8, u10} due to the selection of more credible users as neighbors. (Color figure online)

latent relations between users and items [1]. However, one big issue that has not been touched upon is *how users' rating behavior shall be treated*: taken as they are, ignored, or if weighted, how? and how this will affect the recommendation results. In recommender systems, users' rating scores vary, i.e., some users' scores are widely distributed while others fall in a small range. Some users only rate few items, whereas some users rate a large number of items. Existing CF recommendation approaches largely ignore such differences. In the representative CF approach, all users' ratings are treated as they are, and inaccurate ratings unavoidably affect the recommendation results [6,7]. For instance, the user who gives the same score (e.g. 5.0) to all the items (from the most popular ones to the least popular ones) is not worth taking seriously [8]. In this demo, we provide a way on measuring users' rating credibility by taking their rating distributions into consideration. We believe that incorporating the rating credibility of users can further improve the accuracy and quality of CF-based recommendation.

Contribution. The recommendation quality of the CF method relies highly on selecting appropriate neighbors for the target user. In this work, we propose a method that optimizes the neighbors of an individual user. At first, we develop an algorithm to measure the credibility of users according to their rating behavior. The credibility of each user is measured based on his or her rating behavior. Then, the credibility values are used in the CF algorithm to decrease the impact of the ratings given by neighbors with low credibility. For simplicity, we name this integration of users' credibility and CF approach as "ReInCre" method. Figure 1 shows an example of neighbor optimization in ReInCre. To the best knowledge of the authors, it is for the first time that credibility of users' ratings has been incorporated in a CF approach for optimizing the neighbors. The contributions of this work are: (1) building up a CF-based recommendation solution by incorporating the credibility of users -this model is sufficiently general that it can be applied to any integration of CF-based recommendation approaches-; (2)

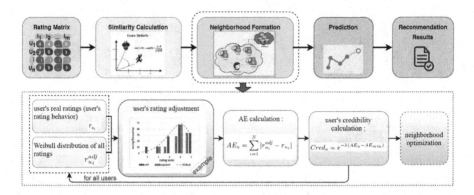

Fig. 2. Framework of our recommendation solution: ReInCre; ReInCre has focused on optimizing neighbors by (1) incorporating the users' rating behavior, (2) adjusting each user's ratings according to its deviation from the total distribution of all ratings, (3) calculating the Absolute Error as *AE*, and (4) calculating each user's credibility as *Cred*.

proposing a method to measure the credibility of users according to their rating behavior; (3) optimizing the neighborhood using the credibility of users in order to decrease the impact of the ratings given by neighbors with low credibility; (4) carrying out a set of experiments using real-world dataset from Yahoo! Movies to show the significant improvement of CF recommendation quality. To show and evaluate the proposed method, we develop a movie-recommendation demo.

2   The ReInCre System

Background. The main components of neighbor-based CF method includes (1) building up the rating matrix by users in rows and movies in columns; (2) measuring the similarity between each pair of users; (3) forming the neighborhood; (4) predicting the ratings of unknown items; and (5) recommending the top-k items that meet the user's interests. As the recommendation quality of CF method relies highly on selecting appropriate neighbors, there have been a lot of recent efforts to optimize the neighbors [9–12]. However, these existing neighbor-selection approaches have not considered users' rating behavior, i.e., the number of ratings a user made, and the rating pattern of a user. Users' rating behavior has been firstly used for the purpose of detecting review dishonesty or spammers [13], and then in social recommendation [8,14]. We believe that considering users' rating behavior is an important factor when selecting appropriate neighbors. In this demo, we calculate users' credibility values according to their rating behavior. We optimize the neighborhood by selecting more credible neighbors and decreasing the impact of the ratings given by neighbors with low credibility.

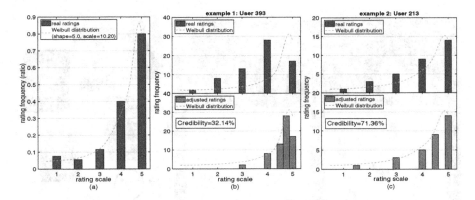

Fig. 3. Rating distribution and two examples of rating adjustment. (Color figure online)

Data[1]. We use the Yahoo! Movies[2] dataset to evaluate our recommendation solution. This dataset consists of 221,367 ratings from 7642 users and 11,915 movies. The users have rated items on a 5-star scale.

Baselines. We compare our method with two baselines: (1) representative CF [6] is a traditional user-based CF approach, which uses the cosine similarity metric, and (2) 2NSCF [11] is a recently-proposed method that aims to improve the recommendation accuracy of the neighbor-based CF through the optimization of neighborhood. They represented a two-layer neighbor-selection method to select the most trustworthy users as neighbors. However, they have not considered users' rating behavior in their method.

Method. Here we explain the framework of the ReInCre which is an enhancement of CF recommendations by incorporating users' rating credibility. Figure 2 shows the main components of the framework of our proposed method. ReInCre is an extendable approach that can be used with any recommendation algorithm to handle variety of different user rating behavior. In ReInCre, each user has assigned with a "credibility value". The credibility of each user is calculated according to his/her rating behavior and its deviation from the total distribution of all ratings; it has a value between 0 and 1. ReIncre optimizes the neighbors according to their credibility values in order to enhance the performance of CF recommendation. This is done through four steps:

Step 1. We fit a Weibull distribution to all ratings. We use 2-parameter Weibull distribution because of its benefit of providing sensibly accurate fitting [15]. "Scipy.stats. weibull_min.fit(data, floc=0)" in python is used to estimate the required parameters *shape* and *scale*, while $floc = 0$ keeps the third parameter, *location*, fixed at zero; and *data* is a Numpy array of ratings;

---

[1] refer to https://github.com/NaimeRanjbarKermany/Cred/ to see the results on other datasets.

[2] http://webscope.sandbox.yahoo.com.

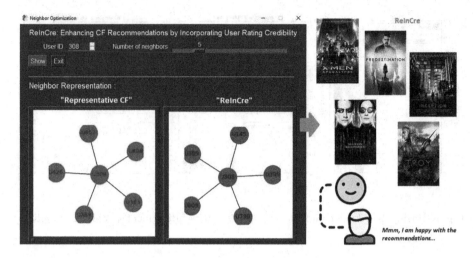

Fig. 4. GUI-based neighbor-optimization system of ReInCre and its positive impact on recommendations; this GUI is designed to compare the neighbors of each user for representative CF and ReInCre simultaneously (refer to Fig. 6 to see the experimental analysis).

Step 2. We adjust each user's rating based on the distribution through $r_{u_i}^{adj} = r_{u_i} * \frac{\widetilde{r}_{u_i}}{O_{Weibull}}$ if $\widetilde{r}_{u_i} > O_{Weibull}$, and $r_{u_i}^{adj} = r_{max} \text{-} (r_{max} \text{-} r_{u_i}) * \frac{\widetilde{r}_{u_i}}{O_{Weibull}}$ if $\widetilde{r}_{u_i} \leq O_{Weibull}$; where the adjusted ratings and the real ratings are denoted by $r_{u_i}^{adj}$ and r_{u_i} respectively, $\widetilde{r}_{u_i}$ is the mean ratings of u_i, $O_{Weibull}$ is the center of the Weibull distribution for all real ratings, and r_{max} is the maximum rating score in the system. The adjusted ratings must fall in the value domain. Note that the adjusted ratings only used to measure the credibility values, and would not change the real ratings;

Step 3. We calculate the difference between the user's ratings and the Weibull curve through $AE_u = \sum_{i=1}^{N} |r_{u_i}^{adj} - r_{u_i}|$, where AE is the Absolute Error and N is the total number of users;

Step 4. We measure users' credibility values through $Cred_u = e^{-\lambda(AE_u - AE_{min})}$, where AE_{min} is the minimum value of AE, and λ is a regulation parameter. A user with a smaller AE has a higher credibility. The credibility values are then utilized in optimizing neighbors, whom chosen by K-Nearest-Neighbors (KNN) algorithm, in order to improve the accuracy/quality of recommendation. As an example, the rating adjustment of users 213 and 393 are shown in Fig. 3, where the green graphs present the real ratings, and the orange graphs shows the after-adjustment ratings. From Fig. 3, it can be seen that the ratings behavior of user 213 are much more compatible with the total distribution (Fig. 3(a)) than that of user 393. User 213, thus, is much more credible to be chosen as a neighbor in recommendation process.

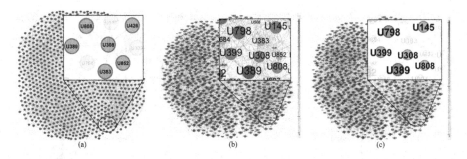

Fig. 5. Partial graph visualization of our neighbor optimization solution for Yahoo! Movies dataset with number of neighbors = 5; (a) U308 and his/her neighbors without considering credibility $\{U_{389}, U_{808}, U_{383}, U_{852}, U_{426}\}$, (b) Users' credibility in different sizes and colors, and (c) U308 and his/her optimized neighbors after considering credibility $\{U_{389}, U_{798}, U_{399}, U_{808}, U_{145}\}$. (Color figure online)

System Architecture. The demo is a GUI-based neighbor-optimization system designed with python, as shown in Fig. 4. We have shown the architecture of neighbor selection with and without using credibility values of users in the video[3] comprehensively.

Discussion. ReInCre aims to optimize the neighbors, as the recommendation accuracy/quality of the CF method relies highly on selecting appropriate neighbors. As we mentioned, the calculated credibility values of users are used in neighbor optimization. It significantly helps to decrease the impact of the ratings given by neighbors with low credibility. Figure 5 provides a partial graph visualization of our neighbor optimization solution on Yahoo! Movies dataset when the number of neighbors (K) is 5; Fig. 5(a) shows the neighbors selection for $user_{308}$ without considering credibility; Fig. 5(b) shows different users' credibility (with different node sizes and colors, low credibility users with smaller size and in light yellow, high credibility users with bigger size and in dark red; and Fig. 5(c) shows the neighbors optimization for $user_{308}$ by considering credibility values of users. Comparing Fig. 5(a) and (c), we can observe that more credible users are selected as the neighbors.

We carry out a set of experiments against dataset Yahoo! Movies and compare our results with the representative CF [6] and 2NSCF [11] as the baselines. The experimental results show the positive effect when user credibility was incorporated into the CF recommendation. Figure 6 shows the differences between real ratings and the predicted ones of the test data through baselines -representative CF and 2NSCF-, and our proposed method -"ReInCre"-. Comparing Fig. 6(b), (c) and (d), we can observe that Fig. 6(d) is left-skewed and more close to real rating patterns (Fig. 6(a)). Moreover, Fig. 6(d) has sharp peaks around the real rating scores because the user credibility is considered in the model. This results in a smaller standard deviation of errors (Fig. 6(g)) as compared to the models

---

[3] https://youtu.be/MyFczz7Vefo.

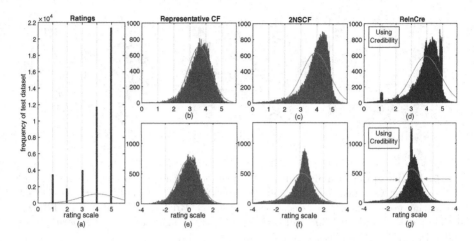

Fig. 6. Frequency of test dataset for (a) real ratings, (b) predicted ratings of representative CF, (c) predicted ratings of 2NSCF (d) predicted ratings of ReInCre -with the use of credibility-, (e) error histogram of representative CF, (f) error histogram of 2NSCF, and (g) error histogram of ReInCre -with the use of credibility-.

Table 1. *Precision* and F_1-*measure* for different Top-K of representative CF, 2NSCF, and ReInCre with the number of neighbors $= 5$

Metric	Model	@K							
		1	3	5	7	9	11	13	15
Precision	*Representative CF*	51.23	47.25	42.89	39.42	34.11	31.01	28.36	25.68
	2NSCF	78.01	74.08	69.59	65.05	60.80	56.89	53.32	50.10
	ReInCre	**85.12**	**81.48**	**76.84**	**70.76**	**68.92**	**65.21**	**60.54**	**56.28**
F_1-*measure*	*Representative CF*	21.51	28.99	30.54	33.15	33.47	33.81	34.12	33.52
	2NSCF	31.03	41.27	47.05	51.57	53.98	56.89	57.02	56.63
	ReInCre	**43.39**	**54.51**	**65.39**	**66.20**	**68.71**	**69.28**	**68.81**	**68.15**

without considering credibility (Fig. 6(e) and (f)). This reduction of standard deviation of errors reflects the improvement of the quality of the recommendation significantly, as shown in Table 1. It means that our proposed method provides more relevant items than baselines for the users. The incorporation of users' credibility helps to provide more accurate recommendations for users.

3   Conclusions

This work has developed ReInCre as a demo solution to enhance CF by incorporating the users' rating credibility. The credibility of users are evaluated based on their rating behavior comparing with the overall distribution of all ratings. A set of experiments has been performed against real-world dataset from Yahoo! Movies. The experimental results show the positive effect when user credibility is incorporated into the CF recommendation systems. Compared with the baselines, the proposed approach has improved the recommendation quality in terms of *precision* and F_1-*measure* significantly. In particular, the incorporation of the rating credibility helps to reduce the standard deviation of errors between the prediction values and real ratings. Because our method involves neighbor optimization, it can be applied to any CF-based recommendation algorithm. For future work, we are going to consider the temporal features of users' ratings in the credibility measurement as users' rating behavior change over time.

References

1. Ricci, F., Rokach, L., Shapira, B.: Recommender systems: introduction and challenges. In: Ricci, F., Rokach, L., Shapira, B. (eds.) Recommender Systems Handbook, pp. 1–34. Springer, Boston (2015). https://doi.org/10.1007/978-1-4899-7637-6_1
2. Kermany, N.R., Alizadeh, S.H.: A hybrid multi-criteria recommender system using ontology and neuro-fuzzy techniques. Electron. Commer. Res. Appl. **21**, 50–64 (2017)
3. Wang, D., Deng, S., Xu, G.: GEMRec: a graph-based emotion-aware music recommendation approach. In: Cellary, W., Mokbel, M., Wang, J., Wang, H., Zhou, R., Zhang, Y. (eds.) WISE 2016. LNCS, vol. 10041, pp. 92–106. Springer, Cham (2016). https://doi.org/10.1007/978-3-319-48740-3_7
4. Rao, J., Jia, A., Feng, Y., Zhao, D.: Taxonomy based personalized news recommendation: novelty and diversity. In: Lin, X., Manolopoulos, Y., Srivastava, D., Huang, G. (eds.) WISE 2013. LNCS, vol. 8180, pp. 209–218. Springer, Heidelberg (2013). https://doi.org/10.1007/978-3-642-41230-1_18
5. Yang, J., et al.: Unified user and item representation learning for joint recommendation in social network. In: Hacid, H., Cellary, W., Wang, H., Paik, H.-Y., Zhou, R. (eds.) WISE 2018. LNCS, vol. 11234, pp. 35–50. Springer, Cham (2018). https://doi.org/10.1007/978-3-030-02925-8_3
6. Huang, Z., Zeng, D., Chen, H.: A comparison of collaborative-filtering recommendation algorithms for e-commerce. IEEE Intell. Syst. **22**(5), 68–78 (2007)
7. Adomavicius, G., Kwon, Y.: New recommendation techniques for multicriteria rating systems. IEEE Intell. Syst. **22**(3), 48–55 (2007)
8. Zhang, Z., Zhao, W., Yang, J., Nepal, S., Paris, C., Li, B.: Exploiting users' rating behaviour to enhance the robustness of social recommendation. In: Bouguettaya, A., et al. (eds.) WISE 2017. LNCS, vol. 10570, pp. 467–475. Springer, Cham (2017). https://doi.org/10.1007/978-3-319-68786-5_37
9. Bai, T., Wen, J.-R., Zhang, J., Zhao, W.X.: A neural collaborative filtering model with interaction-based neighborhood. In: Proceedings of the 2017 ACM on Conference on Information and Knowledge Management, pp. 1979–1982. ACM (2017)
10. Polatidis, N., Georgiadis, C.K.: A multi-level collaborative filtering method that improves recommendations. Expert Syst. Appl. **48**, 100–110 (2016)
11. Zhang, Z., Liu, Y., Jin, Z., Zhang, R.: A dynamic trust based two-layer neighbor selection scheme towards online recommender systems. Neurocomputing **285**, 94–103 (2018)
12. Liji, U., Chai, Y., Chen, J.: Improved personalized recommendation based on user attributes clustering and score matrix filling. Comput. Stand. Interfaces **57**, 59–67 (2018)

13. Fang, H., Zhang, J., Magnenat Thalmann, N.: Subjectivity grouping: learning from users' rating behavior. In: Proceedings of the 2014 international conference on Autonomous agents and multi-agent systems. International Foundation for Autonomous Agents and Multiagent Systems, pp. 1241–1248 (2014)
14. Guo, G., Zhang, J., Thalmann, D.: Merging trust in collaborative filtering to alleviate data sparsity and cold start. Knowl.-Based Syst. **57**, 57–68 (2014)
15. Abernethy, R.B.: The New Weibull Handbook: Reliability and Statistical Analysis for Predicting Life, Safety, Supportability, Risk, Cost and Warranty Claims (2004)

SLIND$^+$: Stable LINk Detection

Ji Zhang[1,2], Leonard Tan[1], Xiaohui Tao[1], Hongzhou Li[3]([✉]), Fulong Chen[4],
and Yonglong Luo[4]

[1] The University of Southern Queensland, Toowoomba, Australia
Ji.Zhang@usq.edu.au
[2] Zhejiang Lab, Beijing, China
[3] Guilin University of Electronic Technology, Guilin, China
homzh@163.com
[4] Anhui Normal University, Wuhu, China

Abstract. Evolutionary behavior of Online Social Networks (OSNs) has not been well understood in many different aspects. Although there have been many developments around social applications like recommendation, prediction, detection and identification which take advantage of past observations of structural patterns, they lack the necessary representative power to adequately account for the sophistication contained within relationships between actors of a social network in real life. In this demo, we extend the innovative developments of SLIND [17] (Stable LINk Detection) to include a novel generative adversarial architecture and the Relational Turbulence Model (RTM) [15] using relational features extracted from real-time twitter streaming data. Test results show that SLIND$^+$ is capable of detecting relational turbulence profiles learned from prior feature evolutionary patterns in the social data stream. Representing turbulence profiles as a pivotal set of relational features improves detection accuracy and performance of well-known application approaches in this area of research.

Keywords: Adversarial learning · Fractal Neural Network · Relational Turbulence Model

1 Introduction

Relational states within an Online Social Network (OSN) play an important role to key applications like event prediction, recommendation, topic modeling, tracking, link prediction, community detection, feature recognition, ranking, knowledge graph embedding, etc. [3]. In industries like fintech [7], telehealth and medicine [2], social and marketing platforms [6], etc. where these applications are used extensively, relationships between nodes and actors pre-exist as binary state link occurances [16]. A key question which has remained unanswered by research, is the ability of machines to represent dynamic relational states that correspond to complex and evolving real-life communication patterns [10]. Detecting and

© Springer Nature Singapore Pte Ltd. 2020
L. H. U et al. (Eds.): WISE 2019, CCIS 1155, pp. 73–80, 2020.
https://doi.org/10.1007/978-981-15-3281-8_8

identifying such patterns can provide valuable insights into the domains where these social technologies are being used [11].

The major drawback of existing methods is that they tend to bias a single feature (often similarity based) heavily when formulating their decisions [1]. This limitation often leads to detection inaccuracies and data misrepresentations [12]. In addition, structural growth, decay and change of a network have not yet been well investigated and understood in literature [5]. In this paper, we develop an extension to the SLIND software and GUI [17] to include novel deep learning techniques that empower the dynamic profiling of relational turbulence [14] between actors of a given network in real time from social data streams.

The novel scientific contribution of our work in this extension involves uncovering and representing the relational states of evolving communication patterns in real life from any online social network architecture by using the innovative Relational Flux Turbulence (RFT) model [15]. Understanding relational states and how they play a role in social communication evolution patterns will improve detection accuracies and reduce misrepresentations of current applications. The innovative features of SLIND$^+$ are summarized as follows:

1. SLIND$^+$ implements the novel idea of running a turing-learning based, Generative Adversarial Fractal Neural Network (GA-FNN) which discriminates the evolution of actor-pair relational states based on observed relational turbulence profiles between generative system and actual model behaviors;
2. SLIND$^+$ features a user-immersive interface that allows for manipulation of various FNN adversarial feature inputs into the analysis of the RFT model. It also provides a rich set of visualization modes to display the final results at either a fixed or continuous time duration through different 3D presentations;
3. SLIND$^+$ is able to adapt to real-time twitter streaming, high dimensional datasets and crawled information from real-life OSNs (e.g. Google, Youtube, etc.). It can also perform stability analysis on small tightly knitted cliques as well. The system model is computationally efficient and versatile;

2   Method and Architecture of SLIND$^+$

In SLIND$^+$, the FNN (Fractal Neural Network) method provides the core capability to scale network depth towards the problem complexity from streaming social data. Through the use of a Generative Adversarial architecture, the descriminator FNN is able to identify and predict relational turbulence profiles and the corresponding communication patterns accurately. The overview of the system architecture of SLIND$^+$ is presented in Fig. 1. Social data is first actively streamed from a query of interest (e.g. geography, topic, hashtag, etc.). Each data stream is first broken down into key relational features - Category confidence, Entity salience, Entity sentiment, Mentions sentiment and Context sentiment using the google NLP API. These features are then fed into the first stage Fractal Neural Network (FNN) with noise to generate a predicted set of relational turbulence profile parameters (Flux intensity, Mention interferences, and Context uncertainty). Then, a synchronized concurrent stream of Relational

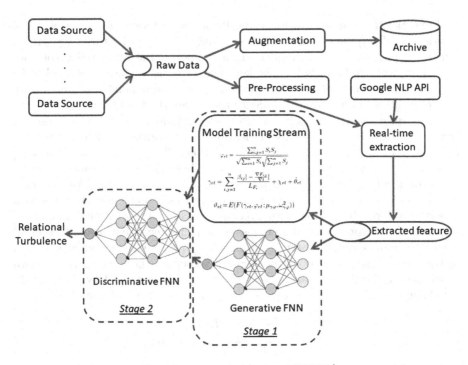

Fig. 1. System architecture of SLIND$^+$

Turbulence Model (RTM) based turbulence profile parameters are fed in simultaneously into the second stage FNN which acts as a discriminator that estimates
the true relational turbulence profile values based on first-stage FNN generative
predictions and RTM model outputs. The FNN is capable of dynamically scaling depth according to representational complexity of relational data contained
within short tweet messages [9]. The fractal recursively evolves its architecture
based on feedback ground truth parameters extracted from the second stage
discriminator FNN.

The dataset chosen for this demo, is streamed live from twitter. It is de-
anonymized to reveal the following relational features in the tweet posts: the
Category confidence, Entity salience, Entity sentiment, Mentions sentiment and
Context sentiment. The Stanford Twitter Sentiment Corpus contains APIs
(http://help.sentiment140.com/api) for classifying raw tweets that allows us to
integrate their classifiers into our deep learning model. Their plug-in module uses
an ensemble of different learning classifiers and feature extractors to deliver the
best outputs with different combinations. In addition to the sentiment results
obtained from their model, we cross validated the output against Google's NLP
API (https://cloud.google.com/natural-language/) to replicate the most accurate sentiment scores and magnitudes of context spaces and mentions. Our twitter dataset was live streamed from a twitter (firehose) API account and contains
a maximum of 1675882 actor / nodes, 851615 circles and 160799842 links.

From the RTM approach, we define Relational Intensity $P(\gamma_{rl})$, Relational Interference $P(\vartheta_{rl})$ and Relational Uncertainty $P(\varphi_{rl})$ to be three key probabilistic outputs of the RFT model which represents the relational turbulence $P_{\tau_{rl}}$ of a given link in an OSN. The key element types we have identified to be contributing features between the duration of the turning point and relationship development (as an unstable/turbulent process) are the Confidence ρ_{ij}, Salience ξ_{ij} and Sentiment λ_{ij} scores in an actor-actor relationship of a social transaction in question. It is noteworthy of mention that the ground truth reciprocities of these element types shared within a relational flux, violates expectancies - $E(\rho_{ij})$, $E(\xi_{ij})$ and $E(\lambda_{ij})$, respectively [14]. These violations (however small), are a contributing factor to temporal representations of relational turbulence - γ_{rl}, ϑ_{rl} and φ_{rl}. Negative expectancy is defined as a polar mismatch between expected reciprocates against actual reciprocates (e.g. Actor i expecting a somewhat positive reciprocation of an egress sentiment stream, but instead, received a negative ingress sentiment stream from actor j). Positive expectancy is defined as the strong cosine similar vector alignment between these reciprocates. Both expectancy violation (EV) extremes however, are characterized by sharp gradient changes of their weighted feature scores. This is given mathematically as:

$$\frac{\partial E_{rl}}{\partial \tau_{rl}} = \sum_{i,j=1}^{n} \prod_{\eta=\rho,\xi,\lambda} \frac{E(\eta_{ji})}{\partial \eta_{ji}} \times \frac{\partial \eta_{ij}}{\partial \tau_{ij}} \tag{1}$$

Where τ_{ij} is also known as the relational turbulence between node i and its surrounding neighbors j.

Relational change or transition - also known as a turning point, defines some state-based critical threshold, beyond which relational turbulence and negative communication is irrevocable [8]. This critical threshold is specific to actor-actor relationships and learned through our model as a conflict escalation minimization function [13]. Conflict escalation is defined as the gradual increase in negative flux $\frac{-\nabla F_{\epsilon}}{\nabla t}$ over time within a classified context area $L_{F_{\epsilon}}$ of interest [13]. The critical threshold parameter is then driven mathematically as:

$$T_{\epsilon} = inf_{t \to \infty} \begin{cases} \frac{1}{2m}(-\frac{\nabla F_{\epsilon}}{\nabla t} \times \log_2(\frac{\nabla F_{\epsilon}}{\nabla L_{F_{\epsilon}}})) & \forall |\frac{\partial E_{rl}}{\partial \tau_{rl}}| > 1 \\ \log_2(|1 - \frac{\nabla F_{\epsilon}}{\nabla L_{F_{\epsilon}}}|) & \forall |\frac{\partial E_{rl}}{\partial \tau_{rl}}| < 1 \end{cases} \tag{2}$$

Where T_{ϵ} is the threshold of interest and m is the total number of training data over the time window t. The equation states simply that the relational transition threshold decreases drastically for strong EVs and gradually for weak EVs.

Our model addresses the prediction problem of relational turbulence by adopting a hybrid (turing-learning based) Fractal Neural Network (FNN) architecture. At the core of the RFT architecture is a stack of Restricted Boltzmann Machines (RBM) which constitutes the essence of a Deep Belief Network (DBN) that pretrains our Deep Neural Network (DNN) structural framework. In our architecture, the generative DBN is used to initialize the DNN weights and the fine-tuning from the backprop is carried out sequentially layer by layer. In order

Table 1. Table of K-fold cross validated MAPE for all three learning models

K	δ_{MAPE} - (SLP)	δ_{MAPE} - (DCN)	δ_{MAPE} - (RFT)
20	0.461	0.189	0.127
30	0.424	0.175	0.131
50	0.420	0.173	0.112
80	0.418	0.169	0.110
100	0.421	0.166	0.107

to tackle the problem of computational efficiency and learning scalability to large data sets, we have adopted the DSN model framework for our study. Central to the concept of such an architecture is the relational use of stacking to learn complex distributions from simple core belief modules, functions and classifiers [4].

3   Preliminary Simulation

Early simulations were conducted on the processed twitter data stream and the contributing feature inputs were tested across three deep architecture models. In addition, the different deep learning approaches were also cross validated using k-fold cross validation techniques. The tests were run across the Single Layer Perceptron (SLP), a 45-layer Deep Convolutional Network (DCN) and a dynamically stacked Fractal Neural Network (FNN). A typical simulation result is summarized and shown in Table 1.

K-fold cross validation is used in our simulation benchmark design to obtain a good estimate of the prediction generalization. It was performed over all deep learning models across the Mean Absolute Percentage Error (MAPE) measurement of each run. Mathematically, MAPE can be expressed as:

$$\delta_{MAPE} = \frac{1}{N} \sum_{i=1}^{N} |\frac{E_i(x) - Y_i(t)}{E_i(x)}| \qquad (3)$$

Where $E_i(x)$ is the expectation at the output of data input set i and $Y_i(t)$ is the corresponding prediction over N total subsamples. As can be seen from Table 1, the RFT model consistently outperforms the SLP model by an average of 72.628% and the DCN model by an average of 32.73% δ_{MAPE}.

4   Human Computer Interaction

SLIND$^+$ extends the original SLIND software platform [17] and was developed to include artificial learning methodologies and the RTM model with extensive human interaction in mind. The software system we have developed runs on a Java engine coded from Netbeans IDE version 8.0.2. The interactive features are displayed in run-time on an 64-bit Intel(R) Core(TM) i7-4710MQ CPU @ 2.50 GHz, 8.00 GB RAM stand-alone machine. In the following subsections, we explore on the major interactive strategies developed in SLIND$^+$.

4.1   Interactions in Adversarial Feature Data Selection

SLIND$^+$ adds important major user interaction control categorizations that enable the seamless modeling and manipulation of data. These major sections include the file operations section, the File section, the visual section, the graph section, the controls section, the model section, the tuning section, the univariate section and the multivariate section. Each of these sections intuitively define a specific use of control which the user can exercise their preferences over.

The Tuning category allows the user to set learning rate parameters to adjust the learning performance of the adversarial model. In addition, it allows the user to specify a sliding window that can be used as a sampling time frame from the data stream that feeds into the RTM model to estimate a model based turbulence profile. In addition, the user is also able to adjust the error tolerance, outlier threshold, valid data range, scaling, vanishing gradient/exploding gradient stochastic decent thresholds, number of layers (upper limit), trust region radius and regularization parameter.

The model category gives the user even more control over the model and provides the user with a wide selection of activation functions that changes the adversarial behavior of the Artificial Neural Network (ANN), improving its capability of adapting to the user application in question. Among the activations covered are the sigmoid, ReLU, Leaky ReLu, Gaussian ReLu, Parametric ReLu, ELU, SoftPlus, Step, sign, tanh and spiking. Switching to spiking activations transforms the ANN into a Spiking Neural Network (SNN) that is able to more efficiently encode deep layered representations of relational information from temporal localities of the cumulative neuron spikes. Features like spiking frequency, mean time to spike, mean time between spikes, spiking signal energy, etc. all become important predicates to representing key relational features of interest. Thus, instead of neuron outputs from a vast array of relational feature inputs, the turbulence profile of relationships within an OSN can be interpreted through these spiking characteristics as: $Fluxintensity \rightarrow spikingsignalenergy$, $Mentioninterferences \rightarrow spikingfrequency$, and $Contextuncertainty \rightarrow meantimebetweenspikes$. In addition, the user is able to adjust the standard deviation and hyper parameter of these activation functions. Furthermore, this section also provides the user with a wide array of starting baseline ANN models to choose from when morphing a fractal structure as the neural network begins learning from continuous OSN data streams. Many of the popular baseline architectures are covered in this categoty and they include: SLP, CRF, DAE, RBM, SPN, RFT, MLP, DBN, HMM, RNN, CNN and DSN. These DNN fractal structures cover generative, discriminative and hybrid architectures.

The controls category allows the user to archive learning metadata into a file for external processing at a later phase. It also provides the user with several key options which enable specific logging functions to be performed on the learning data. These include the convergence, verbose, profile, generate, bias, learn and test.

4.2 Interactions in Data Presentation

There are two presentation modes supported by SLIND$^+$ to display the flux turbulence results, namely the snapshot mode and the timeline mode. In the snapshot mode, the link flux turbulence results are presented at a fixed time frame, while the timeline mode supports the continuous real-time presentation of all the results. The GA-FNN turing learning model can also be toggled to display the evolution of the relational turbulence profile of the graph. Additionally, SLIND$^+$ is able to transform between views for better visualization. Furthermore, users are able to generate plots, run real-time analysis simulations, define labels for links of interest and fill in the markers of detected outliers.

5 Demonstration Plan

The demonstration plan for SLIND$^+$ will consist of the following four major parts. First, we describe to the audience the limitations of the existing relational methods and the main motivations behind using an adversarial FNN model with RTM to identify the relational turbulence profiles in socio-network links. Second, we will showcase the system architecture of SLIND$^+$. Emphasis will be placed on introducing key components of SLIND$^+$, their roles and how they communicate with each other in the software layers of the recursively evolving analysis process. Third, a demonstration on the interactive interfaces developed on SLIND$^+$ will be given. Fourth, a recorded demo of SLIND$^+$ will be played to the audience. Audience interaction with the software platform is encouraged at this stage. Off-site assistance will also be available upon request.

Acknowledgment. This research is partially supported by the National Science Foundation of China (No. 61972438), Capacity Building Project for Young University Staff in Guangxi Province, Department of Education, Guangxi Province (No. ky2016YB149).

References

1. Backstrom, L., Leskovec, J.: Link prediction in social networks using computationally efficient topological features. In: 2011 IEEE Third International Conference on Privacy, Security, Risk and Trust (PASSAT) and 2011 IEEE Third Inernational Conference on Social Computing (SocialCom), pp. 73–80. IEEE (2011)
2. Choi, E., et al.: Multi-layer representation learning for medical concepts. In: Proceedings of the 22nd ACM SIGKDD International Conference on Knowledge Discovery and Data Mining, pp. 1495–1504. ACM (2016)
3. Cordeiro, M., Gama, J.: Online social networks event detection: a survey. In: Michaelis, S., Piatkowski, N., Stolpe, M. (eds.) Solving Large Scale Learning Tasks. Challenges and Algorithms. LNCS (LNAI), vol. 9580, pp. 1–41. Springer, Cham (2016). https://doi.org/10.1007/978-3-319-41706-6_1
4. Deng, L., Yu, D., et al.: Deep learning: methods and applications. Found. Trends® Signal Process. **7**(3–4), 197–387 (2014)

5. Ding, Y., Liu, C., Zhao, P., Hoi, S.C.H.: Large scale kernel methods for online AUC maximization. In: 2017 IEEE International Conference on Data Mining (ICDM), pp. 91–100 (2017)
6. Domingos, P.: Mining social networks for viral marketing. IEEE Intell. Syst. **20**(1), 80–82 (2005)
7. Jin, F., Wang, W., Chakraborty, P., Self, N., Chen, F., Ramakrishnan, N.: Tracking multiple social media for stock market event prediction. Advances in Data Mining. Applications and Theoretical Aspects. LNCS (LNAI), vol. 10357, pp. 16–30. Springer, Cham (2017). https://doi.org/10.1007/978-3-319-62701-4_2
8. Knobloch, L.K., Theiss, J.A.: Relational turbulence theory applied to the transition from deployment to reintegration. J. Family Theory Rev. **10**(3), 535–549 (2018)
9. Larsson, G., Maire, M., Shakhnarovich, G.: FractalNet: ultra-deep neural networks without residuals. arXiv preprint arXiv:1605.07648 (2016)
10. Li, X., Lou, C., Zhao, J., Wei, H., Zhao, H.: "Tom" pet robot applied to urban autism. arXiv preprint arXiv:1905.05652 (2019)
11. Lieberman, E., Hauert, C., Nowak, M.A.: Evolutionary dynamics on graphs. Nature **433**(7023), 312 (2005)
12. Lu, S., Wei, Z., Li, L.: A trust region algorithm with adaptive cubic regularization methods for nonsmooth convex minimization. Computat. Optim. Appl. **51**, 551–573 (2012). https://doi.org/10.1007/s10589-010-9363-1
13. Simeonova, L.: Gradient emotional analysis (2017)
14. Solomon, D.H., Knobloch, L.K., Theiss, J.A., McLaren, R.M.: Relational turbulence theory: explaining variation in subjective experiences and communication within romantic relationships. Hum. Commun. Res. **42**(4), 507–532 (2016)
15. Theiss, J.A., Solomon, D.H.: A relational turbulence model of communication about irritations in romantic relationships. Commun. Res. **33**(5), 391–418 (2006). https://doi.org/10.1177/0093650206291482
16. Wang, P., Xu, B., Wu, Y., Zhou, X.: Link prediction in social networks: the state-of-the-art. Sci. China Inform. Sci. **58**(1), 1–38 (2015)
17. Zhang, J., Tan, L., Tao, X., Zheng, X., Luo, Y., Lin, J.C.-W.: SLIND: identifying stable links in online social networks. In: Pei, J., Manolopoulos, Y., Sadiq, S., Li, J. (eds.) DASFAA 2018. LNCS, vol. 10828, pp. 813–816. Springer, Cham (2018). https://doi.org/10.1007/978-3-319-91458-9_54

The International Workshop on Web Information Systems in the Era of AI

Efficient Privacy-Preserving Skyline Queries over Outsourced Cloud

Lu Li[1,2], Xufeng Jiang[1,4], Fei Zhu[3], and An Liu[3(✉)]

[1] School of Information Engineering, Yancheng Teachers University, Yancheng, China
[2] Suzhou Research Institute, University of Science and Technology of China, Suzhou, China
[3] School of Computer Science, Soochow University, Suzhou, China
anliu@suda.edu.cn
[4] Nanjing Tech University, Nanjing, China

Abstract. In the cloud computing paradigm, data owners could outsource their databases to the service provider, and thus reap huge benefits from releasing the heavy storage and management tasks to the cloud server. However, sensitive data, such as medical or financial records, should be encrypted before uploading to the cloud server. Unfortunately, this will introduce new challenges to data utilization. In this paper, we study the problem of skyline queries in a way that data privacy for both data owner and the client is preserved. We propose a hybrid protocol via additively homomorphic encryption system and Yao's garbled circuits. By taking advantages of Yao's protocol, we design a highly improved protocol which can be used to determine the skyline point and exclude the points dominated by others in an oblivious way. Based on this subroutine, we construct a fully secure protocol for skyline queries. We theoretically prove that the protocols are secure in the semi-honest model. Through analysis and extensive experiments, we demonstrate the efficiency and scalability of our proposed solutions.

Keywords: Privacy-preserving · Skyline queries · Cloud computing · Yao's garbled circuits

1 Introduction

Outsourcing databases to clouds is a cost-effective way for larger scale data storage and management. In the cloud computing paradigm, data owners could outsource their databases to the service provider, and thus reap huge benefits from releasing the heavy storage and management tasks to the cloud server. However, outsourcing the original data directly to the untrusted server provider will cause significant privacy leakage risk. A common solution to prevent the security of sensitive data is to encrypt it before outsourcing. The framework typically consists of three entities, data owner, cloud service provider and users. In the setting of the secure query, data owner publishes an encrypted version

© Springer Nature Singapore Pte Ltd. 2020
L. H. U et al. (Eds.): WISE 2019, CCIS 1155, pp. 83–97, 2020.
https://doi.org/10.1007/978-981-15-3281-8_9

of the original data to the cloud service provider, and the authorized users also submit encrypted query information to the cloud. During the query process, the cloud server should never gain any sensitive information about the query and the original data, whereas the authorized users should only obtain the query result.

For the reason that the ciphertext information is typically computationally indistinguishable with random numbers selected from the same domain, and to ensure the security of sensitive data, the private key should never be revealed to unauthorized community or users, query evaluation on the encrypted data is indeed a very challenging issue. Recently, various solutions have been proposed for different queries over encrypted data, including kNN queries [3–6,11], range queries [7,8] and aggregate queries [9,10]. As an important multi-critical decision query means, the skyline or *Pareto* query is typically used for selecting similar records in the situation that a single similarity metric with all dimensions is hard to define. Moreover, retrieving similar records according to an arbitrary combined attribute set has independent significance.

It is therefore desirable to have efficient protocols to conduct secure skyline queries over encrypted data in the cloud. As mentioned in [2], however, this task is non-trivial. One of the difficulty in technology is to obliviously select a skyline point and eliminate the points that are dominated by the selected skyline point. This will inevitably involve a huge amount of elemental operations in a privacy-preserving way, and require carefully designed to integrate these operations to avoid information leakage. The nature of secure skyline query makes it different from the extensively studied secure queries problems above, and result in the solutions in these studies cannot be applied to the secure skyline query processing.

In a recent piece of work [2], the authors proposed the first fully secure skyline query protocol based purely on additively homomorphic encryption system. This work adopted Paillier encryption system to design secure elemental operations in a secure way, and proposed a secure dominance protocol based on the elemental operations to support obliviously elimination. Although the solution is secure in the presence of semi-honest adversaries, it involves a huge number of public-key style operations, which is prohibitively time-consuming. It turns out that the solution in [2] is not suitable to deal with a large scale database (Fig. 1).

Fig. 1. Secure queries.

The above studies inspire us to design an more efficient privacy-preserving skyline query protocol for encrypted data. The main contributions of our work are as follows:

– We present a hybrid approach to privacy-preserving skyline queries that uses both homomorphic encryption and Yao's garbled circuits. To avoid the huge cost of constructing an entire garbled circuit, we design protocols that invoke small scale garbled circuits as subroutines. By carefully designing, our protocol yields great improvements in computational time compared with existing works.
– By taking advantages of Yao's protocol, we design a highly improved protocol which can be used to determine the skyline point and eliminate the points dominated by others in an oblivious way. This protocol can also be served as key building blocks for the problem of secure kNN query.
– We theoretically prove that our protocol is secure under the semi-honest model. Besides theoretical analysis, we implement a complete privacy-preserving skyline query system on top of FastGC. We extend FastGC with a library that supports minimum value and index search and other necessary arithmetic operations. We also conduct experiments to confirm the performance of our protocols in practice.

The rest of the paper is organized as follows. Section 2 presents the problem statement and Sect. 3 introduces background knowledge. Section 4 presents the protocols for secure skyline query. We analyze the security of the proposed protocols in Sect. 5, and report the experimental results in Sect. 6. Finally, Sect. 7 discusses some related work and Sect. 8 concludes the paper.

2 Problem Statement

2.1 Skyline Computation

Definition 1: (Skyline Query) [12] Given a dataset $\mathbf{P} = \{\mathbf{p}_1, ..., \mathbf{p}_n\}$ and a query q in m-dimensional space. The skyline points in dataset $\mathbf{P}$ with respect to query $\mathbf{q}$ are those points that not dominated by any other point in $\mathbf{P}$. Let $\mathbf{p}_\alpha$ and $\mathbf{p}_\beta$ be two different points in $\mathbf{P}$, we say $\mathbf{p}_\alpha$ dominate $\mathbf{p}_\beta$ with respect to $\mathbf{q}$, denoted by $\mathbf{p}_\alpha \prec p_\beta$, if for all i, $|\mathbf{p}_\alpha[j] - \mathbf{q}[j]| \leq |\mathbf{p}_\beta[j] - \mathbf{q}[j]|$ and for at least one j, $|\mathbf{p}_\alpha[j] - \mathbf{q}[j]| < |\mathbf{p}_\beta[j] - \mathbf{q}[j]|$, where $p_i[j]$ is the jth dimension of $\mathbf{p}_i$, $j = 1, .., m$ and $|x|$ denotes the absolute value of x.

Skyline computation has been extensively studied in the literature [12–14]. For the underlying skyline query algorithm we could have used the efficient divide-and-conquer algorithm [24]; however, this would have required huge additional cost to prevent the intermediate sensitive information during the computation process. Instead, we use the iterative skyline computation algorithm (also used by Liu *et al.*). The general idea of the iterative skyline computation algorithm is to first map the point in dataset P to a new dataset T according with query point q as origin. For example, point $\mathbf{p}_i = \{p_i[1], ..., p_i[m]\}$ will be mapped to $\mathbf{t}_i = \{|p_i[1] - q[1]|, ..., |p_i[m] - q[m]|\}$. Next, it computes the sum $S(t_i)$ of all attributes for each point t_i, and chooses $\mathbf{p}_{min}$ as a skyline point and $\mathbf{t}_{min}$ with smallest $S(t_i)$. It then deletes the tuples dominated by $\mathbf{t}_{min}$. This process is repeated until $\mathbf{T}$ is empty.

2.2 Privacy-Preserving Skyline Queries

Following [2,11], we assume the existence of two non-colluding clouds, C1 and C2. As shown in Fig. 2, the data owner has a database P. To prevent sensitive information leakage, she encrypts each record in P by a public-key cryptosystem under the public key of C2 and outsources the encrypted dataset E(P) to the C1. A client wants to query the skyline points in P to her query q. As q is sensitive information of the client, it is also encrypted by the user before submitted to the C1. Our goal is to construct efficient protocols to enable the client to only obtain the correct answers and keep the clouds from learning any information about the database P and the query q. For technical reasons, we relax the security requirements to admit the cloud to know the number of the query result. Note that this information can be preserved straightforwardly by letting the clouds return a slightly large constant number of points. In the rest of this paper, we will present an efficient solution for this challenging problem.

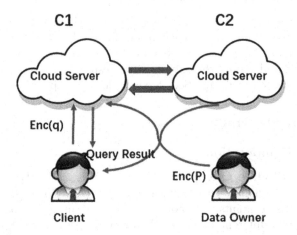

Fig. 2. Secure skyline query framework.

2.3 Security Model

In this paper, we adopt *ideal/real simulation paradigm*, which is a standard security formulation in the area of secure multi-party computation [15,16]. In this formulation, a real protocol execution in a *real world* is mapped to an ideal protocol realization in an *ideal world*. In the ideal world, there exists an external trusted (and incorruptible) party who is willing to help all parties carry out their computation. Consequently, the ideal protocol realization can be implemented as follows: all parties simply send their inputs over perfectly private channels to the trusted party, which then computes the desired function and passes each party its prescribed output. In the real world, however, there is no external party that can be trusted by all parties, so they can only run some protocol amongst themselves without any help. A protocol is said to be *secure* if no adversary can do more harm in a real protocol execution than in an ideal protocol realization. However, successful adversarial attacks cannot be carried out in the ideal protocol realization due to the existence of external trusted party and perfectly private channels. Therefore, we can conclude that all adversarial attacks on the real protocol execution must also fail as long as the protocol is secure.

3 Preliminary

3.1 Yao's Garbled Circtuis

Yao's protocol [16,18] (a.k.a garbled circuits) allows two semi-honest parties respectively holding inputs x and y, to evaluate an arbitrary function $f(x, y)$ without leaking any information about their inputs beyond what can be deduced by the function output. The basic idea is that one party (the garbled-circuit *constructor*) constructs a garbled version of a boolean circuit to compute f, while the other party (the garbled-circuit *evaluator*) then obliviously computes the output of the circuit without learning any intermediate values.

The protocol starts with a boolean circuit evaluating f. To each wire w_i of the circuit, the constructor associates two random cryptographic keys $k_{w_i}^0$ and $k_{w_i}^1$, which are respectively corresponded to the bit-values $b_i = 0$ and $b_i = 1$. For each binary gate g, with input wires (w_i, w_j) and output wire w_k, the constructor first computes four values

$$\varepsilon_{(k_{w_i}^{b_i}, k_{w_j}^{b_j})} k_{w_k}^{g(b_i, b_j)}, b_i, b_j \in \{0, 1\},$$

which in random orders, constitute a *garbled gate*, and then sends it to the evaluator party. Given the pair of keys corresponding to input wires of a binary gate, the evaluator can recover the key of the output wire by decrypting the values. It is worth noting that only the value $k_{w_k}^{g(b_i, b_j)}$ can be obtained, and that no other output values can be recovered for the corresponding gate. Thus, given one key for each input wire of the circuit, the evaluator can securely evaluate all gates in the circuit in topological order to compute one key for each output wire of the circuit.

For a given function $f(x, y)$, the parties first compile it to a boolean circuit. Then, the constructor garbles the circuit by providing each gate four ciphertexts. These values are then send to the evaluator. The only problem is how the evaluator obtains the corresponding keys to each input wire of the circuit. The real inputs are holding by two parties independently. To the values holding by the constructor, she can directly send the appropriate keys to the evaluator. To the values holding by the evaluator, a cryptology tool called *1-out-of-2* oblivious transfer [19,20] can be used to enable the evaluator to obtain the desired keys without leaking her private information. Once obtaining the keys corresponding to all the input wires, the evaluator can locally compute the garbled circuit gate-by-gate. When the keys corresponding to final output are obtained, the evaluator send them to the constructor, who can subsequently resolve the true bit-values. This protocol also enables the evaluator to first obtain the final output by simply modifying the output values using the real bit-values.

At present, Yao's garbled circuits is a very efficient cryptology tools to construct secure protocols. Using Yao's garbled circuits to deal with non-linear operations is much more efficient than using additively homomorphic encryption scheme like Paillier [1]. So, in this paper, we adopt the garbled circuits to conduct the non-linear operations. In this paper, we implement Yao's garbled circuit based on FastGC [17], which is a Java-based open-source framework that enables developers to compute arbitrary circuits using elementary *XOR*, *OR* and *AND* gates and integrate all modules above.

3.2   Paillier Encryption

The encryption function ε is defined as

$$E_{pk}(m, r) = (1 + N)^m \times r^N \quad \mod N^2$$

where $m \in \mathbb{Z}_N$ is a message for encryption, N is a product of two large prime numbers p and q, g generates a subgroup of order N, and r is a random number in $\mathbb{Z}_N^*$. The public key for encryption is (N, g) and the private key for decryption is (p, q). The detail of decryption function D with private key sk can be found in [1]. The properties of the Paillier cryptosystem include homomorphic addition, which means it satisfying

$$D_{sk}(E_{pk}(m_1) * E_{pk}(m_2)) = m_1 + m_2 \quad \mod N$$

where $m_1, m_2 \in \mathbb{Z}_N$.

3.3   Oblivious Transfer

An oblivious transfer protocol [19, 20] allows a receiver to choose one of a possible set of values of a receiver; the receiver selects and learns only one of the values, and the sender does not learn which value the receiver selected. As an important component of Yao's protocol, 1-out-of-2 oblivious transfer protocol, denoted OT_1^2, allows a sender holding strings k_0 and k_1 to interact with a receiver, who holds a selection bit $\delta \in \{0, 1\}$, so the receiver learns b_δ while neither the sender nor receiver learn anything else.

4   Approach

We consider the problem of privacy-preserving skyline queries under the semi-honest adversary model. As shown in Fig. 2, the data owner possesses a database P, encrypts it by the public key provided by cloud C2, and outsources the encrypted database E(P) to C1. To answer the user's query which is also

Table 1. Summary of notations

P	Dataset of n points
$p_i[j]$	The jth attribute of p_i
n	Number of points in P
m	Number of dimensions
k	Number of skyline
l	Number of bits
$\tilde{t}$	Encoded values of t in Yao's circuits
σ	Statistical security parameter
maxt	$2^{ml} - 1$
s_i	$t_i[1] + ... + t_i[m]$
S	$(s_1, ..., s_n)$

encrypted by the public key of C2, C1 and C2 run some secure protocols cooperatively to share the result in exclusive-or secret sharing manner. Finally, they send the shares to the user, who can then straightforwardly obtain the final result. Table 1 shows some notations and symbols that are used extensively in this paper.

4.1 Method Overview

To describe our secure protocols, we first review the underlining iterative skyline computation algorithm, which is shown in Algorithm 1. The general of the iterative skyline computation algorithm is to first map the point in dataset P to a new dataset T according to query point q as the origin. For example, point $\mathbf{p}_i = \{p_i[1], ..., p_i[m]\}$ will be mapped to $\mathbf{t}_i = \{|p_i[1] - q[1]|, ..., |p_i[m] - q[m]|\}$. Next, it computes the sum $S(t_i)$ of all attributes for each point t_i, and chooses p_{min} as a skyline point and t_{min} with smallest $S(t_i)$. It then deletes the tuples dominated by t_{min}. This process is repeated until **T** is empty. Note that although the process for computing the skyline is simple when the dataset is in the clear, it is challenging to devise a corresponding protocol to deal with it securely. The main reason is that the service provider C1 and C2 are not only forbidden to see any useful information about the original data but also cannot get any decision information about which branch will be selected for the next step computation. For example, lines 11 and 12 of Algorithm 1 require the clouds know which row is corresponded to the minimum record, but due to the security consideration, this information should be preserved from the clouds.

A common approach to deal with this kind of problem is first to compute all of the branches and then design secure protocol to select the correct operation numbers(for the further step computation) in an oblivious way. In this paper, we follow this methodology but provide an efficient protocol to reduce the computation cost substantially. Algorithm 2 shows the high-level secure skyline query

---

Algorithm 1. Skyline Computation.

Input: A dataset P and a query q.
Output: Skyline of P with respect to q
 1: **for** $i = 1$ to n **do**
 2:     **for** $j = 1$ to m **do**
 3:         $t_i[j] = |p_i[j] - q[j]|$
 4:     **end for**
 5: **end for**
 6: **while** the dataset T is not empty **do**
 7:     **for** $i = 1$ to size of dataset T **do**
 8:         compute $s_i = \sum_{j=1}^{m} t_i[j]$;
 9:         choose the smallest s_i;
10:         set $min = i$;
11:         add p_{min} to the skyline pool;
12:         delete t_{min} and the tuples dominated by t_{min} for T;
13:     **end for**
14: **end while**
15: **return** skyline pool;

---

protocol. At the very beginning phase, the two servers engage in a secure protocol to convert the encrypted dataset T into an additively secret sharing manner. This phase can be done by letting C1 add masks to the encrypted elements and takes the masks as her shares $P^{(1)}$ and $q^{(1)}$. C1 can perform this process locally, due to the homomorphic property of Paillier encryption system. After that, C1 sends the masked elements to C2, who then decrypts the values to obtain her shares $P^{(2)}$ and $q_{(2)}$, such that $P = P^{(1)} + P^{(2)}, q = q^{(1)} + q^{(2)}$, where the '+' represents matrix add and vector add respectively. Note that this phase can be efficiently done using packing technologies to substantially reduce the computation and communication costs. The rest of our protocol is mainly based on Yao's garbled circuits. We will present detailed solutions in subsequent subsections. Now we itemize the functionalities of some important basic circuits:

- **ST:** This circuit takes as input two l-bit values $\tilde{x}$, $\tilde{y}$ ($\tilde{a}$ denoted the encoded values of a in Yao's garbled circuits), and a extra bit σ, and outputs a bit $\tilde{\delta}$, such that: if $x + \sigma < y$, $\delta = 1$; otherwise, $\delta = 0$. Clearly, σ can be used to control the ST circuit to return the output $x < y$ or $x \leq y$.
- **MUX:** The MUX circuit takes as input two l-bit values $\tilde{x}$, $\tilde{y}$, and an extra bit $\tilde{\sigma}$, and outputs a l-bit values $\tilde{z}$, such that: if $\sigma = 0$, $z = x$; otherwise, $z = y$. In our framework, we also need a modified version of MUX, where one of the values $\tilde{x}$, $\tilde{y}$ will replaced by a value in the clear. For example, we will invoke the MUX circuit using input $\tilde{x}$, 1^l. It is worth noting that knowing $\tilde{z}$ does not means the evaluator has the knowledge of which value she has obtained, even through one of the input values is in the clear. The functionality of MUX is indeed oblivious selection, which is a very useful tool in secure computation.
- **EQ:** The EQ circuit takes as input two l-bit values $\tilde{x}$, $\tilde{y}$, and outputs a bit $\tilde{\delta}$, such that: if $x == y$, $\delta = 1$; otherwise, $\delta = 0$. We will sometimes invoke the

EQ circuit analogously to the MUX circuit, with one of the input is the clear value. Moreover, we also need the circuit output the clear value at times. This means that we need the output δ, not $\tilde{\delta}$.

- **MIN:** The MIN circuit takes as input two $s+l$-bit values $\tilde{i}||\tilde{x}$, $\tilde{j}||\tilde{y}$, where the s represents the bit length of i(which represents the index), and l the bit length of x(which represents value), and outputs an $(s+l)$-bit value $\tilde{k}||\tilde{z}$, such that: $k = i, z = x$, if $(x \le y)$; $k = j, z = y$, otherwise. This circuit can be flexibly controlled to output the index or the value only.
- **ADD:** The ADD circuit takes as input two l-bit values $\tilde{x}$, $\tilde{y}$, and outputs a $l+1$-bit values $\tilde{z}$, such that: $z = x + y$.
- **ABSSUB:** The ABSSUB circuit takes as input two l-bit values $\tilde{x}$, $\tilde{y}$, and outputs a l-bit values $\tilde{z}$, such that: if $z = |x - y|$.

The simple circuit library provided by FastGC also contains elemental circuits, such as *and*, *or* and *xor*, etc. It is straightforward to understand the functionalities of these operations, so we omit here due to space limitation. It is worth noting that the modules of the garbled circuits can be composed to perform more complex tasks. For examples, two clouds can invoke n-1 ADD circuits to evaluate the sum of n numbers in an oblivious way. We use the symbol nADD to denote the corresponding composite circuit.

Algorithm 2. Secure skyline query (high-level).

Input: C1: $E(P), E(q), pk$ C2: (pk, sk)
Output: client: Skyline of P with respect to q
 1: convert the encrypted dataset into an additively secret sharing manner;
 2: compute $\tilde{T}$;
 3: set $flag = 0$;
 4: **while** $flag == 0$ **do**
 5:    **for** $i = 1$ to n **do**
 6:       compute $\tilde{s_i}$, where $s_i = t_i[1] + ... + t_i[m]$;
 7:    **end for**
 8:    choose the minimum sequence $\widetilde{p_{min}}||\widetilde{t_{min}}$ with respect to $s_i, i = 1, ..., n$;
 9:    add $\widetilde{p_{min}}$ to the skyline pool;
10:    set $flag = (t_{min} == maxt)?1 : 0$;
11:    update $\tilde{T}$ using $\widetilde{t_{min}}$;
12: **end while**
13: send the results to the client;

4.2 Privacy-Preserving Skyline Query

Upon receiving the random shares of **P** and **q**, two clouds leverage Yao's protocol to perform the secure query. We let C1 act as the *constructor* and C2 the *evaluator*. C1 and initialize an ADD circuit, and then invoke an OT protocol to enable C2 get the tokens of $P^{(1)}, P^{(2)}, q^{(1)}, q^{(2)}$, namely, $\widetilde{P^{(1)}}, \widetilde{P^{(2)}}, \widetilde{q^{(1)}}, \widetilde{q^{(2)}}$.

Then, they cooperatively execute Yao's protocol on the ADD circuit. After that, C2 obtains the values $\widetilde{P}$ and $\widetilde{q}$. Meanwhile, C1 holds the map table, which can be used to efficiently get the corresponding values in the clear. The values $\widetilde{T}$ and $\widetilde{S}$ can also be obtained by C2 by executing Yao's protocol on ABSSUB and ADD circuits with C1. As mentioned above, the difficult part of performing skyline queries securely is how to choose the skyline and eliminate the points in the dataset which are dominated by the selected point in an oblivious way. In the following, we will present our solutions to these problems one by one, which together forms the foundation of our privacy-preserving skyline queries protocol.

We dub the problem oblivious selection. The protocol is shown in Algorithm 3. To perform the minimum number selection in an oblivious way, we first let C2 bind the elements of each row. For example, considering the i-th row, the binding result will be $\widetilde{p_i}||\widetilde{t_i}||\widetilde{s_i}$. Then, they use a composite MIN circuit to let C2 obtain the encoding information of the first two parts of the tuple(that is $\widetilde{p_{min}}||\widetilde{t_{min}}$) which has the minimum s_i. Note that this information does not help C2 to know which tuple has the minimum s_i, because the encoding information has been updated using fresh randomness. Although this encoding data contains no sensitive information about the original data, it can be used for the next step computation. In the following, we show how to use this intermediate information to conduct efficient elimination. First, we make use of $\widetilde{t_{min}}$ to determine whether the selected $\widetilde{p_{min}}$ is a skyline point. We do this by testing whether t_{min} equals 1^{ml}, which means that the tuple of this row had been eliminated. The testing result in the clear will be published to the servers, which can also be used to identify whether all the skyline points have been found. Next, we show how to take advantage of $\widetilde{t_{min}}$ to delete the points dominated by the just selected skyline. According to the definition of skyline, $\mathbf{p}_\alpha$ dominates $\mathbf{p}_\beta$ iff for all i, $t_\alpha \le t_\beta$ and for at least one j, $t_\alpha < t_\beta$, we first compute the former expression and then perform equality determination about t_α and t_β. It is clear that if the first result is 1 and the second result is 0, then this tuple is dominated by $\widetilde{p_{min}}$, and should be deleted. We observe that we can simply set the t_i part to all 1s. This process can be done by setting lm 1s in the clear as the other part of the input to MUX circuit. In this way, this tuple will never be selected as skyline in future query process. It is worth noting that $\widetilde{p_{min}}$ should also be eliminated for the next step query. A natural idea is to use the result from the equality determination to serve as the *flag* bit, and then leverage MUX circuit to obliviously resetting the tuple. This method is correct in some cases, however, it is not valid in the case that there are multiple tuples that equal to t_{min} . For this case, only the first tuple (which is indeed t_{min}) should be deleted. So, we adopt a method that works by setting another *flag* bit to identify whether the current is the first tuple equal to t_{min}.

The remaining problem is how to let the client obtain the final result. Note that in current situation C2 holds the encoding information of all the skyline points and C1 holds the mapping table. Although they can directly send this information to the client, who can get the final result based on this information, it will cause unnecessary computation tasks to the client. To deal with this

Algorithm 3. Oblivious Selection.

Input: C1: *constructor* C2: *evaluator*,$\widetilde{P}$, $\widetilde{T}$
Output: C2: skyline pool ($\widetilde{ps_k}$)
1: $flag = 0, k = 0$;
2: **while** $flag == 0$ **do**
3:     $d = 1$;
4:     **for** $i = 1$ to n **do**
5:         $\widetilde{s_i} = \text{mADD}(\widetilde{t_i}[1], .., \widetilde{t_i}[m])$;
6:     **end for**
7:     $\widetilde{p_{min}}||\widetilde{t_{min}} = \text{nMIN}(\widetilde{p_1}||\widetilde{t_1}||\widetilde{s_1}, ..., \widetilde{p_n}||\widetilde{t_n}||\widetilde{s_n})$;
8:     $f = \text{EQ}(1^{lm}, \widetilde{t_{min}})$
9:     **if** f==1 **then**
10:        **break**;
11:    **end if**
12:    **for** $i = 1$ to n **do**
13:        **for** $j = 1$ to m **do**
14:            $\widetilde{r_j} = \text{ST}(\widetilde{t_{min}}[j], \widetilde{t_i}[j])$;
15:        **end for**
16:        $\widetilde{b} = \text{mAND}(\widetilde{r_1}, ..., \widetilde{r_m})$;
17:        $\widetilde{c} = \text{EQ}(\widetilde{t_{min}}, \widetilde{t_i})$;
18:        $\widetilde{r} = 3\text{AND}(\widetilde{b}, \widetilde{c}, \widetilde{d})$
19:        $\widetilde{\delta} = \text{OR}(\text{AND}(\widetilde{b}, !\widetilde{c}), \widetilde{r})$;
20:        $\widetilde{d} = \text{AND}(\widetilde{d}, !\widetilde{r})$;
21:        $\widetilde{t_i} = \text{MUX}(\widetilde{t_i}, 1^{lm}, \widetilde{\delta})$;
22:    **end for**
23:    k++;
24:    $\widetilde{ps_k} = \widetilde{p_{min}}$;
25: **end while**

problem, we let the clouds to execute an XOR circuit, where C1 takes as input a random sequence r and chooses the sequence as the share of the result, and C2 takes as input the encoding information of the skyline points. The mapping table of the result is then sent to C2, who can obtain the other part of shares. Then they take the shares as query results and return them to the client.

5 Theoretical Analysis

5.1 Computational Complexity

In the initial phase, C1 needs to do mn encryptions and multiplications for the ciphertext, and C2 need to do mn decryptions. The remaining cost in the protocol is to execute Yaos garbled circuits. Because the XOR gate is nearly free [21], the computation cost of Yao's protocol is typically determined by the number of non-XOR gates. We first present a detailed analysis of Algorithm 3. As the executing time of Algorithm 3 directly depends on the number of skyline points which is uncertain, we give a complete analysis for one-time execution.

The mADD circuit on l-bit (line 5) needs to be done n times, which leads to at most $(m+l)n$ non-XOR gates. The nMin circuit on $(2ml+l+m)$-bit (line 7) needs to be done once, where will cost at most $(2ml+l+m)n$ non-XOR gates. Lines 8 and 17 both require executing the EQ circuit of lm-bit once, which leads to at most $2lm$ non-XOR gates. Line 14 requires mn ST circuit on l-bit, which leads to mnl non-XOR gates. Line 16 costs mn non-free gate. Line 21 requires executing the MUX circuit of ml-bit n times, which leads to mnl non-XOR gates. The rest in Algorithm 3 only involves a constant number of non-XOR operations, thus can be ignored. Therefore, the main cost of Algorithm 3 is about $3mnl$ non-free gates. Supposing that the number of skyline points is k, then the total cost of Algorithm 3 is $3mnlk$. Besides, the protocol requires to execute mnADD circuit on l-bit, which leads to the total cost of the protocol $3mnlk + mnl$ non-free gate and mn public-key operations.

5.2   Security

Based on the security definition in the semi-honest model, we need to construct efficient simulators to simulate the intermediate information during the protocol execution. However, in our protocol, the intermediate information only contains garbled information which has been proved in [18] that this kind of information can be efficiently simulated, and random shares of sensitive data. Therefore, we only need to prove that this information can be efficiently generated from only the input and the output of the protocol. We do this by presenting a more general proof.

Theorem 1. *Suppose that A has run the key generation algorithm for a semantically secure homomorphic public-key encryption scheme, and has given her public-key to B. Further suppose that A and B run Protocol P, for which all messages passed from A to B are encrypted using this scheme, and all messages passed from B to A are uniformly distributed (in the range of the ciphertext) and are independent of Bs inputs. Then Protocol P is secure in the semi-honest adversary model.*

Proof. Two participants in P are asymmetric, therefore, we construct simulators in two distinct cases, which is subject to which party was corrupted.

Case 1: A is corrupted by an adversary. We construct a simulator S1 to simulate A's view. To do this, every time A receives message from B, S1 randomly picks a number from $\mathbb{Z}_N$ and encrypts it. Then, the simulation is perfect due to the fact that any PPT adversary cannot distinguish the simulators encryption of a random number from B's encryption of the correct computation that has been shifted by randomness of B's choice.

Case 2: B is corrupted by an adversary. We construct a simulator S2 to simulate the messages sent by A. For each encryption that A is supposed to send to B, we let the simulator S2 pick a random element from $\mathbb{Z}_N$, and send an encryption of this element. Any adversary who can distinguish between interaction with A verses interaction with S2 can be used to break the security assumptions. Thus, no such PPT adversary exists can distinguish them with a significant probability.

6   Performance Evaluation

In this section, we evaluate the performance of the proposed protocols. Our protocols are implemented on top of FastGC and tested on two computers (2 GHz CPU and 4 GB RAM) connected by a 100 Mbps LAN. The default experimental setting is as follows: the encryption key length in Paillier is 1024, the bit length l is 8. We evaluate our protocols by varying the number of tuples (n), the number of dimensions (m), and the number of skyline points (k) on datasets randomly generated depending on the parameters values in consideration. The main cost of the protocol is due to Yao's protocol.

Figure 3(a), (b) and (c) show the time cost of different m, n and k, respectively. We observe that the time cost increases approximately linearly with the number of tuples n, the number of dimensions m and the number of skyline points, respectively, which is consistent with our complexity analysis. As shown in Fig. 3(b), when m = 2, the cost of our protocol ranges from 29 to 387 seconds as n changes from 2000 to 10000, while the best previous protocol takes more than 1 h in all cases. Our work provides order-of-magnitude improvements in computation time than previous work.

(a) the impact of m   (b) the impact of n   (c) the impact of k

Fig. 3. Computation time cost (l = 8)

7   Related Work

As kNN queries are the most relevant to the skyline queries, so we first review some recent achievements on secure kNN computation. Wong et al. [3] develop an symmetric-scalar-product preserving (ASPE) encryption function that preserves scalar products between query point q and any point p_i for distance comparison (i.e., $p_i q = E(p_i)E(q)$ where E is an ASPE encryption function), based on which the kNN can be found directly. However, the solution cannot be used to support skyline queries. Hu et al. [4] devise a secure kNN protocol by adopting probably secure privacy homomorphism [22] which supports modular addition and multiplication over encrypted data. The weakness of privacy homomorphism (a.k.a. fully homomorphic encryption [23]), is its low efficiency which restricts its use mostly as a reference for theoretical interest. Yao et al. [5] propose a partition-based secure Voronoi diagram (SVD) method which returns a relevant partition E(G) that is guaranteed to contain the answer for the kNN query. As an improvement, Elmehdwi et al. [6] design a secure kNN protocol to return the exact answer. This protocol is built on a set of basic secure protocols including secure squared Euclidean distance (SSED), secure minimum (SMIN), secure bit-decomposition (SBD) and secure bit-or (SBOR), which are implemented using the Paillier cryptosystem. The most relevant work to ours is [2]. Although the solution is secure in the presence of semi-honest adversaries, it involves huge number of pubic-key style operations, which is prohibitively time-consuming.

8   Conclusions

In this paper, we studied the problem of secure skyline queries of encrypted dataset outsourced to the cloud. By taking advantages of Yao's protocol, we design a highly improved protocol which can be used to determine the skyline point and exclude the points dominated by others in an oblivious way. Based on this subroutine, we construct a fully secure protocol for skyline queries. We theoretically prove that the protocols are secure in the semi-honest model. Through analysis and extensive experiments, we have shown that our approach provides order-of-magnitude improvements than previous work.

Acknowledgment. This work was partially supported by Natural Science Foundation of China (Grant No. 61602400) and Jiangsu Provincial Department of Education (Grant No. 16KJB520043).

References

1. Paillier, P.: Public-key cryptosystems based on composite degree residuosity classes. In: Stern, J. (ed.) EUROCRYPT 1999. LNCS, vol. 1592, pp. 223–238. Springer, Heidelberg (1999). https://doi.org/10.1007/3-540-48910-X_16
2. Liu, J., Yang, J., Xiong, L., Pei, J.: Secure skyline queries on cloud platform. In: ICDE, pp. 633–644 (2017)
3. Wong, W.K., Cheung, D.W.-L., Kao, B., Mamoulis, N.: Secure kNN computation on encrypted databases. In: SIGMOD, pp. 139–152 (2009)
4. Hu, H., Xu, J., Ren, C., Choi, B.: Processing private queries over untrusted data cloud through privacy homomorphism. In: ICDE, pp. 601–612 (2011)
5. Yao, B., Li, F., Xiao, X.: Secure nearest neighbor revisited. In: ICDE, pp. 733–744 (2013)
6. Elmehdwi, Y., Samanthula, B.K., Jiang, W.: Secure k-nearest neighbor query over encrypted data in outsourced environment. In: ICDE, pp. 664–675 (2014)
7. Hore, B., Mehrotra, S., Canim, M., Kantarcioglu, M.: Secure multidimensional range queries over outsourced data. VLDB J. **21**(3), 333–358 (2012)
8. Wang, P., Ravishankar, C.V.: Secure and efficient range queries on outsourced databases using Rp-trees. In: ICDE, pp. 314–325 (2013)
9. Wong, W.K., Kao, B., Cheung, D.W.-L., Li, R., Yiu, S.-M.: Secure query processing with data interoperability in a cloud database environment. In: SIGMOD, pp. 1395–1406 (2014)

10. Hacıgümüş, H., Iyer, B., Mehrotra, S.: Efficient execution of aggregation queries over encrypted relational databases. In: Lee, Y.J., Li, J., Whang, K.-Y., Lee, D. (eds.) DASFAA 2004. LNCS, vol. 2973, pp. 125–136. Springer, Heidelberg (2004). https://doi.org/10.1007/978-3-540-24571-1_10

11. Liu, A., Zheng, K., Li, L., Liu, G., Zhao, L., Zhou, X.: Efficient secure similarity computation on encrypted trajectory data. In: ICDE, pp. 66–77 (2015)

12. Dellis, E., Seeger, B.: Efficient computation of reverse skyline queries. In: VLDB, pp. 291–302 (2007)

13. Bentley, J.L.: Multidimensional divide-and-conquer. Commun. ACM **23**(4), 214–229 (1980)

14. Li, C., Zhang, N., Hassan, N., Rajasekaran, S., Das, G.: On skyline groups. In: CIKM, pp. 2119–2123 (2012)

15. Goldrich, O.: Foundations of Cryptography: Volume 2, Basic Applications. Cambridge University Press

16. Yao, A.C.-C.: How to generate and exchange secrets. In: FOCS 1986, pp. 162–167 (1986)

17. Huang, Y., Evans, D., Katz, J., et al.: Faster secure two-party computation using garbled circuits. In: USENIX Security Symposium (2011)

18. Lindell, Y., Pinkas, B.: A proof of Yao's protocol for two-party computation. J. Cryptol. **22**, 161–188 (2009)

19. Rabin, M.: How to exchange secrets by oblivious trarnsfer. Technical Report TR-81, Aiken Computation Laboratory, Harvard University (1981)

20. Even, S., Goldreich, O., Lempel, A.: A randomized protocol for signing contracts. Commun. ACM **28**(6), 637–647 (1985)

21. Kolesnikov, V., Schneider, T.: Improved garbled circuit: free XOR gates and applications. In: Aceto, L., Damgård, I., Goldberg, L.A., Halldórsson, M.M., Ingólfsdóttir, A., Walukiewicz, I. (eds.) ICALP 2008. LNCS, vol. 5126, pp. 486–498. Springer, Heidelberg (2008). https://doi.org/10.1007/978-3-540-70583-3_40

22. Domingo-Ferrer, J.: A provably secure additive and multiplicative privacy homomorphism[*]. In: Chan, A.H., Gligor, V. (eds.) ISC 2002. LNCS, vol. 2433, pp. 471–483. Springer, Heidelberg (2002). https://doi.org/10.1007/3-540-45811-5_37

23. Gentry, C.: Fully homomorphic encryption using ideal lattices. In: STOC, pp. 169–178 (2009)

24. Kung, H.T., Luccio, F., Preparata, F.P.: On finding the maxima of a set of vectors. JACM **22**, 469–476 (1975)

Leveraging Pattern Mining Techniques for Efficient Keyword Search on Data Graphs

Xinge Lu[1]([⊠]), Dimitri Theodoratos[1], and Aggeliki Dimitriou[2]

[1] New Jersey Institute of Technology, Newark, NJ 07102, USA
{xl368,dth}@njit.edu
[2] National Technical University of Athens, Athens, Greece
angela@dblab.ntua.gr

Abstract. Graphs model complex relationships among objects in a variety of web applications. Keyword search is a promising method for extraction of data from data graphs and exploration. However, keyword search faces the so called performance scalability problem which hinders its widespread use on data graphs.

In this paper, we address the performance scalability problem by leveraging techniques developed for graph pattern mining. We focus on avoiding the generation of redundant intermediate results when the keyword queries are evaluated. We define a canonical form for the isomorphic representations of the intermediate results and we show how it can be checked incrementally and efficiently. We devise rules that prune the search space without sacrificing completeness and we integrate them in a query evaluation algorithm. Our experimental results show that our approach outperforms previous ones by orders of magnitude and displays smooth scalability.

Keywords: Graph data · Keyword search · Tree encoding · Canonical form

1 Introduction

Graphs model complex relationships among objects in a variety of applications including communication and computer systems, the World Wide Web, online social networks, biological networks, transportation systems, epidemic networks, and chemical networks. These systems can be modeled as graphs, where different components interact with other components resulting in massive networks. The tremendous success of the internet search engines over flat documents has triggered, in the last years, intense research activity on searching with keywords databases and datasets with some form of structure. The ambition is to allow users to extract information deeply hidden in these data sources with the simplicity offered by keyword search. The target datasets of this research involve different data models including fully structured relational databases, tree structured databases, key-value stores, RDF data graphs, and entity databases among

© Springer Nature Singapore Pte Ltd. 2020
L. H. U et al. (Eds.): WISE 2019, CCIS 1155, pp. 98–114, 2020.
https://doi.org/10.1007/978-981-15-3281-8_10

others, but most databases can be modelled directly or indirectly as graphs. We focus here on datasets which are in the form of a graph.

There are at least three major reasons for this strong interest from the database and IR communities on keyword search over data with some structure. First, the users can retrieve information without mastering a complex structured query language (e.g., SQL, XQuery, SPARQL). Second, they can issue queries against the data without having full or even partial knowledge of the structure (schema) of the data source. Third, they can query different data sources in an integrated way. This is particularly important in web environments where the data sources are heterogeneous and even if some of them adopt the same data model, they do not necessarily have the same structure/schema.

The Problem. There is a price to pay for the simplicity, convenience and flexibility of keyword search. Keyword queries are imprecise and ambiguous in specifying the query answer. They lack expressive power compared to structured query languages. Consequently, they generate a very large number of candidate results. This is a typical problem in IR. However, it is exacerbated in the context of data with some structure. Indeed, in this context the result to a keyword query is not a whole document but a data fragment (e.g., a subtree, or a subgraph) and this exponentially increases the number of results. This weakness incurs the performance scalability problem: existing algorithms for keyword search are of high complexity and they cannot scale satisfactorily when the number of keywords and the size of the input dataset increase. Note that top-k processing algorithms [7,13] do not solve the performance scalability problem as they still generate, in most cases, a large number of results or rely on specialized indexes which cannot be assumed to be available in practice. Another way to address the problem is exploratory search where the system directs the search of the user in a sequence of interaction steps [2]. Even though exploratory search is capable of reducing the number of results, it requires the involvement of the user. Therefore, the performance scalability problem has hindered the widespread use of keyword queries over data with some structure.

Contribution. In this paper, we consider the problem of efficiently computing the results of keyword queries over a data graph. We assume that the results are structured as undirected, unordered trees. This setting is general as it does not only represent keyword search over genuinely graph databases but also keyword search over relational databases which, or their schemas, are commonly modelled as graphs [3,10,11,13,15]. We observe that existing algorithms generate and process redundant intermediate results and/or produce duplicate final results. Duplicate results are the isomorphic ordered representations of an unordered result tree. Both problems substantially increase the memory footprint of the algorithms. In order to avoid the processing of duplicate intermediate results they employ time consuming intermediate result comparisons. In order to avoid returning duplicate results, they recur to an expensive post-processing redundant result elimination step. These techniques, though, prohibitively increase the execution time of the algorithms and negatively affect their time scalability.

To address these problems, we use and adapt pattern mining techniques developed for extracting tree-patterns from data structures. We further devise heuristics by observing the properties and construction process of intermediate result trees. We combine those in the design of a novel algorithm which minimizes the generation and avoids the processing of redundant intermediate results (and therefore, of duplicate final results). As it turns out, our algorithm outperforms by orders of magnitude previous algorithms. The main contributions are the following.

- We define a canonical form for result trees. The canonical form of a result tree is one of its automorphic representations. Its utility lies on the fact that by considering and expanding only intermediate result trees in canonical form we can still guarantee correct computation of all results trees. We provide a way for encoding result trees and for efficiently checking result trees for canonicity incrementally during the expansion of intermediate result trees (Sect. 3).
- We devise rules for expanding intermediate results which guarantee the correct computation of all the results while avoiding the generation of many redundant intermediate result trees. These rules are compatible and complement the result tree canonical form (Sect. 4).
- The above techniques are implemented in the design of a novel algorithm for computing the results of a keyword query on a data graph. The main feature of the algorithm is that it minimizes the processing of redundant intermediate results. Contrary to its competitors, it does not require intermediate (or final) result comparison and elimination (Sect. 4).
- We implemented our approach and run extensive experiments to evaluate its execution time and memory consumption performance and scalability. We also compared with two other previous well-known approaches which treat intermediate results differently to compute the same result set. Our experiments show that our algorithm outperforms the other approaches up to two orders of magnitude in terms of both query execution time and memory consumption and scales smoothly (Sect. 5).

2   Data Model and Query Semantics

Data Model. We consider a data graph $G = (V, E, l)$, where V is a set of nodes, E is a set of directed edges and l is a labeling function assigning distinct labels to all the nodes and edges in $V \cup E$. Labels on edges are useful for distinguishing two distinct edges between the same nodes. Set $labels(V)$ denotes the set of the labels of the nodes in V. Every node label l in $labels(V)$ is associated with a set $terms(l)$ of keywords from a finite set of keywords $\mathcal{K}$. The same keyword can appear in the sets $terms(l_1)$ and $terms(l_2)$ for two distinct node labels $l_1, l_2 \in labels(V)$. Figure 1(a) shows a data graph with six nodes. The labels and their termsets are shown by the nodes.

Queries and Query Semantics. A *query* is a set of keywords from $\mathcal{K}$. The answer of a query is defined based on the concept of query result. As is usual [3,9,10,12,13], we define the result of a query on a graph to be a tree.

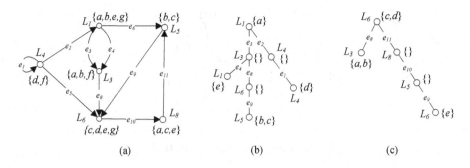

Fig. 1. (a) Data graph, (b) and (c) Results for the keyword query $\{a, b, c, d, e\}$

Definition 1 (Query Result). *Given a graph G, a result of a query Q on G is a node and edge labeled undirected tree R such that:*

(a) Every node of R is labeled with a label from labels(V). A function keys on the nodes of R assigns to every node n in R a (possibly empty) set of keywords from $Q \cap$ terms(label(n)). Function keys satisfies the following two conditions:
(i) for every two nodes $n_1, n_2 \in R$,
$keywords(n_1) \cap keywords(n_2) = \emptyset$ (unambiguity), and
(ii) $\bigcup_{n \in R} keywords(n) = Q$ (completeness).
(b) If there is an l-labeled edge between nodes n_1 and n_2 in R, then there is also an l-labeled edge between nodes labeled by label(n_1) and label(n_1) in G.
(c) There is no leaf node (i.e., a node with only one incident edge) n such that keywords(n) = $\emptyset$ (minimality).

Figure 1(b) and (c) show two results for the keyword query $\{a, b, c, d, e\}$ on the data graph of Fig. 1(a). The keyword set of every node is shown by the node. Observe that label L_4 appears twice in the result tree of Fig. 1(b), and in one occurrence the corresponding node has an empty keyword set.

We can now define the answer of a query.

Definition 2. *The* answer *of a query Q on a data graph G is the set of results of Q on G.*

The results of a keyword query Q represent different interpretations of Q. Function *keywords* assigns a meaning to a keyword in Q by associating it with a result node whose label l contains this keyword in its term set *term(l)*. A keyword can appear in the keyword set of only one of a result to guarantee that only one meaning is assigned to each query keyword in a query result. This is the unambiguity property of a query result. We adopt AND semantics [11] for queries: all the keywords of Q should appear in a result of Q. This is guaranteed by the completeness property of a query result. The minimality property guarantees that a query result does not have redundant nodes.

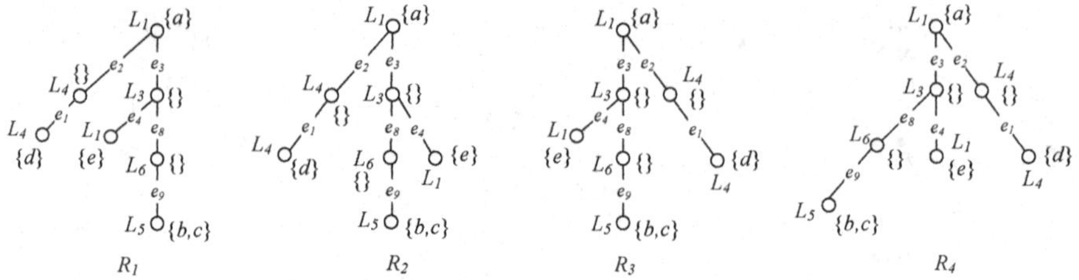

Fig. 2. Four isomorphic result trees

Note that this definition of a query result is general: the result does not need to have an embedding to the data graph. That is, it does not need to be a subtree of the data graph (though it can be restricted to be). As a consequence, the same label can label multiple nodes in the result. A node n in a result which does not have any keyword associated to it (that is, $keywords(n) = \emptyset$) is called *empty* node. Based on the definition above, a query result cannot have empty nodes as leaf nodes.

A result tree can be of unrestricted size. Given a result tree R, $size(R)$ denotes the number of nodes in R. To constraint the number of results, it is common to restrict the size of the result tree. This is a meaningful constraint since results which bring the keywords closer are commonly assumed to be more relevant [5,11,16]. It is also required for performance reasons since the number of results can be very large. Other constraints can also be used for performance and/or results relevance reasons.

3   A Canonical Form for Result Trees

In this section, we leverage results obtained in the field of tree pattern mining to define a canonical form for result trees and to check whether a result tree is in canonical form.

Our algorithm for computing query answers constructs query result trees starting from a root node. Therefore, query results are generated as rooted trees. In the rest of the discussion in this section we focus on rooted trees.

Unordered and Ordered Trees. Rooted result trees are unordered trees. However, the trees that are generated by all the algorithms are ordered since a representation order is imposed to the nodes. Two labeled rooted trees R and S are *isomorphic* to each other if there is a one-to-one mapping from the nodes of R to the nodes of S that preserves node labels, edge labels, adjacency and the roots. An *automorphism* is an isomorphism that maps a tree to the same unordered tree. Figure 2 shows four isomorphic results trees R_1, R_2, R_3 and R_4 which form one automorphic group.

To reduce the generation of isomorphic trees (which are redundant since they represent the same unordered tree) and produce only one tree for every automorphic group we use a canonical form for result trees. In the rest of this section, we consider ordered trees. Given a node n in a tree R, let $root(R)$ denote the root of R and $subtree(n)$ denote the subtree of R rooted at n.

An Order for Labels and Trees. We first define an order for trees. Let $\leq$ be a linear order on the label set $label(V)$. Abusing notation, we also denote as $\leq$ an order on trees defined recursively as follows:

Definition 3 (Tree Order). *Given two trees R and S, let $r = root(R)$ and $s = root(S)$, respectively. Let also $r_1, \ldots, r_m$ and $s_1, \ldots, s_n$ denote the list of the children of r and s, respectively. Then, $R \leq S$ iff either:*

1. *$label(r) \leq label(s)$, or*
2. *$label(r) = label(s)$ and either:*
   (i) $m \geq n$ and $\forall i \in [1, n], subtree(r_i) = subtree(s_i)$, or
   (ii) $\exists k \in [1, min(m, n)]$ such that: $\forall i \in [1, k - 1], subtree(r_i) = subtree(s_i)$ and $subtree(r_k) \leq subtree(s_k)$.

The tree order above is essentially the same as the one introduced in [18, 20]. In the context of result trees, in order to take into account the labels of the edges in result trees, we view a labeled edge as two unlabeled edges incident to a node which has the label of the edge. Further, in order to take into account the keyword sets of the result tree nodes, we assume that the label of a result tree node n is the concatenation of the label $label(n)$ and of the keywords in $keywords(n)$ (if any) in alphabetical order. For instance, for the result trees of Fig. 2, one can see that $R_1 \leq R_2 \leq R_3 \leq R_4$.

A Tree canonical Form. We can define now the canonical form adopted for a tree [4, 18, 20].

Definition 4 (Tree Canonical Form). *A tree R is in canonical form if for every tree S which is automorphic to R, $R \leq S$.*

As an example, consider the four trees of Fig. 2. These are all the automorphic representations for the corresponding unordered tree. As $R \leq S$, for every tree S in the automorphic group, R is in canonical form.

To check whether a tree is in canonical form, the following proposition [18, 20] can be used.

Proposition 1. *A tree R is in canonical form iff for every node n in R, $subtee(n_i) \leq subtree(n_{i+1})$, $i \in [1, m - 1]$, where $n_1, \ldots, n_m$ is the ordered list of children of n.*

Therefore, we can check whether a tree is in canonical form if we can decide about the order of a given pair of trees.

Exploiting a String Representation for Trees. Checking the order of a pair of trees can be done efficiently leveraging a string representation for trees. One such representation can be produced through a depth-first preorder traversal of the tree by adding the node label to the string at the first encounter and by adding a special symbol, say $, whenever we backtrack from a child to a parent node [4, 19]. For instance, the string representation for the tree of Fig. 1(c) (ignoring, for simplicity, edge labels and the node keyword sets) is $L_6 L_3 \$ L_8 L_5 L_6 \$\$\$$. Let's extend the linear order $\leq$ defined on labels to include $\$$ and let's assume that every label precedes $\$$ in this order.

The string representation for the trees is useful for checking the order of trees because of the following proposition [18, 20]:

Proposition 2. *Given two trees R and S, $R \leq S$ iff string$(R) \leq$ string(S).*

Therefore, well known string comparison algorithms and implementations can be employed to efficiently check the order of two trees.

4   The Algorithm

Our algorithm for computing keyword query answers takes as input a data graph G, a keyword query Q and a size threshold T for the query results. It starts by choosing randomly a keyword k from the input keyword query Q and by constructing intermediate result trees with a single node. For every node labeled by L_n in the data graph which contains k in its term set one node n labeled by L_n is constructed. Node n is associated with keyword sets and the resulting single node intermediate result trees are pushed into a stack. The keyword sets *keywords*(n) associated with n: (a) contain keyword k and (b) are subsets of the set of *terms*(L_n) of label L_n in the data graph, and of the keyword query Q. The query results are constructed by expanding these initial single node intermediate results.

Unconstrained Expansion. In the absence of any expansion constraint, the expansion process can be outlined as follows: a node n labeled by L_n is expanded by adding an adjacent node m labeled by L_m if the node labeled by L_m in the data graph is adjacent to the node labeled by L_n. The set of keywords of m is selected from the set of terms of the node L_m of the data graph which: (a) appear in the keyword query and (b) do not appear in the keyword set of other nodes of the intermediate result tree. The set of keywords of a node can also be empty. All the nodes in the intermediate result can be considered for expansion and a node is expanded in all possible ways. Intermediate results which contain all the keywords of Q in the keyword sets of their nodes are characterized as final results and are returned to the user if they do not have empty leaf nodes (minimality condition of a query result). If they do not satisfy the minimality condition, they are discarded. Intermediate results whose size is equal to the given size limit and are not final are not expanded anymore and they are discarded. Note that this process will generate duplicate results (isomorphic ordered versions of unordered trees). Hence, the results will have to be compared for isomorphism with previous results before returned to the user if an answer without duplicates is sought.

The expansion process can be constrained without missing any results. We show below how this can be achieved.

Considering Only Intermediate Result Trees in Canonical Form. For the result trees, it is sufficient to have result trees in canonical form (the other isomorphic versions of the result are redundant). It turns out that intermediate results which are not in canonical form do not need to be considered in the expansion process. This is shown by the next proposition.

Proposition 3. *All the results of a query on a data graph can be computed by considering, during the expansion process, only intermediate result trees in canonical form.*

Therefore, intermediate result trees which are not in canonical form can be discarded. Clearly, eliminating non-canonical intermediate result trees from the search space allows a significant reduction of the number of intermediate results generated. Note that the expansion of intermediate result trees can generate trees which are not in canonical form (even if the initial tree was in canonical form). We have presented in the previous section a technique for efficiently checking result trees for canonicity. We will show below how this technique can be further improved.

Empty Node Expansion. It can be further observed that if an intermediate result tree has an empty leaf node, it can be chosen for expansion without missing any results. This is shown by the next proposition.

Proposition 4. *All the results of a query Q on a data graph G can be computed by expanding only empty leaf nodes in the result trees under construction (if empty leaf nodes exist).*

Following this remark, if an empty node exists in an intermediate result, it should be chosen for expansion.

Rightmost Path Node Expansion. By default, in the absence of an empty leaf node, all the nodes of intermediate result tree need to be expanded to guarantee the computation of all the results. The next proposition shows that many intermediate result tree nodes can be excluded from expansion without affecting the completeness of the result set.

Proposition 5. *All the results of a query Q on a data graph G can be computed by expanding only the nodes on the rightmost path of the result trees under construction.*

If this expansion strategy is followed, in most cases, most of the intermediate result tree nodes (those which are not on the rightmost path) are not expanded.

Checking the Canonicity of Result Trees Incrementally. In order to check whether a tree is in canonical form we can use Proposition 1 (and also Proposition 2 to perform the comparisons of trees efficiently). However, as mentioned above: (a) only trees which are in canonical form are expanded, and (b) only nodes in the rightmost path of a intermediate result tree are expanded. These remarks allow for an incremental checking of the canonicity of the newly generated intermediate

---

Algorithm 1. *CFS*

Input: data graph G, query Q, size limit T
Output: query results of Q on G of size up to T
1: $E := \emptyset$ /* E is a queue of query results */
2: Chose a keyword k in Q
3: **for** every node n in G s.t. $k \in terms(n)$ **do**
4:    **for** every set $K \in \mathcal{P}(terms(n) \cap Q)$ such that $k \in K$ **do**
5:       Construct a single-node result R labeled by $label(n)$
6:       $keywords(R) = K$
7:       $enqueue(R, E)$
8: **while** $E \neq \emptyset$ **do**
9:    $R := dequeue(E)$
10:   **if** R has an empty leaf node q **then**
11:      $ExpandList := \{q\}$
12:   **else**
13:      $ExpandList := \{$ nodes in the rightmost path of R $\}$
14:   **for** every node $l \in ExpandList$ **do**
15:      **for** every node m adjacent to the node labeled by $label(l)$ in G **do**
16:         $D := (Q \cap terms(m)) - keywords(R)$
17:         **for** every set $K \in \mathcal{P}(D)$ **do**
18:            Add a node p with $label(p) = label(m)$ and $keywords(p) = K$ and an edge (l, p) to R.
19:            **if** R is in canonical form and satisfies the structural constraints **then**
20:               **if** $keywords(R) = Q$ **then**
21:                  output R
22:               **else**
23:                  **if** $size(R) < T$ **then**
24:                     $enqueue(R, E)$

---

result tree: only the trees rooted at the rightmost child of the expanded node n and the trees rooted at the rightmost child nodes of the ancestor nodes of n need to be compared to the tree rooted at their immediate left sibling. No other comparisons are needed.

Correctness of the Algorithm. The pseudo code for our algorithm is shown in Algorithm 1. This algorithm integrates in the unconstrained expansion described in the beginning of this section the three expansion constraints described subsequently. The algorithm is named CFS (for 'Canonical Form-based Search').

Theorem 1. *Algorithm CFS correctly computes all the results of a keyword query Q on a data graph G given a size threshold T.*

The correctness of the theorem results from the correctness of the expansion constraining Propositions 3, 4 and 5 and the fact that in the absence of expansion constraints the algorithm exhaustively expands all intermediate results.

Checking the canonicity of an intermediate result tree R can be done in $O(N)$, where n is the number of nodes of R. Let m be the number of nodes in the data graph G that contain the initially chosen keyword k in their term

Table 1. Queries on the (a) IMDB and (b) TPC-H database

	Keywords
Q_1	cuadro, Alex
Q_2	cuadro, Alex, Rafael
Q_3	cuadro, Alex, Rafael, 173
Q_4	Musical, Anne, Bauman
Q_5	17485, Anne, Bauman, David
Q_6	Aabel, Steve, 352881, crime, Kodanda
Q_7	Brown, grandfather, Tony, Musical
Q_8	Anne, Adams, Rafael, Musical, cuadro, 1664
Q_9	Halloween, 2000, Musical, Comedy
Q_{10}	2012, David, Musical, Grandfather, Alex, Tony

(a)

	Keywords
Q_1	Supplier, clerk
Q_2	carefully, express
Q_3	truck, regular, customer
Q_4	Morocco, packages, return
Q_5	foxes, Brand, small
Q_6	return, spring, yellow
Q_7	Indian, Burnished, India, Brand
Q_8	Manufacturer#3, Manufacturer#4, large
Q_9	special, France, Brand#22, India
Q_{10}	yellow, green, Brand#23, ironic, clerk

(b)

set, and d be the average degree of the nodes in G (number of incident edges). Since Algorithm CFS expands nodes in all possible ways through the incident edges of a node, its worst case complexity is $O(m(T-1)!d^{T-1})$, where T is the size threshold. The worst case complexity is of little help here: in practice, Algorithm CFS takes advantage of the canonical form and the result expansion constraints to substantially reduce the number of intermediate results and this feature allows for superior performance compared to its competitors.

5   Experimental Evaluation

We run experiments to evaluate the efficiency, the memory consumption and the scalability of our algorithm. We also compared with the techniques employed for computing all the results by two previous keyword search algorithms on graphs derived from relational databases. As mentioned in Sect. 6, these algorithms compute similar types of results on the data graphs. To allow for a fair comparison, given a keyword query, we generate a data graph to evaluate the query the way it is generated in the context of the previous algorithms from relational schema graphs. Our implementation was coded in Java. All the experiments reported here were performed on a workstation having an Intel(R) Core(TM) i7-7500 CPU @ 2.70 GHz processor with 8 GB memory.

Datasets. We used a benchmark and two relational databases to generate data graphs: the *TPC-H* benchmark database and the *IMDB* database. The *TPC-H* benchmark is a decision support database. The data are chosen to have broad industry wide relevance. The schema of the dataset[1] used here comprises eight relation schemas and eight foreign keys. Its tables contain 866,602 tuples. The *IMDB* database is a repository of films, actors, reviews and related information.

---

[1] http://www.tpc.org/tpch/.

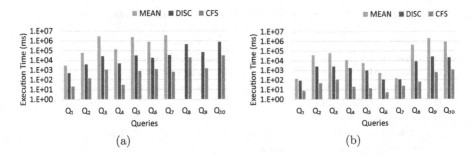

Fig. 3. Execution time for the queries on the (a) IMDB, and (b) TPC-H database

The schema of the dataset[2] used here comprises seven relation schemas and six foreign keys. Its tables contain 5,694,919 tuples. The data graphs used in the experiments are generated separately for each keyword query as explained below in the paragraph discussing the queries.

Queries. We generated different queries to evaluate on the datasets and we report on 10 of them for each dataset. They are displayed in Table 1. The queries have from one to six keywords. Given a dataset and a keyword query, the data graph to evaluate the query is an extension of the schema graph of the relational database generated as follows: for every relation R in the schema of the relational database, additional nodes are added to the schema graph for every combination of query keywords appearing in a tuple of relation R which does not have other query keywords. Edges are added between these nodes mirroring the key-foreign key edges between the corresponding relations in the database schema.

Statistics about the queries including the total number of keyword instances in the generated graphs (#Ins) and the number of results (#Results) are provided in Tables 2. The number of nodes and edges of the generated (extended

Table 2. Statistics for the queries on the (a) IMDB and (b) TPC-H database

	#GNodes	#GEdges	#Ins	#Results		#GNodes	#GEdges	#Ins	#Results
Q_1	13	19	6	89	Q_1	10	12	2	14
Q_2	17	27	10	883	Q_2	30	54	22	618
Q_3	17	27	10	6695	Q_3	20	32	12	267
Q_4	20	30	13	1238	Q_4	19	31	11	45
Q_5	27	43	20	9147	Q_5	18	26	10	47
Q_6	24	46	14	411	Q_6	12	13	4	19
Q_7	26	45	19	8802	Q_7	13	15	5	12
Q_8	32	55	25	27837	Q_8	29	51	21	1
Q_9	31	54	24	12086	Q_9	30	56	22	2337
Q_{10}	34	59	27	52515	Q_{10}	35	58	27	408
		(a)					(b)		

---

[2] https://relational.fit.cvut.cz/dataset/IMDb.

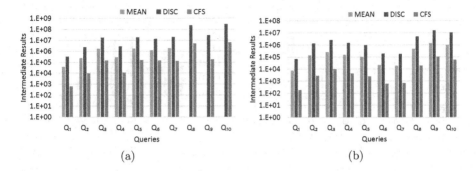

Fig. 4. Number of intermediate results produced for the queries on (a) the IMDB database, and (b) the TPC-H database

schema) data graphs for every query are also shown in these tables in the columns '#GNodes' and #GEdges, respectively.

Algorithms in Comparison. We compared our algorithm with the algorithm designed for the $DISCOVER$ system [11] (adopted also in other systems [10, 15]). We also compared with the meaningful keyword search algorithm used in [13]. We refer to them as $DISC$ and $MEAN$, respectively. Both of them search on graphs which are extended relational schemas constructed, for every query, as described above in the paragraph "Queries". The DISCOVER approach imposes some additional constraints on the query results which are ignored here to secure the computation of similar results by all three algorithms. Our interest on these algorithms in on the way they guarantee result sets without duplicates (that is, without isomorphic ordered result trees). Different approaches are followed by these two algorithms. Algorithm $DISC$ computes the results and removes duplicate results at the end with a post-processing step to guarantee that there are not duplicates. Algorithm $MEAN$ is similar to $DISC$ but excludes duplicates by comparing intermediate results, while they are generated, with previously generated intermediate results. For the needs of the comparison, it assigns an ID to every generated tree based on tree isomorphism during the execution of the algorithm. The ID of a tree is compared with the IDs of the trees that are generated so far and the current tree is accepted only if it has not been generated previously. Algorithm $MEAN$ computes top-k results. Therefore, for the needs of the comparison we assume that k is larger than the number of the query results so that all results are computed. We refer to our algorithm as CFS.

Experiments on the Execution Time. In our first experiment we measured the efficiency of our algorithm in terms of execution time and we compared these numbers with those achieved by $DISC$ and $MEAN$. The size limit was set to 6 edges. Figure 3 shows the execution time of the algorithms on the IMDB and the TPC-H datasets, respectively. Note that the scale of the y-axis is logarithmic.

One can see that Algorithm CFS is much faster than both $DISC$ and $MEAN$. Algorithm CFS outperforms $DISC$ by at least one order of magnitude in all

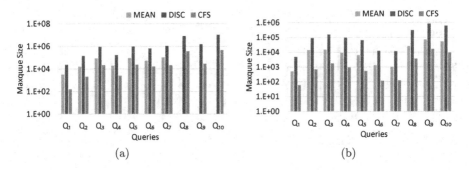

Fig. 5. Memory consumption for the queries on the (a) IMDB and (b) TPC-H database

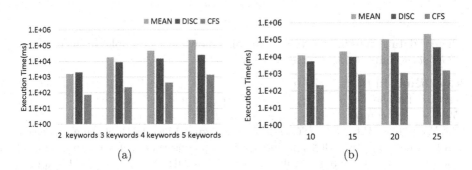

Fig. 6. Average execution time vs. number of keywords and (b) Average execution time vs. number of keyword instances

cases. Algorithm *MEAN* is much slower than the other two. It is two orders of magnitude slower than *CFS* in most cases and in several cases slower by more than three orders of magnitude. Note than in several cases, *MEAN* could not finish within a reasonable amount of time and therefore, no value is displayed in the plots for the corresponding queries (queries Q_8, Q_9 and Q_{10} on IMDB).

Experiments on the Number of Intermediate Results. In this experiment we measured the performance of the algorithms in terms of the number of inter-mediate results generated. Figure 4 shows the number of intermediate results produced on the IMDB and TPC-H databases, respectively. The intermediate results are the partial or complete result trees generated by the algorithms. Algo-rithm *DISC* pushes all the intermediate results into the queue maintained by the algorithm as long as they satisfy the size constraint. Algorithm *MEAN* pushes intermediate results into the queue if they satisfy the size constraint and no iso-morphic intermediate result is found in the queue. Finally, algorithm *CFS* pushes intermediate results into the queue if they are in canonical form and satisfy the size restriction.

As one can see, algorithm *CFS* produces the smallest and *DISC* the largest number of intermediate results in all cases on both datasets. Algorithm *DISC*

produces at least one and in most cases two orders of magnitude more intermediate results than *CFS*. The number of intermediate results produced by
MEAN falls between the numbers produced by the other two algorithms. This is
expected since *DISC* does not filter intermediate results and eliminates duplicate
results only at the end through a post-processing step. *MEAN* filters intermediate results by comparing with other intermediate results stored in the queue
while *CFS* filters intermediate results by producing only trees in canonical form.
However, *DISC* and *MEAN* generate result trees by expanding all the nodes of
a given intermediate result tree while *CFS* expands preferably an empty node
and nodes in the rightmost path of an intermediate result tree. The sophisticated intermediate result expansion method of *CFS* and its intermediate result
pruning technique based on canonical form explain the superior performance of
CFS.

We can also observe that for a given algorithm, the execution time and the
number of intermediate results are very closely correlated metrics. However, the
number of intermediate results does not determine the execution time among different algorithms. Algorithm *CFS* produces less intermediate results than *DISC*
and it is also faster. On the other hand, *MEAN* produces less intermediate results
than *DISC* and it is much slower. The reason is that *MEAN* has to compare every
qualified intermediate result with all the intermediate results currently stored in
the queue. As the next experiment shows, there can be many intermediate results
in the queue and this comparison can take a lot of time. This explains the inferior
time performance of *MEAN* compared to *DISC*.

Experiments on Memory Consumption. We also measured the memory
consumption of the three algorithms in terms of the maximum number of intermediate results put in the queue. Figure 5 shows the measured values. In order
to minimize the memory footprint, in every algorithm, every occurrence of the
query keyword selected to initiate the algorithm is added to the queue as a single
node intermediate result only after all the intermediate results from the previous
single node intermediate result have been processed and the queue is emptied.

As we can see *DISC* consumes one to two orders of magnitude more memory
on the average than *CFS*. The difference between *MEAN* and *CFS* is not so
pronounced. It is on the average less than one order of magnitude in favor of
CFS. This difference is not expected since *MEAN* compares every produced
intermediate result against all stored intermediate results and discards it if is
found there. Nevertheless, *MEAN* expands intermediate results using all the
nodes in the result tree as opposed to *CFS* which restricts this expansion to the
empty node or the nodes in the rightmost path of the tree. This is the reason of
the superior performance of *CFS* over *MEAN*.

Scalability Experiments. We also measured how the execution time evolves
when the number of query keywords and the number of keyword instances
increases. For this experiments we used a synthetic data set whose schema is
similar to the IMDB data set. We generated ten queries each with 2, 3, 4 and 5
keywords and measured the average execution time when the number of keywords
in the query increases. The results are shown in Fig. 6(a). We also considered

ten five-keyword queries and we increased the total number of instances of each query from 10 to 25. The measured average execution time when the total number of instance increases is shown in Fig. 6(b). It can be observed that overall, *CFS* scales smoother than the other two approaches as it avoids the expensive comparisons for removing isomorphic intermediate and final results.

6   Related Work

Keyword search on graphs can be classified in three categories based on the schema constraints on the underlying graph data and the features of the results: (a) keyword search on tree data [14], (b) keyword search over relational databases viewed as graphs [1,3,9–11,13,15,17], and (c) keyword search on genuine graph data/networks [6,8,12].

Banks [3] evaluates a keyword query by exploring the data graph backwards starting from the nodes containing at least one query keyword. This strategy is not optimal and can lead to poor performance in certain graphs. To address this problem bidirectional search [12] offers the option of exploring the graph by following forward edges as well starting from potential roots. Both forward and backward expansions explore the graph edge by edge without having any knowledge of the structure of the graph and the distribution of the keywords in the graph. Blinks [9] proposed a bi-level index to store reachability information in advance. The index helps avoiding aimless exploration of the graph and improves the performance of keyword search. These techniques are not useful in our context as they cannot be used for undirected result trees.

Keyword search on graphs generated by relational databases falls in the category of schema-based or tuple-based keyword search. A well-known schema based approach is DISCOVER [11] which generates result trees (called candidate networks) and uses them to generate SQL statements. Discover exhaustively searches the schema graph constraining the candidate networks with a size limit. Similar algorithmic approaches are followed by [1,10,15]. Meaningful keyword search [13] also follows a schema-based approach for keyword search on relational databases and computes candidate networks. This approach identifies roles for the matches of the keywords. It presents a ranking technique and a top-k algorithm. The candidate networks are similar to the undirected result trees we have defined in this paper. Therefore, we experimantally compare with those two approaches in Sect. 5.

S-KWS [17] focuses on keyword search over relational data streams. In addition, it proposes a technique to reduce the number of partial results generated during the computation of candidate networks over a data graph. This technique shares the same goal as our approach but it is not complete and it does not use the notion of canonical form which we leverage in this paper.

7   Conclusion

We have addressed the problem of efficiently evaluating keyword queries on graph data. We observed that existing algorithms generate numerous intermediate results and this negatively affects their execution time and memory consumption. We defined a canonical form for result trees and we showed how it can checked incrementally and efficiently. We devised rules that prune the intermediate result search space without sacrificing completeness. These rules were integrated in a query evaluation algorithm. Our experimental results show that our approach largely outperforms previous ones in terms of execution time and memory consumption and scales smoothly when the number of keywords and the number of keyword instances increases.

We are currently working on designing algorithms which efficiently compute keyword queries enhanced with constraints that bridge the gap between keyword and structured queries. We also work on incremental keyword query evaluation for graph data exploration.

References

1. Agrawal, S., Chaudhuri, S., Das, G.: DBXplorer: a system for keyword-based search over relational databases. In: IEEE ICDE, pp. 5–16 (2002)
2. Bao, Z., Zeng, Y., Jagadish, H.V., Ling, T.W.: Exploratory keyword search with interactive input. In: ACM SIGMOD, pp. 871–876 (2015)
3. Bhalotia, G., Hulgeri, A., Nakhe, C., Chakrabarti, S., Sudarshan, S.: Keyword searching and browsing in databases using banks. In: ICDE, pp. 431–440 (2002)
4. Chi, Y., Yang, Y., Xia, Y., Muntz, R.R.: CMTreeMiner: Mining both closed and maximal frequent subtrees. In: Dai, H., Srikant, R., Zhang, C. (eds.) PAKDD 2004. LNCS (LNAI), vol. 3056, pp. 63–73. Springer, Heidelberg (2004). https://doi.org/10.1007/978-3-540-24775-3_9
5. Dimitriou, A., Theodoratos, D., Sellis, T.K.: Top-k-size keyword search on tree structured data. Inf. Syst. **47**, 178–193 (2015)
6. Elbassuoni, S., Blanco, R.: Keyword search over RDF graphs. In: ACM CIKM, pp. 237–242 (2011)
7. Feng, J., Li, G., Wang, J.: Finding top-k answers in keyword search over relational databases using tuple units. IEEE ICDE **23**(12), 1781–1794 (2011)
8. Golenberg, K., Kimelfeld, B., Sagiv, Y.: Keyword proximity search in complex data graphs. In: Proceedings of the ACM SIGMOD, pp. 927–940 (2008)
9. He, H., Wang, H., Yang, J., Yu, P.S.: BLINKS: ranked keyword searches on graphs. In: ACM SIGMOD, pp. 305–316 (2007)
10. Hristidis, V., Gravano, L., Papakonstantinou, Y.: Efficient ir-style keyword search over relational databases. In: VLDB, pp. 850–861 (2003)
11. Hristidis, V., Papakonstantinou, Y.: DISCOVER: keyword search in relational databases. In: VLDB, pp. 670–681 (2002)
12. Kacholia, V., Pandit, S., Chakrabarti, S., Sudarshan, S., Desai, R., Karambelkar, H.: Bidirectional expansion for keyword search on graph databases. In: VLDB, pp. 505–516 (2005)
13. Kargar, M., An, A., Cercone, N., Godfrey, P., Szlichta, J., Yu, X.: Meaningful keyword search in relational databases with large and complex schema. In: IEEE ICDE, pp. 411–422 (2015)
14. Le, T.N., Ling, T.W.: Survey on keyword search over XML documents. SIGMOD Rec. **45**(3), 17–28 (2016)

15. Liu, F. Yu, C., Meng, W., Chowdhury, A.: Effective keyword search in relational databases. In: ACM SIGMOD, pp. 563–574 (2006)
16. Liu, Z., Chen, Y.: Processing keyword search on XML: a survey. World Wide Web **14**(5–6), 671–707 (2011)
17. Markowetz, A., Yang, Y., Papadias, D.: Keyword search on relational data streams. In: ACM SIGMOD, pp. 605–616 (2007)
18. Nijssen, S., Kok, J.N.: Efficient discovery of frequent unordered trees. In: MGTS, pp. 55–64 (2003)
19. Zaki, M.J.: Efficiently mining frequent trees in a forest. In: ACM SIGKDD, pp. 71–80 (2002)
20. Zaki, M.J.: Efficiently mining frequent embedded unordered trees. Fundam. Inform. **66**(1–2), 33–52 (2005)

Range Nearest Neighbor Query with the Direction Constraint

Xue Miao[1], Xi Guo[1], Xiaochun Yang[2], Zhaoshun Wang[1(✉)], and Peng Lv[1(✉)]

[1] Beijing Key Laboratory of Knowledge Engineering for Materials,
University of Science and Technology Beijing, Beijing, China
xuemiao@xs.ustb.edu.cn, xiguo@ustb.edu.cn, zhswang@sohu.com,
lvpeng2035@163.com
[2] School of Computer Science and Technology, Beijing Institute of Technology,
Beijing, China
yang.x.chun@gmail.com

Abstract. In this paper, we study a direction-aware spatial data query method, i.e., range nearest neighbor query with the direction constraint (Range-DCNN query). Traditional DCNN query retrieves the top-k nearest neighbors within an angular range. Our Range-DCNN query finds all nearest neighbors within an angular range for all points in a rectangle. Dissimilar to the traditional DCNN query, the user's location in the Range-DCNN query is abstracted to a rectangle rather than a point and the user's location can be anywhere in the rectangle. In doing so, the user's precise location will not be leaked, which ensures an effective privacy protection of user's location. In Range-DCNN query, an observation is made that splitting points can be utilized to obtain all query results without having to search for all points. We propose some properties of locating splitting points. According to these properties, efficient algorithms are designed with the assistance of the R-tree. Extensive experiments have been conducted on both real and synthetic datasets. The experimental results demonstrate that our algorithms are capable of locating all results precisely and efficiently.

Keywords: Location-based services · Location privacy protection · Direction constraint · Range nearest neighbor query · Spatial databases

1 Introduction

With the rapid development and application of wireless communication and mobile location technologies, location-based services (LBSs) have been rapidly developed and popularized. In LBSs, sometimes the simple nearest neighbor query methods without considering direction attribute don't work well [14]. Users query information of interest by providing their geographical locations to the server. Meanwhile, service providers can easily acquire users' locations and accumulate users' historical trajectories. The leakage of user's location information may bring potential security hazards to the user. Consequently, the spatial

© Springer Nature Singapore Pte Ltd. 2020
L. H. U et al. (Eds.): WISE 2019, CCIS 1155, pp. 115–131, 2020.
https://doi.org/10.1007/978-981-15-3281-8_11

direction attribute and the location privacy protection are two extremely important factors in LBSs.

We focus on the range nearest neighbor query with the direction constraint (Range-DCNN query), where user utilizes a rectangle to blur his exact location and user's location may be anywhere in the rectangle. Range-DCNN query finds all nearest point-of-interests (POIs) within an angular range for all points in the rectangle. It considers not only the direction attribute, but also the distance attribute. Additionally, it gives a consideration to the user's location privacy protection. Conventional range nearest neighbor (Range-NN) query [1] finds all nearest neighbors for all points in a rectangle. Traditional direction-constrained nearest neighbor (DCNN) queries, such as [2] and [15], find the top-k nearest neighbors within an angular range. Their shortcomings are that Range-NN query doesn't consider the spatial direction attribute and DCNN query doesn't consider user's location privacy protection. Based on these two queries, we propose the Range-DCNN query. Figure 1(a) gives an example of the Range-DCNN query. Given an exact location q and an angular range ($area_i$), conventional DCNN query [2] finds the nearest restaurant (p_i) within $area_i$. Given a rectangle Ω and an angular range $[0°, 25°) \cup (343°, 360°)$, Range-DCNN query finds the nearest restaurant within the angular range for each point in Ω. The result of [2] is p_i and the results of our Range-DCNN query are p_m, p_n and p_i.

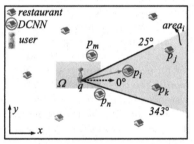

(a) Range-DCNN and DCNN queries

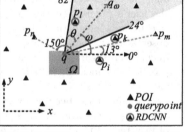

(b) R-DCNN query and $RDCNNs$

Fig. 1. Visualization of range-DCNN and DCNN queries

The contributions made in this paper are summarized as follows:

- Our Range-DCNN query is an extension of the DCNN query [2]. The query on a point is extended to the query on a rectangular area, which is an effective way to protect the privacy of the user's location.
- In Range-DCNN query, the challenge is that there are countless points in the rectangular query area, and not all points should be searched. Therefore, we propose efficient algorithms that help us to find all results for all points in the area but with only a small number of queries.
- We evaluate our algorithms. Experimental results show that our algorithms are capable of solving Range-DCNN query in an accurate and efficient way.

The remaining sections in this paper are structured as follows. The formal definition of the Range-DCNN query is raised in Sect. 2.1 and the related work is summarized in Sect. 2.2. In Sect. 3, the framework of the Range-DCNN query is presented. Some properties are proposed in Sect. 4. Our algorithms are proposed in Sect. 5. The experimental results are displayed in Sect. 6.

2   Preliminaries

In two-dimensional Euclidean space, $P = \{p_1, p_2, ..., p_n\}$ is a POIs set and Ω is a rectangle. User's exact location q can be any point in Ω. A polar coordinate system is established by using q as the pole and positive x-axis as the polar axis.

2.1   Problem Definitions

Definition 1 (Favorite Direction). A ray emitted from q is used to visualize the favorite direction, the size of it is the angle between the ray and the polar axis. Let q_ω denote the favorite direction and $\omega \in [0, 2\pi)$ is q_ω's size.

Definition 2 (Favorite Angle). The angles deviating from the left and the right sides of q_ω are all the user's favorite angles. Let $\theta \in (0, \pi/4]$ denote it.

Definition 3 (Query Angular Range). Given q_ω and θ, the query angular range can be figured out using the following formula. Let $(\omega_\perp^\theta, \omega_\top^\theta)$ denote the query angular range.

$$(\omega_\perp^\theta, \omega_\top^\theta) = \begin{cases} (\omega - \theta, \omega + \theta), & \theta \leq \omega, \omega + \theta \leq 2\pi \\ [0, \omega + \theta - 2\pi) \cup (\omega - \theta, 2\pi), & \theta < \omega, \omega + \theta > 2\pi \\ [0, \omega + \theta) \cup (2\pi + \omega - \theta, 2\pi), & \theta > \omega \end{cases} \quad (1)$$

In Fig. 1(b), Ω is a rectangular query area and $q \in \Omega$ is a possible exact location of the user. The red ray is user's favorite direction (q_ω) w.r.t. q. θ in Fig. 1(b) is user's favorite angle and the blue area is user's query angular range.

Each POI $p_i \in P$ has a vector $\overrightarrow{qp_i}$. The **relative direction** of p_i is the orientation of $\overrightarrow{qp_i}$ and let δ_i denote it. p_i's **relative distance** is the Euclidean distance from q to p_i, let $dist(q, p_i)$ denote it.

$$\forall p_i \in P, \exists (dist(q, p_i), \delta_i), i \in \{1, 2, ..., n\} \quad (2)$$

Definition 4 (RDCNN). A RDCNN is the nearest POI within the query angular range w.r.t. a possible exact location $q \in \Omega$.

In Fig. 1(b), the nearest POI p_l in the blue area is a RDCNN w.r.t. q.

Definition 5 (Range-DCNN Query). Given Ω, ω and θ, a Range-DCNN query retrieves all RDCNNs for all points in Ω.

For simplicity, Range-DCNN query is abbreviated as R-DCNN query. Let $R\text{-}DCNN(\Omega)$ denote the results set of a R-DCNN query and let $RDCNN(q)$ denote q's $RDCNN$.

$$R\text{-}DCNN(\Omega) = \{RDCNN(q)|\ q \in \Omega\} \qquad (3)$$

Figure 1(b) depicts a R-DCNN query. Ω is the grey area, $\omega = 53°$, $\theta = 29°$ and the query angular range is $(24°, 82°)$. The R-DCNN query finds all $RDCNN$s for all points in Ω and the results set of it is $R\text{-}DCNN(\Omega) = \{p_l, p_k, p_i\}$. Table 1 describes some of the symbols used in this paper.

Table 1. Symbols and descriptions

Symbols	Descriptions
Ω	A given rectangle and user's location may be any point in it
q	User's exact location, it may be any point in Ω
$q_\omega\ (\theta)$	Favorite direction (angle), the size of it is $\omega \in [0, 2\pi)(\theta \in (0, \pi/4])$
$\delta_i(dist(q, p_i))$	POI p_i's relative direction (distance) w.r.t. q and $\delta_i \in [0, 2\pi)$
$(\omega_\perp^\theta, \omega_\top^\theta)$	User's query angular range
$RDCNN$	The nearest POI within user's query angular range

2.2 Related Work

As a supporting technology of LBSs, nearest neighbor (NN) query [3] was suggested by Knuth in 1973. It's a significant and basic query type supported by many spatial databases [4–6]. At present, the research of NN query in Euclidean space is more abundant and mature [4,5,7–13]. Direction and distance are very important spatial attributes in LBSs. However, this simple NN query doesn't consider the direction attributes of spatial objects. The existing direction-aware spatial queries considering both direction and distance attributes are limited to [2] and [14–19].

DCNN query [2] studies a direction-aware spatial data query technology. When user gives his moving direction and acceptable angle, an angular range can be calculated, it finds the top-k nearest POIs within the angular range. There are two obvious shortcomings in DCNN query. Firstly, the angle between user's favorite direction and the segment where he is located can only be 0°. Such restriction could hamper practical applications. Secondly, what it gets is the exact location of the user, which will reveal the location information. Consequently, a more general form of DCNN query is proposed, i.e., the R-DCNN query. On the one hand, the angle between the favorite direction and the segment is extended to any angle in [0°, 90°]; On the other hand, allowing for the user's location privacy protection, R-DCNN query substitutes the precise location of the user with a rectangular area. In sum, the R-DCNN query is of more practical significance than the DCNN query.

It's worth noting that R-DCNN query is fundamentally different from [18] and [19]. [18] searches for the nearest neighbors around a rectangle, while our R-DCNN query searches for nearest neighbors in a given direction range. We cannot solve our problem by using the techniques proposed in [18], because the objects don't have domination relationships like the objects in [18]. In R-DCNN, the user (i.e., the query point) issues his favorite direction, while in [19] the objects (i.e., the query targets) have specific orientations themselves. Additionally, our problem cannot be solved by using the multiple granularity index structure (MULTI) proposed in [19], because in R-DCNN the user's exact location is blurred by a rectangle and each object does not have inherent orientation.

3   Query Framework

In this section, an analysis is conducted of the R-DCNN query. We propose some lemmas and give the proofs. According to these lemmas, a framework of answering the R-DCNN query is raised.

The angle between the favorite direction q_ω and an edge of the rectangle Ω is $\alpha \in [0, \pi/2]$. According to α, two spatial relationships between user's query angular range and Ω are observed.

- **Type 1.** For each edge of Ω, there is $\alpha \in [\theta, \pi/2]$ (As shown in Fig. 2(a));
- **Type 2.** For a pair of parallel edges of Ω, there is $\alpha \in [\theta, \pi/2]$ (Such as L_{bc} and L_{ad} in Fig. 2(b)), and for another pair of parallel edges, there is $\alpha \in [0, \theta)$ (Such as L_{ab} and L_{dc} in Fig. 2(b)).

Definition 6 (Safe Edge). For each point on an edge of Ω, if the two boundary lines of the point's query angular range are oriented towards the interior of Ω, then the edge is a safe edge.

Definition 7 (Unsafe Edge). For each point on an edge of Ω, if there is at least one boundary line of the point's query angular range is oriented towards the outside of Ω, then the edge is an unsafe edge.

In Fig. 2(a), edges L_{ab} and L_{ad} are safe edges and L_{bc} and L_{dc} are unsafe edges. In Fig. 2(b), L_{ad} is a safe edge and L_{ab}, L_{bc} and L_{dc} are unsafe edges.

Lemma 1. If the $RDCNN$ of a point on a safe edge is outside Ω, there must be another point on an unsafe edge that has the same $RDCNN$.

Proof. Figure 3(a) visualizes the proof process. The user is on the safe edge L_{ad} and his $RDCNN$ p_m is outside Ω. Segment $\overline{qp_m}$ ($\overline{op_m}$) is the radius of the circle q (o), o is the intersection of $\overline{qp_m}$ and the unsafe edge L_{dc}. The intersections of the boundary lines of q's (o's) query angular range and the circle q (o) are u (u') and l (l'). The two circles are tangent at p_m and the sector $u'ol' \in$ sector uql. As p_m is q's $RDCNN$, there are no other points in sector uql. Consequently, there are no other points in sector $u'ol'$, so p_m is also o's $RDCNN$.

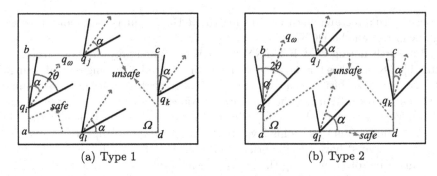

(a) Type 1   (b) Type 2

Fig. 2. Visualization of two spatial relationships

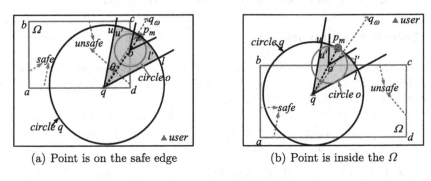

(a) Point is on the safe edge   (b) Point is inside the Ω

Fig. 3. Proofs of Lemmas 1 and 2

Lemma 2. A point is inside Ω, if the $RDCNN$ of the point is outside Ω, there must be another point on an unsafe edge that has the same $RDCNN$.

As Fig. 3(b) shows, the proof of the Lemma 2 can be easily inferred from the proof of the Lemma 1. Here we no longer give the proof of the Lemma 2.

Lemma 3. The POIs in Ω (including four edges) must be $RDCNN$s.

Obviously, a POI in Ω must be the $RDCNN$ of the point where it is located.

$$RDCNN(p_i) = \{p_i|\ p_i \in P, L_{p_i} \in \Omega\} \tag{4}$$

L_{p_i} is the location of POI p_i. Therefore, for a POI p_i in P, if p_i is in Ω, then p_i must be in set $R\text{-}DCNN(\Omega)$.

$$\forall p_i \in P, if\ L_{p_i} \in \Omega, \exists p_i \in R\text{-}DCNN(\Omega) \tag{5}$$

A range query could be applied to search for all POIs in Ω. The crucial of the R-DCNN query is to *find $RDCNN$s for all points on the unsafe edges*. Based on q_ω and θ, the unsafe edges can be identified. Each edge of Ω contains countless points and it's impractical to issue countless queries to find all $RDCNN$s. Our observation is that a limited number of queries can be used to find all $RDCNN$s for all points on the unsafe edges. Algorithm 1 is the framework of the R-DCNN query. Unsafe edges of Ω are identified and stored in a list *edgesList* (Line 1). Finding all *RDCNN*s for all points on each unsafe edge (Line 2 and 3). A range query is performed to find all POIs in Ω (Line 4).

Algorithm 1. R-DCNN Query

Input: Ω, ω, θ
Output: All *RDCNN*s for all points in Ω
1 *edgesList*←get unsafe edges ►lemma 1 and 2
2 **for** *edge* in *edgesList* **do**
3 $\quad \lfloor \quad$ *resultSet*←find all *RDCNN*s for the unsafe edge
4 *resultSet*←find all POIs in Ω ►lemma 3

---

4   Unsafe Region

Unsafe regions and some geographical properties are proposed in this section. According to the properties, POIs in unsafe regions may generate new splitting points on the unsafe edges.

It is discovered that there are three cases of α. **Case 1.** $\alpha = 0$, such as Fig. 4(a); **Case 2.** $\alpha \in (0, \theta)$, such as Fig. 4(b); **Case 3.** $\alpha \in [\theta, \pi/2]$, such as Fig. 4(c). R-DCNN query displays different geographical properties when α varies. The property corresponding to the case 1 is the Property 1 [2], i.e., according to the *RDCNN*s of the current real splitting point and the possible splitting point, the location of the new splitting point can be located. Based on the case 2, the Properties 1 and 2 are inferred. According to the case 3, the Property 3 is inferred.

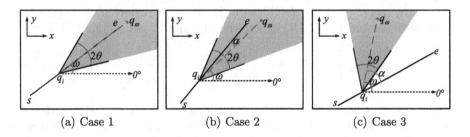

(a) Case 1   (b) Case 2   (c) Case 3

Fig. 4. Three cases of the angle α

In R-DCNN query, if a current real splitting point is q_i, it's *RDCNN* is p_i and the next possible splitting point is q_{i+1}. Two circles are made with centers being q_i and q_{i+1}, and radii being segments $\overline{q_i p_i}$ and $\overline{q_{i+1} p_i}$, respectively. The boundary lines of the circle q_i's (q_{i+1}'s) query angular range are l_{ub} (l'_{ub}) and l_{lb} (l'_{lb}). d (d') is the intersection between l_{lb} (l'_{lb}) and the circle q_{i+1}. If circles q_i and q_{i+1} have two intersections, one of them is p_i and it is assumed that the other is o. According to the location of o, the definitions of the unsafe regions are presented. We use Fig. 5 to visualize our description above.

Definition 8 (Unsafe Region a). When $\alpha \in (0, \theta)$, if o is in the query angular range of q_{i+1}, the unsafe region a is comprised of two circles q_i and q_{i+1}.

Let UR_a denote the unsafe region a and let $\odot q_{i+1}$ and $\odot q_i$ denote the circles q_{i+1} and q_i. There is

$$UR_a = \odot q_{i+1} - (\odot q_i \cap \odot q_{i+1}), \quad l'_{lb} \leq o < l'_{ub} \tag{6}$$

As Fig. 5(a) shows, the $l'_{lb} \leq o < l'_{ub}$ denotes o is between the boundary lines l'_{ub} and l'_{lb}. And the yellow area is the unsafe region a, i.e., UR_a.

Property 1. For each point between q_i and q_{i+1}, UR_a is always in the query angular range. If q_{i+1}'s $RDCNN$ is in UR_a, then there may be new splitting point between q_i and q_{i+1}.

Proof. Figure 5(a) visualizes the proof process. q_{i+1}'s $RDCNN$ is p_m and it is in UR_a. The line l_{im} is the vertical bisector of the segment $\overline{p_i p_m}$. The point $q_i^m \in \overline{q_i q_{i+1}}$ is the intersection between l_{im} and segment $\overline{q_i q_{i+1}}$. For each point between q_i and q_{i+1}, POIs p_i and p_m are always in the angular range. For the segment $\overline{q_i q_i^m}$, the $RDCNN$ is POI p_i, and for $\overline{q_i^m q_{i+1}}$, the $RDCNN$ is POI p_m. Therefore, the intersection q_i^m is a new splitting point.

Definition 9 (Unsafe Region b). When $\alpha \in (0, \theta)$, if o is below l'_{lb}, the unsafe region b is comprised of two circles and the boundary lines l_{lb} and l'_{lb}.

Let UR_b denote the unsafe region b. The F_{q_i} ($F_{q_{i+1}}$) denotes the fan-shaped area $q_i l_{ub} l_{lb}$ ($q_{i+1} l'_{ub} l'_{lb}$). Let IR_q denote the irregular region in circle q_{i+1} but not in circle q_i. And we let IR_d denote the irregular region $q_{i+1} q_i d d'$. There is

$$UR_b = \begin{cases} IR_q - (F_{q_{i+1}} - (F_{q_i} \cap F_{q_{i+1}})), & l_{lb} \leq o < l'_{lb} \\ IR_d - (F_{q_i} \cap IR_d), & o < l_{lb} \end{cases} \tag{7}$$

$l_{lb} \leq o < l'_{lb}$ denotes that o is between l'_{lb} and l_{lb}. As Fig. 5(b) shows, the red and the yellow areas together constitute IR_q. The red area is the unsafe region b, i.e., UR_b. $o < l_{lb}$ denotes that o is below l_{lb}. In Fig. 5(c), the red area is UR_b.

Property 2. For all points between q_i and q_{i+1}, the closer to q_{i+1}, the smaller the size of UR_b is. If it exists POIs in UR_b, then there may be new splitting points between q_i and q_{i+1}.

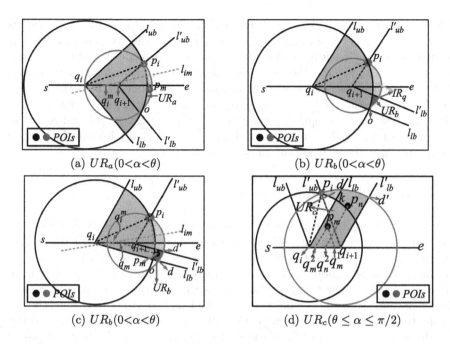

(a) $UR_a(0<\alpha<\theta)$

(b) $UR_b(0<\alpha<\theta)$

(c) $UR_b(0<\alpha<\theta)$

(d) $UR_c(\theta \leq \alpha \leq \pi/2)$

Fig. 5. Unsafe regions (Color figure online)

Proof. Figure 5(c) visualizes the proof process. If there is only one POI p_m in the UR_b. The segment $\overline{q_m p_m}$ ($q_m \in L_{se}$) is parallel to l_{lb}. Lines l_{im} and L_{se} intersect at q_i^m and l_{im} is the vertical bisector of the segment $\overline{p_i p_m}$. From q_i to q_i^m, only two POIs p_i and p_m are in the query angular range and the nearest one is p_i; From q_i^m to q_m, p_i and p_m are still in the angular range but the nearest one is p_m; From q_m to q_{i+1}, only one POI p_i is in the angular range, so POI p_i is the $RDCNN$. Therefore, q_i^m and q_m are new splitting points. If the $RDCNN$ of q_{i+1} is in the yellow region, consideration needs to be given to q_{i+1}'s $RDCNN$.

Definition 10 (Unsafe Region c). When $\alpha \in [\theta, \pi/2]$, the unsafe region c is comprised of the two circles and the boundary lines l_{lb} and l'_{lb}.

Let UR_c denote the unsafe region c. The IR_k denotes the irregular region $p_i kd$ and IR_d denotes the irregular region $q_{i+1} q_i dd'$. There is

$$UR_c = IR_k \cup IR_d, \quad \alpha \in [\theta, \pi/2] \qquad (8)$$

k is the intersection between l_{lb} and the circle q_i. In Fig. 5(d), the yellow area and the grey area together comprise the unsafe region c, i.e., UR_c. The yellow area is the IR_k and the grey area is the IR_d.

Property 3. For all points between q_i and q_{i+1}, IR_k is always in the angular range. The closer to q_{i+1}, the bigger the size of UR_c is. If it exists POIs in UR_c, then there may be new splitting points between q_i and q_{i+1}.

Proof. Figure 5(d) visualizes the proof process. For each point on $\overline{q_i q_{i+1}}$, IR_k is always in the query angular range. From q_i to q_{i+1}, the grey area IR_d in the angular range has been increasing. An assumption is made that there are only POIs p_m and p_n in IR_d. We make auxiliary lines for them, which are parallel to the boundary lines of the angular range. For $\overline{q_i q_m^2}$, only p_i is in the angular range and p_i is the $RDCNN$; For $\overline{q_m^2 q_n^2}$, p_m enters the angular range and p_m is the nearest one; For $\overline{q_n^2 q_m^1}$, p_n enters the angular range, p_i, p_m and p_n are in the angular range and p_m is the nearest one; For $\overline{q_m^1 q_{i+1}}$, p_m isn't in the angular range and p_n is the nearest one, so p_n is the $RDCNN$.

5   Query Algorithm

According to the properties, algorithms are designed to answer the query on the unsafe edges. There are three cases of the query angular range. For the sake of simplicity, we are limited to presenting the algorithms corresponding to $\omega < \theta$, the algorithms corresponding to the other two cases can be easily inferred from the case of $\omega < \theta$. The toughest challenge is that there are innumerable points on the unsafe edge and each point may be the user's location. Consequently, it's impractical to search each point to find all results. Our method is to find the unsafe region. Based on POIs in the unsafe region, we find the splitting points on the unsafe edge and find all results for the edge. We take Fig. 6(a) and (b) as examples to visualize the processes of our algorithms.

5.1   R-DCNN Query Algorithm $(0 < \alpha < \theta)$

When the angle between the favorite direction q_ω and an unsafe edge (L_{se}) is $\alpha \in (0, \theta)$, we design the unsafe edge query algorithm based on properties 1 and 2. A priority queue que is used in the algorithm. Initially, que stores the root node of the R-tree. The shorter the distance from the node to the query point, the higher the priority is. If the type of the node popped from que is a non-leaf node or a leaf node, the operations are same as [2]'s Algorithm 1. If the type of the *node* popped from the que is a point, the operations are as follows.

In Algorithm 2, (s_x, s_y) and (e_x, e_y) are starting and ending coordinates of L_{se}. As Fig. 6(a) shows, the current query point is q and the boundary lines of its query angular range are l_{ub} and l_{lb}. The *node* is the $RDCNN$ of q. The lines l_{ub}' and l_{lb}' are the boundary lines of q''s angular range. l_{ub} and l_{ub}' (l_{lb} and l_{lb}') are parallel, and point *node* is on l_{ub}'. We store the $RDCNN$ *node* in the set *resultSet2* (Line 2). We judge whether the end condition is satisfied (Line 3), if it's satisfied, we execute line 4, otherwise we execute lines 5 to 17. The center of $circle_1$ ($circle_2$) is q (q') and its radius r_1 (r_2) is the distance from q (q') to the current $RDCNN$ *node*. And *node* is one of the intersections of the two circles, and we calculate another intersection *newp* and judge its location (Line 6). In Fig. 6(a), *newp* is below the boundary line l_{lb}. As Fig. 6(a) shows, according to *node*, *newp* and r_2, we can calculate the MBR *mbr* of the candidate region (Line 7). We use a range query to find all points that are in the *mbr* and store them

---

Algorithm 2. $EdgeQuery^{(0<\alpha<\theta)}(que, q)$

Input: s_x, s_y, e_x, e_y, ω, θ
Output: All $RDCNN$s for all points on the unsafe edge L_{se}
1 $q' \leftarrow$ calculate the intersection between l'_{ub} and L_{se}
2 $resultSet2 \leftarrow (node.x, node.y)$
3 **if** $dist(s,q) \geq dist(s,e)$ **then**
4 $\quad$ show $resultSet2$ and end the program

5 **else**
6 $\quad$ $newp \leftarrow$ calculate another intersection and judge its location
7 $\quad$ $mbr \leftarrow$ compute the MBR of the candidate region
8 $\quad$ $set1 \leftarrow$ execute range query on mbr
9 $\quad$ **if** there are points in $area_1$ **then**
10 $\quad\quad$ $tempList1 \leftarrow$ find q''s $RDCNN$
11 $\quad$ $tempList1 \leftarrow$ find all points in $area_2$
12 $\quad$ $tempList2 \leftarrow$ execute a LNN search for $tempList1$
13 $\quad$ **for** ele in $tempList2$ **do**
14 $\quad\quad$ **if** $ele[2][0] \in [q[0], q'[0]]$ **then**
15 $\quad\quad\quad$ $resultSte2 \leftarrow ele[0], ele[1]$

16 $\quad$ $q \leftarrow q'$
17 $\quad$ empty and initialize the priority queue que

---

in the set $set1$ (Line 8). For points in $set1$, if they are in the $area_1$, we find the nearest one to q' and store it in list $tempList1$ (Line 10). We find all points in $area_2$ and store them in the $tempList1$ (Line 11). The $area_2$ is unsafe region b i.e., UR_b. We execute a LNN search [1] for all points in $tempList1$ and store the results in $tempList2$ (Line 12). The elements in the list $tempList2$ are in the form of (p_1, p_2, q_{12}), the point q_{12} is the intersection of the vertical bisector

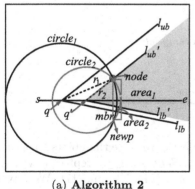

(a) **Algorithm 2**

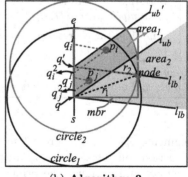

(b) **Algorithm 3**

Fig. 6. Visualization analyses of the Algorithms 2 and 3

Algorithm 3. $EdgeQuery^{(\theta \leq \alpha \leq \pi/2)}(prioque, q)$

Input: $s_x,\ s_y,\ e_x,\ e_y,\ \omega,\ \theta$

Output: All $RDCNNs$ for all points on the edge L_{se}

1 $r_1\ (r_2) \leftarrow dist(q, node)\ (dist(q', node))$

2 $mbr \leftarrow$ compute the MBR of unsafe region

3 $set2 \leftarrow$ execute range query on mbr

4 **for** p_i in $set2$ **do**

5 $\quad$ $q_i^2 \leftarrow \overline{q_i^2 p_i}$ is parallel to l_{ub} and the q_i^2 is on line L_{se}

6 $\quad$ $q_i^1 \leftarrow \overline{q_i^1 p_i}$ is parallel to l_{lb} and the q_i^1 is on line L_{se}

7 $\quad$ **if** $q[1] \leq q_i^2[1] \leq q'[1]$ and $dist(p_i, q') \leq r_2$ **then**

8 $\quad\quad$ $que1 \leftarrow ((dist(q_i^2, q), p_i, q_i^2, 1), dist(q_i^2, q))$

9 $\quad\quad$ **if** $q[1] \leq q_i^1[1] \leq q'[1]$ **then**

10 $\quad\quad\quad$ $que1 \leftarrow ((dist(q_i^1, q), p_i, q_i^1, 0), dist(q_i^1, q))$

11 $\quad$ **if** $q_i^2[1] < q[1]$, $r_1 \leq dist(p_i, q)$, $dist(p_i, q') \leq r_2$ **then**

12 $\quad\quad$ $tempSet, tempList5 \leftarrow p_i$

13 $tempList3 \leftarrow$ do an operate on the priority queue $que1$

14 **for** $ele1$ in $tempList3$ **do**

15 $\quad$ $tempList4 \leftarrow$ do a LNN search for $tempList5$

16 $\quad$ **for** $ele2$ in $tempList4$ **do**

17 $\quad\quad$ **if** $ele1[0][0][1] \leq ele2[2][1] < ele1[1][0][1]$ **then**

18 $\quad\quad\quad$ $que1 \leftarrow ((dist(q, ele2[2]), (ele2[0], ele2[1]), ele2[2], 2),\ (dist(q, ele2[2])))$

19 $\quad$ **if** $ele1[1][2] == 1$ **then**

20 $\quad\quad$ $tempList5 \leftarrow ele1[1][1]$

21 $\quad$ **else**

22 $\quad\quad$ $tempList5.remove(ele1[1][1])$

23 **while** $que1.size() != 0$ **do**

24 $\quad$ $bestp \leftarrow que1.pop()$

25 $\quad$ **if** $bestp[3] == 1$ **then**

26 $\quad\quad$ $tempSet.add(bestp[1])$

27 $\quad$ **if** $bestp[3] == 0$ **then**

28 $\quad\quad$ $tempSet.remove(bestp[1])$

29 $\quad$ $nnp \leftarrow$ find the nearest one to $bestp[2]$ in $tempSet$

30 $\quad$ $resultSet3 \leftarrow nnp$

31 $q \leftarrow q'$

32 *empty and initialize the priority queue* prioque

---

of segment $\overline{p_1 p_2}$ and L_{se}. From line 13 to line 15, we store the points that their intersections on the segment $\overline{qq'}$ in the $resultSet2$. Next, we replace q with q', and empty and initialize the priority queue que (Lines 16 and 17). We repeat the above operations until the end condition is satisfied.

Table 2. Synthetic and real datasets

Dataset size (real and synthetic)	Region size (real and synthetic)	Data type (real)
$0.1K$	[0, 100]*[0, 100]	Hotels
$1K$	[0, 1000]*[0, 100]	Gas stations
$10K$	[0, 1000]*[0, 1000]	Banks
$100K$	[0, 10000]*[0, 1000]	Restaurants

5.2   R-DCNN Query Algorithm ($\theta \leq \alpha \leq \frac{\pi}{2}$)

When $\alpha \in [\theta, \pi/2]$, the unsafe edge query algorithm based on Property 3 is designed. A priority queue is used to assist with implementing the algorithm. If the type of the element popped from the queue is a point, then we store it in the set $resultSet3$ and calculate the next possible splitting point q'. Subsequently, we determine whether the end condition $dist(s,q) \geq dist(s,e)$ is satisfied. If it is satisfied, we end the program and output $resultSet3$. Otherwise, we execute the Algorithm 3.

In Algorithm 3, starting and ending coordinates of L_{se} are (s_x,s_y) and (e_x,e_y). Favorite direction and favorite angle are q_ω and θ. We calculate the radii of the two circles ($circle_1$ and $circle_2$) (Line 1). As Fig. 6(b) shows, "$area_1$" and "$area_2$" together constitute the unsafe region c (UR_c). We compute the MBR of the unsafe region (Line 2). A range query can be used to find all points in the mbr and storing them in the set $set2$ (Line 3). For each point p_i in $set2$, we calculate q_i^1 and q_i^2 for p_i (Lines 5 and 6). Line 7, we determine whether q_i^2 is on the segment $\overline{qq'}$ and the p_i is in the $circle_2$, and if so, we execute lines 8 to 10. We push a tuple associated with q_i^2 into the priority queue $que1$ (Line 8). If q_i^1 of p_i is on the segment $\overline{qq'}$, we push the tuple $((dist(q_i^1,q),p_i,q_i^1,0),dist(q_i^1,q))$ into the $que1$ (Line 10). If the q_i^2 of p_i is below the point q, and p_i is within the "$area_2$", we store p_i in the set $tempSet$ and the list $tempList5$ (Line 12). We do a operation for all elements in the priority queue $que1$ and get the list $tempList3$ (Line 13). Let's take Fig. 6(b) as an example to illustrate the elements stored in the List $tempList3$, which is $[((q,none,none), (q_j^2,p_j,1)), ((q_j^2,p_j,1), (q_j^1,p_j,0)),$ ..., $((q_i^2,p_i,1), (q',none, none))]$. For every element $ele1$ in the $tempList3$, we do a LNN search [1] for all points in $tempList5$ and store the results in $tempList4$ (Line 15). For every element $ele2$ in $tempList4$, if LNN search [1] generates new splitting points on the element, we execute the line 18. From line 19 to line 22, we update the list $tempList5$ according to the marking of the element $ele1$. The priority queue $que1$ stores all splitting points. For every splitting point, we execute the line 23 to the line 30 to find all $RDCNNs$ and store them in the $resultSet3$.

6   Experiments

In this section, we give the evaluations of the proposed algorithms. All algorithms are implemented in Python and all experiments are conducted on the ubuntu

16.04 system. The datasets used in our experiments are presented in Table 2 and the datasets include real and synthetic datasets. Synthetic datasets are generated on a random basis. Real datasets are crawled from the High German map involving the data of the hotels, gas stations, banks and restaurants in Beijing, China.

Baseline Algorithm. When a search is conducted on an unsafe edge L_{se} of Ω, our baseline method is to have random selection of some points on L_{se} and perform snapshot DCNN queries [2] for these points to find their $RDCNN$s. A comparison of the efficiency is drawn of the baseline method to the proposed R-DCNN query method. Experimental results demonstrate that our method is not only capable of a higher accuracy rate than the baseline method, but also more efficient than it.

6.1   Experiments on R-DCNN Query ($0 < \alpha < \theta$)

In this section, we show the experimental results of the R-DCNN query algorithm ($0 < \alpha < \theta$). We evaluate the effect on varying the sizes of the favorite angle θ and the dataset. The favorite angles in the experiments include $10°, 20°, 30°$ and $40°$. In addition, an evaluation is made of the effect on varying the fan-out size of the R-tree. When the node is a leaf, the fan-out size is the number of the points in MBR. If the node is an internal node, the fan-out size is the number of branches. In our experiments, "BSL" is used to indicate the baseline method, and "R-DCNN" is used to indicate the R-DCNN query algorithm. Let vertical axis denote the query time (second) and let horizontal axis denote the dataset size (Fig. 7(a), (b), (e) and (f)), or the favorite angle size (Fig. 7(c) and (d)).

Figure 7(a) and (b) show the experimental results of variation in the dataset sizes. Obviously, R-DCNN query method is more efficient than the baseline method on both real and synthetic datasets when the size of the dataset varies. The θ is $40°$ and fan-out size is 25. In Fig. 7(c) and (d), they are the experimental results of varying sizes of the favorite angle θ. It is discovered that the R-DCNN query method is more efficient as compared to the baseline method on both real and synthetic datasets when the sizes of favorite angle θ vary. Dataset size is $100K$ and fan-out size is 25. Figure 7(e) and (f) exhibit the experimental results (R-DCNN query) of varying the fan-out size of the R-tree. It has been observed that the efficiency of the R-DCNN query algorithm varies when the fan-out size is different, whether it's on real or synthetic datasets. When dataset size equals $1K$ or $10K$ and fan-out size is 25, R-DCNN query has the highest efficiency. When dataset size is $0.1K$ and fan-out size is 15, the algorithm exhibits the highest efficiency. The fan-out sizes we selected are 15, 25 and 35 and θ is $30°$.

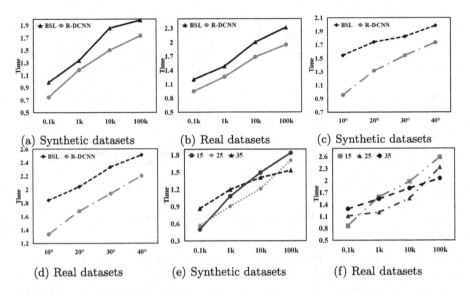

Fig. 7. Experiments on R-DCNN query $(0 < \alpha < \theta)$

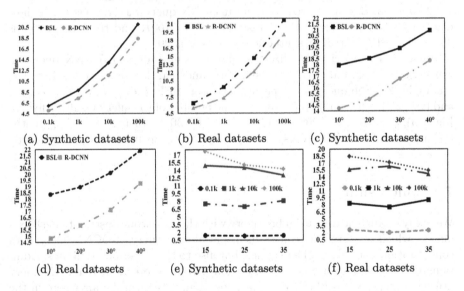

Fig. 8. Experiments on R-DCNN query $(\theta \leq \alpha \leq \pi/2)$

6.2 Experiments on R-DCNN Query $(\theta \leq \alpha \leq \pi/2)$

Figure 8(a) and (b) are experimental results obtained from varying the dataset size. R-DCNN algorithm is more efficient than the baseline method when the dataset size is different, whether it's on real or synthetic datasets. θ is 40° and fan-out size is 25. Figure 8(c) and (d) show experimental results of vary-

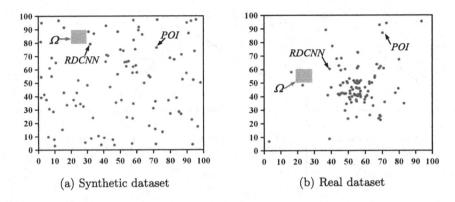

(a) Synthetic dataset   (b) Real dataset

Fig. 9. Query results of R-DCNN query

ing θ. Apparently, when the size of θ varies, the efficiency of the R-DCNN query is higher than that of the baseline method, whether it's on real or synthetic datasets. Fan-out size is 25 and dataset size is $100K$. Figure 8(e) and (f) exhibit experimental results of varying fan-out size. The fan-out sizes we selected are 15, 25 and 35. It's discovered that the R-DCNN query method has the highest efficiency when the size of the dataset is $10K$ or $100K$ and the fan-out size is 35, whether it's on real or synthetic datasets. θ is $20°$.

Figure 9(a) and (b) visualize the query results of the R-DCNN query on synthetic and real datasets. Both synthetic and real dataset sizes are 100. The rectangle Ω is the query area specified by user. In Fig. 9(a), $q_\omega = 10°$, $\theta = 15°$ and $(\omega_\perp^\theta, \omega_\top^\theta) = [0°, 25°) \cup (355°, 360°)$. The number of the query results is five. In Fig. 9(b), $q_\omega = 10°$, $\theta = 20°$ and $(\omega_\perp^\theta, \omega_\top^\theta) = [0°, 30°) \cup (350°, 360°)$. Apparently, the number of the $RDCNNs$ is five. Fan-out size on both real and synthetic datasets is 15.

7   Conclusion

We study a range nearest neighbor query with the direction constraint (R-DCNN query), which is a direction-constrained spatial data query. R-DCNN query gives consideration not only to the distance, but also to the direction attributes. Additionally, it takes into account the location privacy protection. R-DCNN query utilizes a rectangle to blur user's exact location, which can be anywhere in the rectangle. Consequently, the exact location of the user will not be exposed. R-DCNN query finds the nearest POI in the query angular range for each point in the rectangle. According to some properties we design effective algorithms and experimental results indicate that our algorithms are accurate and efficient.

Acknowledgment. This work is supported by the National Natural Science Foundation of China (No. 61602031). This work is also supported by Research into the High-Definition Remote Sensing-Based Critical Intelligent Monitoring Technology for Spatial Planning and its Model Applications (Dedicated Project of East-West Cooperation) (No. 2018YBZD1629).

References

1. Hu, H., Lee, D.L.: Range nearest-neighbor Query. IEEE Trans. Knowl. Data Eng. **18**(1), 78–91 (2006)
2. Miao, X., Guo, X., Wang, H., Wang, Z., Ye, X.: Continuous nearest neighbor query with the direction constraint. In: Kawai, Y., Storandt, S., Sumiya, K. (eds.) W2GIS 2019. LNCS, vol. 11474, pp. 85–101. Springer, Cham (2019). https://doi.org/10.1007/978-3-030-17246-6_8
3. Knuth, D.E.: The art of computer programming volume 3 sorting and searching. Comput. J. **17**(4), 324–324 (1998)
4. Korn, F, Sidiropoulos, N.D., et al.: Fast nearest neighbor search in medical image databases. In: Proceedings of International Conference on Very Large Data Bases, pp. 215–226 (1996)
5. Seidl, T., Kriegel, H.: Optimal multi-step k-nearest neighbor search. ACM SIGMOD Rec. **27**(2), 154–165 (1998)
6. Cui, B., Ooi, B.C., et al.: Contorting high dimensional data for efficient main memory KNN processing. In: ACM SIGMOD International Conference on Management of Data, pp. 479–490 (2003)
7. Roussopoulos, N., Kelley, S.: Nearest neighbor queries. In: ACM SIGMOD International Conference on Management of Data ACM, vol. 24, no. 2, pp. 71–79 (1995)
8. Hjaltason, G.R., Samet, H.: Distance browsing in spatial databases. ACM Trans. Database Syst. **24**(2), 265–318 (1999)
9. Berchtold, S., Ertl, B., et al.: Fast nearest neighbor search in high-dimensional space. In: Proceedings of the ICDE, 209–218 (1998)
10. Belussi, A., Bertino, E., et al.: Using spatial data access structures for filtering nearest neighbor queries. Data Knowl. Eng. **40**(1), 1–31 (2002)
11. Henrich, A.: A distance scan algorithm for spatial access structures. Int. J. Geogr. Inform. Sci. 136–143 (1994)
12. Sharifzadeh, M., Shahabi, C.: VoR-tree: R-trees with voronoi diagrams for efficient processing of spatial nearest neighbor queries. In: VLDB, pp. 1231–1242 (2010)
13. Zhu, H., Yang, X., et al.: Range-based obstructed nearest neighbor queries. In: Proceedings of the SIGMOD, pp. 2053–2068 (2016)
14. Guo, X., Zheng, B., et al.: Direction-based surrounder queries for mobile recommendations. VLDB J. **20**(5), 743–766 (2011)
15. Li, G., Feng, J., et al.: DESKS: direction-aware spatial keyword search. In: IEEE International Conference on Data Engineering, vol. 1084, no. 4627, pp. 474–485 (2012)
16. Chen, L., Li, Y., et al.: Direction-aware why-not spatial keyword top-k queries. In: ICDE, pp. 107–110 (2017)
17. Chen, L., Li, Y., et al.: Towards why-not spatial keyword top-k queries: a direction-aware approach. IEEE Trans. Knowl. Data Eng. **30**(4), 796–809 (2018)
18. Guo, X., Yang, X.: Direction-aware nearest neighbour query. IEEE Access **7**, 30285–30301 (2019)
19. Lee, J.M., Choi, W.D., et al.: The direction-constrained k nearest neighbor query. GeoInformatica **20**(3), 471–502 (2016)

Cloud Service Access Frequency Estimation Based on a Stream Filtering Method

Shiting Wen[1,2(✉)], Jinqiu Yang[1], Chaoyan Zhu[1], and Genlang Chen[1,2]

[1] Ningbo Insitute of Technology, Zhejiang Uiniversity, Ningbo, China
{wensht,jqyang,zcy,cgl}@nit.zju.edu.cn
[2] Ningbo Research Institute, Zhejiang University, Ningbo, China

Abstract. Cloud service discovery forms the foundation of the efficient and agile implementation of complex business processes. The core problem of existing QoS-aware cloud service discovery mechanisms is that the process of cloud service QoS acquisition is difficult. The issue of how to obtain the number of times a cloud service has been accessed over a period of time needs to be addressed, and the access information for the cloud service needs to be fully recorded. It is difficult to adapt traditional means of data processing to the concurrent access requirements of a massive cloud service, resulting in a lack of accurate QoS information support for cloud service aggregation. This paper proposes a method based on bucket filtering to collect cloud service access flow log information. It then explores a way of abstracting cloud service access flow into a binary bit stream, and uses the DGIM algorithm to carry out an approximate evaluation of cloud service access to analyse cloud service access flow. Our approach enables an estimation of cloud service access frequency and balances the space and time overheads of cloud service access log storage and calculation. Theoretical analysis and experimental verification prove that our access has good universality and good performance.

Keywords: Cloud service · QoS-aware estimation · Services composition

1 Introduction

Cloud services are a new type of software usage that relies on the Internet to provide software services. Compared with traditional software applications, cloud services are characterised by pay-on-demand, platform independence and flexible combinations, and have become the most commonly used software delivery and usage mode [11,15,18], as shown in Fig. 1.

In order to make cloud services widely available, providers typically limit their functions and provide only atomic cloud services (such as weather forecasts, airline tickets, hotel reservations, etc.). However, the customer's business needs

L. H. U et al. (Eds.): WISE 2019, CCIS 1155, pp. 132–141, 2020.
https://doi.org/10.1007/978-981-15-3281-8_12

Fig. 1. Cloud service application scenario

are usually more complex, requiring multiple component cloud services to be combined to fulfil these needs.

However, users face problems when selecting multiple component cloud services in order to combine them. The issue of how to objectively select the appropriate component cloud service is a very challenging one, and if the selection of a component cloud service is inappropriate, it may reduce the efficiency of the entire business package. Each cloud service provides services to users via interfaces, and users are not aware of the details of the implementation inside the component cloud services. Many users do not have professional knowledge, and cannot understand these details, and it is therefore often necessary to monitor the component cloud to help users select appropriate services. Cloud services are chosen based on the quality of service (such as the response time, error rate, reliability or throughput) of their component services during service execution.

We therefore need to use an effective method to monitor the operation of cloud services. However, cloud services provide services to the entire Internet, with large numbers of users and an uneven distribution of execution frequency. We therefore need to be able to use effective measures to record key metrics, such as the number of visits to a cloud service and the response time of each call. The management and analysis of the historical execution of cloud services faces the following challenging problems:

- **Large amounts of data:** Cloud services are provided to users throughout the Internet. The frequency of use of some cloud services may be very high, and the amount of logged information may be very large. It is almost impossible to record all the information on call history.
- **Unpredictable access:** User access to cloud services is random, and the frequency of access does not follow a probability distribution. It is difficult to estimate user access over a period of time using probabilistic methods.

– **Diversity of queries:** Users often initiate query requests such as "the average execution time over the last N calls", although the values of N sent by different users are completely different, and the differences are very large. The issue of how to answer this is not straightforward, and the problem of "anytime multiple queries recently" remains a huge challenge.

This paper proposes a new method for recording log information about cloud service execution, and can offer a feasible solution to these problems given the error boundary. In Sect. 2, we review relevant research work; Sect. 3 gives details about the background and the methods used in this paper; Sect. 4 describes the problem-solving steps used in the specific application model; Sect. 5 presents an analysis and an experimental evaluation of the proposed method; and Sect. 6 gives a summary of the work carried out in this paper.

2   Related Works

Cloud service is currently one of the most popular software delivery and delivery methods. It is an Internet-based, pay-as-you-go, dynamic expansion, cross-platform software usage model. The cloud is widely used in online services, travel services, public services, e-commerce and other applications. The main difficulty in cloud service applications is that of how to find cloud services that meet the user's requirements. In recent years, research related to cloud service selection has been based on the choice of service quality perception, QoS-driven cloud service discovery is still the focus of current research [7,17]. This mainly focuses on QoS acquisition, weight calculation, and factors affecting QoS. Ma et al. examined a combination of configurable cloud services and proposed the concept of reconfigurable services; they then developed a reconfigurable service for specifying QoS attributes, and considered a problem involving reconfigurable services [8]. Kumara et. al. proposed a QoS-aware service clustering method to improve the performance of service selection. This method generates an affinity matrix based on QoS profit value and the algorithm aggregates services on the service domain based on QoS values [5].

The discovery and recommendation of cloud services based on collaborative filtering is also the focus of many researchers. The authors of a proposed mobile service use a multidimensional space-time model to analyse the service consumption relationship due to a change in the client's location, in which the recommender considers the service request time and the location of the target client in order to effectively predict the unknown quality of service (QoS) [12]. The author of this model proposes the use of collaborative filtering to achieve a service recommendation based on QoS attribute values. A ratio-based approach has also been proposed to calculate the similarity, which is used as the basis for a new method for predicting unknown values [16]. In another study, a framework is developed for modelling the dependencies between different QoS parameters of component services. Collaborative filtering is used to predict the QoS values of different services to develop an optimised solution [4].

In another work, a QoS-based cloud service automation portfolio solution is developed that pre-generates all possible service combinations and stores them in a relational database. When the user request is received, the SQL retrieves the top-K combination scheme in response to the user's needs [6]. Service selection based on top-K and skyline has also been studied by the current authors in relation to how to solve the problem of service choice for uncertain QoS [14]. In other work, a scheme is proposed that can automatically combine a set of skyline combination schemes in response to user requests [13].

The characteristics of the mobile Internet environment, such as mobility, rapid changes in the network environment and so on, are considered in a new cloud service composition problem for mobile devices [3]. A hybrid approach has been put forward for the automatic composition of Web services that combines a set of graph optimisations with a local global search to extract the best components from the graph [9]. Another study addresses the efficiency issues of cloud services when dealing with large-scale data, and the author divides the parallel execution strategy of atomic services into three different categories: a slow strategy, a restriction strategy, and a penalty policy. Based on these strategies, the proposed predictive model can calculate the execution time of the composite service when using parallel execution and can estimate the optimal parallelism of the composite service [10].

3   Preliminaries

3.1   Motivation

Cloud services provided on the Internet are charged according to their usage. In order to obtain the trust of the users, the providers must do their utmost to ensure the quality of these services (such as the response time). However, the QoS changes with alterations in the network environment and the number of user requests. Before using the cloud service, the user needs to have an objective understanding of the historical execution of the cloud service. We must therefore be able to accurately answer a user's query about the execution of the cloud service within a certain time window, for example: "How many times has cloud service S been successfully accessed in the last K transactions?".

We can abstract such problems into a statistical counting problem for binary streams. We define a query for the most recent N transactions by setting a window of size N. When the cloud service S is successfully accessed, the equivalent bit 1 enters the stream; otherwise, a bit equivalent to 0 enters the stream. When a new binary bit is entered, the new bit data is directly inserted into the end of the stream unless the stream has reached the maximum limit of the window. If the stream window is full, the bit that is furthest from the current time is discarded, and the new bit is inserted at the end of the stream. To answer the questions discussed above, we simply need to summarise the data elements in the stream, as shown in Fig. 2.

3.2   Problem Statement

Since it is not possible to control external requests to access cloud services, external requests are infinite and non-stationary. To answer the above questions accurately, the provider must be able to record all user requests and service execution information. If the size of the window N is very large (for example $N = 1$ billion), we do not have enough storage space to store such large user log records.

We propose a statistical query method for cloud service access based on bucket management. The proposed method implements a query for cloud service access within a set window, and can be used to request a query evaluation of the cloud service access in the case of non-uniform arrival.

Definition 1. *(Binary Stream): A binary bit stream $(<..., b_i, ..., b_2, b_1>)$ is a stream data type where each element b_i is a binary bit (with value 1 or 0).*

Definition 2. *(Bucket): A bucket is a two-tuple $bucket_i = <ts_i, size_i>$ where:*

- *ts_i: is the timestamp of the $i - th$ bucket, which is the deadline timestamp of all elements in the bucket;*
- *$size_i$: indicates the number of elements in the $i - th$ bucket.*

4   Cloud Service Usage Query Model

4.1   Cloud Service Query Modeling

The bucket management uses the DGIM algorithm, which is widely used to count binary streams [1,2]. For a cloud service S, if a user's access attempt is successful, a binary bit is used to record this. A bucket is then used to organise and store the binary bit stream generated by this user access. Here, we do not store the fixed-length binary bit stream in each bucket, but instead store the cut-off timestamp of this sub-stream element and the number of bit elements with value one contained in this sub-stream. For the partitioning of buckets, we have a mandatory constraint that requires the size of each bucket (the number of binary bits with value 1 stored in the bucket) to be a power of two, as shown in Fig. 2.

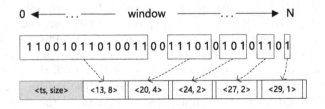

Fig. 2. Buckets

Each bit has a unique timestamp in the stream, such as $1, 2, 3, ...N$. In our system, an older time stamp indicates an earlier entry of the binary bit; otherwise, a larger timestamp value indicates a later entry of the bit into the system (no timestamp values exceed the window size N). In each bucket, we need to save the stop timestamp of the binary bits in the bucket and the total number of bits with value one in the bucket.

In addition, the following constraints must be met for each bucket: (i) the number of bits in the bucket with value one must be an exponential multiple of two; (ii) the number of buckets containing the same number of bits with value one can only be one or two; (iii) there is no repetition of the time stamp for any element between buckets; (iv) the buckets are sorted according to the number of bits they hold with value 1, and a bucket formed earlier contains no fewer than the number of bits with value 1 contained in the newly generated bucket; (v) when the deadline timestamp of bits with value 1 in the bucket exceeds the maximum timestamp number N, then the bucket is discarded.

4.2   Bucket Creation and Update Algorithm

When a new bit arrives, a timestamp must be assigned to it (the timestamp is allocated using an auto-increment mode). If the arriving bit is zero, then no processing is required, but if the arriving bit is one, then a new bucket of size one needs to be created for the newly arrived bit. The timestamp of the bucket is the same as this bit (as shown in lines 3 to 8 of Algorithm 1). Secondly, all buckets are traversed in order of size, from small to large. When the number of buckets with the same size is greater than two, the first two buckets to be created need to be merged. The size of this merged bucket is equal to that of two buckets, and its timestamp is the timestamp of whichever bucket was created later (see lines 9 to 14 of Algorithm 1). Thirdly, if the timestamp of a bucket exceeds the window, i.e. the bucket's timestamp is less than the current timestamp minus N (the window size), then the bucket is discarded (as shown in lines 15 to 19 of Algorithm 1).

4.3   Cloud Service Access Query

In this section, we answer the question of how many times the most recent N visits of a cloud service were successfully called. The provider of the cloud service is usually a clustered service. In order to obtain as many users as possible, the service provider will provide several different types of interface, parameters and levels of QoS, but the cloud services will function similarly for each type of user. In order to effectively evaluate the appeal of these cloud services to users, we need to perform a statistical analysis and to query the user's call status over a period of time, in order to better arrange resources and optimise the user experience. As shown in the model in Fig. 3, a virtual bit stream is maintained for each cloud service access log, and the bit stream is managed by applying the bucket model mentioned above. When a user needs to know the success rate of a recent cloud service access, only the bit stream of the corresponding cloud

Algorithm 1. Cloud Service Access Log Stream Data Processing

---

    input : 0 *or* 1 *bit stream data*
    output: *A List of Buckets:* $\{bucket_i\}$
1 **Init:** *set* $ts = -1$;
2 **begin**
3   **foreach** $\forall b$ *received from Users* **do**
4         $ts \leftarrow (ts + 1)\% N$;
5   **if** b *equals to* 1 **then**
6   *create a newbucket bucket';*
7             $bucket' \leftarrow \{timestamp = ts, size = 1\}$;
8             $ListBucket \leftarrow ListBucket \cup \{bucket'\}$;
9   **while** $count\{ListBucket, size = i(i \in [1, N])\} > 2$ **do**
10                $\{bucket_a, bucket_b\} \leftarrow Max : ListBucket\{size = i\}(b > a)$;
11                $ListBucket \leftarrow ListBucket - \{bucket_a\}$;
12                $bucket_b \leftarrow \{timestamp_b, size_a + size_b\}$;
13                $i \leftarrow i + 1$;
14   **end**
15   **foreach** $bucket \in ListBucket$ **do**
16   **if** $bucket.timestamp < ts - N$ **then**
17                   $ListBucket \leftarrow ListBucket - \{bucket\}$;
18   **end**
19   **end**
20   **else**
21   *discard* b_i;
22   **end**
23   **end**
24 **end**

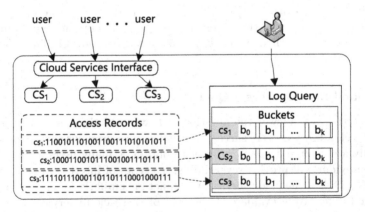

Fig. 3. Cloud service query model

service needs to be queried. More specifically, the total number of successful cloud service accesses within a given window is given by summing all the bits of the bucket in the current window and adding half of the bit stream of the boundary bucket. The ratio of this value to the window size gives the success rate of access.

5   Experimental Evaluation

We performed experiments on a server with a Windows 10 64-bit system, 8 GB memory (1600 MHz), Intel(R) Core(TM) i5-5300U CPU 2.30 GHz (2295 MHz). We deployed six functionally identical cloud services, and simulated 600 users who randomly requested six cloud services. These 600 users were divided into 10 groups.

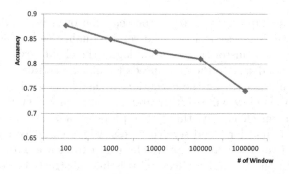

Fig. 4. Accuracy of prediction of cloud service access frequency

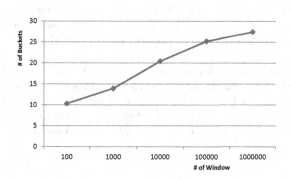

Fig. 5. Number of buckets for different window sizes

Figure 4 shows the average prediction accuracy based on the proposed method (where the ordinate is the accuracy of the cloud service access prediction, and the abscissa is the window size). The accuracy of the window class is statistically measured at different times. As the window becomes larger, the accuracy rate shows a linear downward trend, and the overall accuracy still reaches about 75% when the window reaches a size of 1 million. The accuracy is close to 90% when the window is small. This is because as the window grows larger, the number of elements stored in the oldest bucket class increases exponentially, causing the total elements of the statistics. As the proportion increases, the statistical error increases accordingly.

Figure 5 shows the number of buckets that need to be saved for different window sizes. The number of buckets increases as the window becomes larger, in a relatively linear manner. When the window size reaches 1 million, the number of buckets does not exceed 30, which shows that the algorithm has good robustness.

6   Conclusion

QoS is the most important factor in the selection of cloud services by a user. However, the user's assessment of cloud service quality mainly depends on statistical queries of the historical execution log of the cloud service. The platform providing the cloud service therefore needs to allocate certain resources to save historical log information on the execution of the cloud service. Maintaining a large log query window will exert greater pressure on the system. In order to solve this problem effectively, this paper proposes a bucket-based log stream management method for cloud service access, which can effectively reduce the consumption of resources and improve the user experience of querying logs. In our proposed method, cloud service access is first abstracted into a bit stream, and the DGIM bit stream management algorithm is then applied to manage the log bit stream accessed by the cloud service. Experimental verification shows that the accuracy of our method in estimating cloud service access can reach more than 75%, and that the storage resources that need to be allocated can be greatly reduced. The user query experience can also be significantly improved. In future work, we intend to perform bit-stream-based estimation of other QOS execution information, such as the historical execution time.

Acknowledgment. This work was supported in part by the Natural Science Foundation of China with No.61802344, in part by Zhejiang Provincial Natural Science Foundation of China with No. LY16F030012 and LY15F030016, in part by Humanities and Social Science Foundation of Ministry of Education of China with No. 16YJCZH112 and in part by Ningbo Science and Technology Special Projects of China with No. 2016C11024 and 2017C110002.

References

1. Babcock, B., Babu, S., Datar, M., Motwani, R., Widom, J.: Models and issues in data stream systems. In: Proceedings of the Twenty-First ACM SIGMOD-SIGACT-SIGART Symposium on Principles of Database Systems, pp. 1–16. ACM (2002)
2. Datar, M., Gionis, A., Indyk, P., Motwani, R.: Maintaining stream statistics over sliding windows. SIAM J. Comput. **31**(6), 1794–1813 (2002)

3. Deng, S., Huang, L., Hu, D., Zhao, J.L., Wu, Z.: Mobility-enabled service selection for composite services. IEEE Trans. Serv. Comput. **9**(3), 394–407 (2016)
4. Hashmi, K., Malik, Z., Erradi, A., Rezgui, A.: Qos dependency modeling for composite systems. IEEE Trans. Serv. Comput. **11**(6), 936–947 (2018)
5. Kumara, B.T.G.S., Paik, I., Siriweera, T.H.A.S., Koswatte, K.R.C.: QoS aware service clustering to bootstrap the web service selection. In: 2017 IEEE International Conference on Services Computing (SCC), pp. 233–240 (2017)
6. Li, J., Yan, Y., Lemire, D.: Full solution indexing for top-k web service composition. IEEE Trans. Serv. Comput. **11**(3), 521–533 (2018)
7. Liu, A., Li, Q., Huang, L., Ying, S., Xiao, M.: Coalitional game for community-based autonomous web services cooperation. IEEE Trans. Serv. Comput. **6**(3), 387–399 (2013)
8. Ma, H., Bastani, F., Yen, I., Mei, H.: Qos-driven service composition with reconfigurable services. IEEE Trans. Serv. Comput. **6**(1), 20–34 (2013)
9. Rodríguez-Mier, P., Mucientes, M., Lama, M.: Hybrid optimization algorithm for large-scale qos-aware service composition. IEEE Trans. Serv. Comput. **10**(4), 547–559 (2017)
10. Trang, M.X., Murakami, Y., Ishida, T.: Policy-aware service composition: predicting parallel execution performance of composite services. IEEE Trans. Serv. Comput. **11**(4), 602–615 (2018)
11. Wang, H., Wang, L., Yu, Q., Zheng, Z., Bouguettaya, A., Lyu, M.R.: Online reliability prediction via motifs-based dynamic Bayesian networks for service-oriented systems. IEEE Trans. Softw. Eng. **43**(6), 556–579 (2017)
12. Wang, S., Ma, Y., Cheng, B., Yang, F., Chang, R.N.: Multi-dimensional QoS prediction for service recommendations. IEEE Trans. Serv. Comput. **12**(1), 47–57 (2019)
13. Wen, S., Li, Q., Tang, C., Liu, A., Huang, L., Liu, Y.: Processing mutliple requests to construct skyline composite services. J. Web Eng. **13**(1–2), 53–66 (2014)
14. Wen, S., Tang, C., Li, Q., Chiu, D.K.W., Liu, A., Han, X.: Probabilistic top-K dominating services composition with uncertain QoS. SOCA **8**(1), 91–103 (2014)
15. Wen, S., Yang, J., Chen, G., Tao, J., Yu, X., Liu, A.: Enhancing service composition by discovering cloud services community. IEEE Access **7**, 32472–32481 (2019)
16. Wu, X., Cheng, B., Chen, J.: Collaborative filtering service recommendation based on a novel similarity computation method. IEEE Trans. Serv. Comput. **10**(3), 352–365 (2017)
17. Zeng, L., Benatallah, B., Ngu, A.H.H., Dumas, M., Kalagnanam, J., Chang, H.: QoS-aware middleware for web services composition. IEEE Trans. Softw. Eng. **30**(5), 311–327 (2004)
18. Zhu, J., He, P., Zheng, Z., Lyu, M.R.: Online QoS prediction for runtime service adaptation via adaptive matrix factorization. IEEE Trans. Parallel Distrib. Syst. **28**(10), 2911–2924 (2017)

Influence Maximization Based on Community Closeness in Social Networks

Qingqing Wu, Lihua Zhou$^{(\boxtimes)}$, and Yaqun Huang

School of Information, Yunnan University, Kunming 650091, China
wuqing@mail.ynu.edu.cn, {lhzhou,yqhuang}@ynu.edu.cn

Abstract. The research of Influence maximization (IM) has always been a hot research topic in network analysis, which aims to find the most influential users in social networks to maximize the reach of influence. In recent year, many studies have focused on the problem of IM to improve efficiency by taking advantage of the small-scale community structures. However, the existing community-based methods only consider the number of nodes in a community and ignore the density of edge connections in a community. In addition, existing method can only be applied to non-overlapping community structures. In this paper, we propose community closeness-based influence maximization algorithm (CCIM) to select most influential nodes. CCIM considers the influence of point-to-point and point-to-community, reflecting the micro-level and meso-level influence. The experimental results on synthetic and three real datasets verify CCIM outperforms the state-of-the-art baselines.

Keywords: Influence maximization · Community closeness · Information diffusion

1 Introduction

In recent years, the rapid advance of internet technologies promoted the development of social networks, such as Twitter, Weibo and WeChat. Social network is an intricate network of relationships among individuals, which facilitates the spread of information among them. Influence maximization (IM) aims to identify a set of most influential users with limited budget such that the expected number of influenced users is maximized. Due to its wide range of practical applications such as viral marketing [1, 2], rumor control [3, 4] and cascade detection [5], influence maximization draws tremendous attention to both researchers and experts.

The IM problem is first formulated by Kempe et al. [6] who proved its NP-hardness and proposed the greedy algorithm with guaranteed solution accuracy. Traditional greedy algorithm has high time complexity causing it cannot be applied to large networks. To solve this problem, many approximation algorithms and heuristic methods have been proposed in recent years, such as simulation-based algorithms [5, 7], centrality-based algorithms [8–10], path-based algorithms [11–13], and community-based algorithms [14–18]. Community-based algorithms usually take advantage of the influence of a node in a community to approximate its influence on the entire network.

The original version of this chapter was revised: missing reference has been added, minor typographical errors and inaccuracies in content were corrected. The correction to this chapter is available at https://doi.org/10.1007/978-981-15-3281-8_16

© Springer Nature Singapore Pte Ltd. 2020, corrected publication 2020
L. H. U et al. (Eds.): WISE 2019, CCIS 1155, pp. 142–156, 2020.
https://doi.org/10.1007/978-981-15-3281-8_13

Community structure [19] is one of the most prominent features of the network. It is described as a special group, where nodes are densely connected in intra-communities and sparsely connected in inter-communities. It reveals the organizational structure and functional components of the network, and describes the structure of the network from the meso-level. For the two nodes in a community, even if they have only weak relationships in the micro-structure due to data sparsity, the influence between them will be strengthened by the constraints of the community structure. In addition, since the scope of one's influence is limited, it is feasible to approximate its influence on the entire network with the influence in a community. Taking the advantages that the size of community is usually much smaller than the entire network, the influence of a node can be calculated more efficiently under guaranteed solution accuracy. Existing community-based IM algorithms have achieved promising results, such as CoFIM [17] and IMPC [18]. However, these algorithms only consider the number of nodes in a community and ignore the density of edge connections in a community. As Fig. 1(a) describing a network with community structure, there are the same number of nodes in the community C_3 and C_4, but the number of edges in C_4 is more than that in C_4. Considering only the number of nodes, the influence of the two communities is the same. However, more the number of edges in a community indicates a higher possibility of interaction amongst nodes, which may contribute to more chances for an inactive node to be activated. This suggests that it is necessary to distinguish the influence of C_3 and C_4.

In addition, existing methods can only be applied to non-overlapping community structures. But in real world, communities are usually overlap, i.e. a node may belong to many communities. For example, in Fig. 1(b), node v_1 belongs to C_1, C_2 and C_4 three communities, thus it has influence to nodes of the three communities.

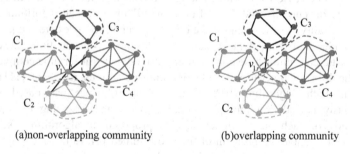

(a)non-overlapping community   (b)overlapping community

Fig. 1. The network with community structure

In this paper, we propose community closeness-based influence maximization algorithm (CCIM) to select most influential nodes. CCIM considers the influence of point-to-point and point-to-community, reflecting the micro-level and meso-level influence. The major contributions of this paper are summarized as follows:

- We define the concept of community closeness to describe the close relationship of nodes within a community.
- An influence measure based on micro-influence and meso-influence is proposed. The proposed measure considers the number of nodes and the density of edge connections in a community at the same time, thus the measure of influence is more accurate.

- We propose CCIM algorithm to effectively select seed nodes, which adopts the incremental computation of the marginal gain to avoid influence overlap.
- Extensive experiments are conducted on synthetic and three real datasets to verify the performance of our method. The experiment results show that our method outperforms the state-of-the-art methods.

The rest of this paper is organized as follows: Sect. 2 reviews the related work, Sect. 3 details our community closeness-based IM (CCIM) framework, Sect. 4 gives the experiment and results, Sect. 5 summarizes the work.

2 Related Work

As a widely studied field, IM is first studied by Domingos and Richardson [1]. And then, Kempe et al. [6] formulated the problem as an optimization problem and proved it is NP-hard. They provided a greedy algorithm which iteratively selects the seed nodes with the maximum marginal gain and theoretically proved that the solution can be approximated to within a factor of $(1 - 1/e - \varepsilon)$ (about 63%). After then, a significant number of studies have improved the efficiency and scalability of IM problem. Leskovec et al. [5] proposed CELF algorithm to greatly improve the time efficiency of the traditional greedy algorithm by using submodularity property. Since the method obtains an approximate objective function undergo a large number of Monte Carlo (MC) simulation, it is prohibited for applying in large-scale networks. Chen et al. [8] proposed the Single Discount (SD) that is a node centrality-based algorithm. To avoid the influence overlaps, once a node is chosen as seed nodes, the degree of its neighbor nodes will be decreased by 1. which taking into consideration the effect of previously chosen seeds on current candidates. Liu et al. [9] proposed an algorithm based on closeness centrality, which extended the closeness centrality index from one node to a group of nodes and defined the generalized closeness concentration index (GCC). These heuristic algorithms based on centrality usually have linear time complexity, but ignoring the diffusion process will lead to inaccurate solutions. Kim et al. [11] proposed Independent Path Algorithm (IPA), which is an influence path-based algorithm simultaneously considering multiple influence paths and assuming they propagate independently of each other. Liu et al. [12] proposed an algorithm based on the influence path to solve the problem of time-constrained IM. In this method, influence diffusion paths are firstly constructed, and then some paths are pruned to reduce excessive computation. Influence path-based algorithms show better performance in running time and solution quality. However, these algorithms require a large amount of memory to maintain the influence path, resulting in a large space consumption.

Recently, community-based methods for solving IM problem have been proposed. Community structure [19] is defined as the partition of network nodes into groups, within which nodes are densely connected while between which they are sparely connected. Galstyan et al. [14] firstly made use of the network topological property (community structure) to solve the IM problem. The approach was restricted to random networks composed of only two communities. Cao et al. [15] view the IM problem in community-based social networks as resource allocation problem and give a dynamic programming algorithm (OASET) to solve the problem. Wang et al. [16] first detected community structure of a social network by taking into account information diffusion and proposed a CGA algorithm for finding top-k influential nodes. Shang et al. [17] proposed CoFIM algorithm which combine number of neighbors and the number of neighbor communities to measure the influence of nodes. After then, Shang et al. [18] also proposed IMPC algorithm which evaluate the influence of the node based on multi-neighbor potential in community networks.

However, the above community-based methods consider only the number of nodes in a community and ignore the density of edge connections in a community. In addition, these studies work on the non-overlapping community structure, and cannot be applied on the networks with overlapping community structure.

3 Community Closeness-Based Influence Maximization Framework

Given a network $G(V, E)$, where V is a set of nodes and E is a set of edges. Suppose a network is divided into M communities, denoted as $C = \{C_1, C_2, ..., C_M\}$, where nodes are densely connected within communities and sparsely connected amongst communities. For any node $u \in V$, it may belong to one or more communities. If $u \in C_i$, C_i is called the belonging community of u. Let $BC(u)$ denote the collection of belonging communities of u, $|BC(u)| \geq 1$. If node v is directly connected with node u in G, v is called the neighbor of u, or one-hop neighbor. A neighbor of the neighbor of a node is called two-hop neighbor of the node. Let $N(u)$ denote one-hop neighbor set of u, $N(N(u))$ denote two-hop neighbor set of u. If $u \in C_i$, $u \notin C_j$ but its neighbor node $v \in C_j$ $(i \neq j)$, C_j is called the neighbor community of u. Let $NC(u)$ denote the collection of neighbor communities of u, $|NC(u)| \geq 0$.

In information diffusion process, each node takes one of two states, active or inactive. The active state means that the node has accepted the information exposed to it and may retweet the information to its neighbors, while the inactive state means that the node has not accepted the information yet. When the inactive nodes are affected by the diffusion of active nodes, they change their states from inactive to active, but not vice versa. An active node u first tries to affect its neighbor nodes, and the activated neighbor $v \subseteq N(u)$ affect its neighbors $N(v)$ further.

3.1 Problem Statement

Given a network G, our goal aims to select a set of the most influential nodes S, such that the expected number of overall activated nodes $\sigma(S)$ is maximized under a specific diffusion model:

$$S^* = \arg_S \max \sigma(S) \qquad (1)$$

The key to solving the above problem is how to measure the influence of nodes.

3.2 Influence Measure

In this paper, we suppose influence diffusion process of an active node u is divided into two phases, one is called as multi-neighbor propagation and the other is called as community propagation. Multi-neighbor propagation considers the influence of point-to-point, thus it reflects the micro-level influence. Community propagation considers the influence of point-to-community, reflecting meso-level influence. Considering the micro-level and meso-level influence at the same time is beneficial to measure the influence of a node in the network accurately from multiple levels and views.

3.2.1 Multi-neighbor Influence

In the multi-neighbor propagation process, we focus on two steps of influence propagation. First, the influence propagates from u to $N(u)$, which is the direct effect of u on $N(u)$. Then the influence will continue propagate from activated nodes in $N(u)$ to $N(N(u))$, which is the indirect effect of u on $N(N(u))$ through $N(u)$. For each node u, we only consider its influence on one-hop neighbors $N(u)$ and two-hop neighbors $N(N(u))$ in this paper, because we assume the active node u has less effect on more than two-hop neighbors through this way of information cascading diffusion and it is difficult to indirectly activate them.

Let P_{uv} represent the influence probability of u on v, $IN_1(u)$ and $IN_2(u)$ represent the influence of node u on one-hop neighbors and two-hop neighbors respectively, then $IN_1(u)$ and $IN_2(u)$ are defined as Eq. (2) [20] and (3).

$$IN_1(u) = \sum_{v \in N(u)} p_{uv} \tag{2}$$

$$IN_2(u) = \sum_{v \in N(u)} p_{uv} IN_1(v) \tag{3}$$

Then, the multi-neighbor influence of node u is represented as $f_1(u)$, it can be approximated by:

$$f_1(u) = IN_1(u) + IN_2(u) \tag{4}$$

Since $N(u)$ and $N(N(u))$ are direct and indirect neighbors of u, the influence of u on $N(u)$ is direct, while the influence of u on $N(N(u))$ is indirect. In general, the direct influence is greater than the indirect influence, so nodes in $N(u)$ are more likely to be activated by u. If only the influence of active node u is considered, $N(u)$ includes a larger proportion of active nodes than $N(N(u))$ after multi-neighbor propagation.

3.2.2 Community Influence

After multi-neighbor propagation, some nodes in $N(u)$ and $N(N(u))$ are activated. These nodes will spread influence to the rest of the network further. The nodes in $N(u)$ and $N(N(u))$ may scatter in different communities, so that influence can be spread to different communities. The crucial problem in this phase is how to analytically computer the influence spread from $N(u)$ and $N(N(u))$ to different communities. The nodes in $N(u)$ may scatter in $BC(u)$ (the collection of belonging communities of u) and $NC(u)$ (the collection of neighbor communities of u), while the nodes in $N(N(u))$ may scatter in $BC(u)$, $NC(u)$ and other communities. For simplify, we ignore the influence of nodes in other communities except $BC(u)$ and $NC(u)$. In this paper, the influence of active nodes in $BC(u)$ is called intra-community influence, while the influence of active nodes in $NC(u)$ is called inter-community influence.

The influence of a node in a community not only depends on the number of nodes in the community, but also on the relationship between nodes in the community. The more nodes in a community, the wider the scope of influence; the closer the relationship between nodes, the greater the intensity of the influence. In order to quantitatively measure the observation, we define the concept of the community closeness based on the average shortest distance between nodes in a community. And then, we give the definitions of intra-community influence and inter-community influence.

Definition 1. Community Closeness. Let C_i be a community, and $d(u,v)_{\min}$ be the shortest path between node u and v, $u,v \in C_i$, then the closeness of the community C_i is defined as: $close(C_i) = \dfrac{\sum\limits_{u \in C_i} \sum\limits_{v \in C_i/u} d(u,v)_{\min}}{|C_i| \cdot (|C_i|-1)}$.

$close(C_i)$ is the average shortest path of nodes in C_i, which reflects the density of edges connections in C_i, and the small $close(C_i)$ indicates the more influence in C_i.

- **Intra-community influence**

The intra-community influence measures the influence of active nodes in $BC(u)$ to the inactive nodes in $BC(u)$. Let A_i represent the active nodes in $C_i \in BC(u)$, then the influence will spread from A_i to inactive nodes in C_i.

In cascade diffusion process, the influence decreases with the increasing length of the path. It is obvious that the short the path between A_i and the inactive nodes in C_i indicates the inactive nodes are activated more easily. The average path from the inactive nodes in C_i to A_i is represented as $cd(u, C_i, A_i)$, it is defined as:

$$cd(u, C_i, A_i) = \frac{\sum\limits_{v \in C_i/(u \cup A_i)} d(v, A_i)_{\min}}{|C_i/(u \cup A_i)|} \qquad (5)$$

where $d(v, A_i)_{\min}$ represents the shortest path from v to A_i, $|C_i/(u \cup A_i)|$ represents the number of inactive nodes in C_i. The $cd(u, C_i, A_i)$ is a variant of the community closeness with respect to A_i. The small the value of $cd(u, C_i, A_i)$ indicates great the influence of A_i in community C_i due to the close connection of nodes in community C_i.

When the influence spreads in a community, the influence in the community not only depends on community closeness, but also on the number of nodes in the community. The large number of nodes in the community implies the more nodes likely to be activated. Therefore, we normalize the number of nodes in a community as the weight of the community, denoted as W_{C_i}. Thus, the large W_{C_i} and the small $cd(u, C_i, A_i)$ suggest the more influence in community C_i. Therefore, we measure the intra-community influence of node u by combining the weight and the closeness of community, which is denoted as $IC_1(u)$, it is defined as:

$$IC_1(u) = \sum_{C_i \in BC(u)} W_{C_i} \cdot cd(u, C_i, A_i)^{-1} \tag{6}$$

- **Inter-community influence**

The inter-community influence measures the influence of active nodes in $NC(u)$ to the inactive nodes in $NC(u)$. Due to the sparse connection between node $u \in C_i$ and the neighbor community $C_j \in NC(u)$, for each C_j, the number of active nodes in C_j (A_j) is small, so A_j has little influence in community C_j. Therefore, in order to improve computational efficiency, we lose sight of the spread process from A_j to $NC(u)$, and estimate the inter-community influence with influence of community itself. We also combine the weight and the closeness of community to measure the influence of community C_j, denoted as $I(C_j)$, it is defined as:

$$I(C_j) = W_{C_j} \cdot close(C_j)^{-1} \tag{7}$$

The inter-community influence of node $u \in C_i$ is denoted as $IC_2(u)$, it can be approximated by:

$$IC_2(u) = \sum_{C_j \in NC(u)} I(C_j) \tag{8}$$

Then, we combine the intra- and inter-community influence as the community influence of the node u, denoted as $f_2(u)$.

$$f_2(u) = \alpha \cdot IC_1(u) + \beta \cdot IC_2(u) \tag{9}$$

Where α and β denote the weight of the intra-community influence $IC_1(u)$ and inter-community influence $IC_2(u)$ respectively.

3.2.3   Total Influence

Eventually, we integrate multi-neighbor influence and community influence as the total influence of the node u in the entire network, denoted as $f(u)$, which facilitates a more comprehensive measurement of the influence of a node.

$$\begin{aligned} f(u) &= f_1(u) + f_2(u) \\ &= [IN_1(u) + IN_2(u)] + [\alpha \cdot IC_1(u) + \beta \cdot IC_2(u)] \end{aligned} \tag{10}$$

3.3 CCIM Algorithm

In this section, we propose the community closeness-based influence maximization (CCIM) algorithm to effectively select seed nodes. Algorithm 1 shows the pseudo-code of CCIM algorithm. First, divide the network $G(V, E)$ into M communities by community detection algorithm, and then calculate the influence of the nodes and find the next seed node with max influence. In order to avoid repeated calculations, we adopt the incremental computation of the marginal gain strategy. After selecting a seed node, remove the overlapping influence and recalculate the influence of the remaining nodes. Finally, the seed nodes spread influence in the network under a diffusion model to maximize the reach of influence.

Algorithm 1: The CCIM algorithm

Input: A network $G(V, E)$, number of seed nodes k, parameter α, β

Output: The seed set S

1: Divide $G(V, E)$ into M community by community detection algorithm

2: Initialize: $S = \phi$

3: **for** $i = 1$ to k **do:**

4:     **for** each $u \in V$ **do:**

5:         calculate multi-neighbor influence $f_1(u)$ by Equ. (4)

6:         calculate community influence $f_2(u)$ by Equ. (9)

7:         calculate total influence $f(u)$ by Equ. (10)

8:     **end for**

9:     $v = \max_u f(u)$

10:     $S \leftarrow S \cup \{v\}$

11: **end for**

12: **return** S

The time complexity of our CCIM algorithm is $O(n + k(d + m))$, where k is the number of seed nodes, $n = |V|$ is the number of nodes in network, $m = |E|$ is the number of edges in network, d is the average node degree.

4 Experiments

In this section, we verify the effectiveness of CCIM algorithm, explore the impact of algorithm parameters, and investigate the impact of community weight and closeness.

4.1 Experimental Preparation

- **Datasets**

    In the process of experiments, we use four datasets including three real-world datasets (NetHEPT [18], NetPHY [18] and Epinions [18]) and one synthetic dataset

(SNOCS) with overlapping community structure. NetHEPT and NetPHY are the collaboration networks, where the nodes represent scholars and the edges represent the relation of cooperation amongst scholars. Epinions is a social network, where the nodes represent users, and the edges represent the trust relationship amongst users. We use the LFR [21] algorithm to generate the SNOCS with specific community structure. The parameters of LFR are set as follows: the number of node $N = 5000$, the average degree $k_{avg} = 15$, the maximum degree $k_{max} = 60$, the mixing parameter $\mu = 0.01$, the minus exponent for the degree sequence $t_1 = 2$, minus exponent for the community size distribution $t_2 = 1$, the minimum for the community sizes $C_{min} = 10$, the maximum for the community sizes $C_{max} = 80$, the number of overlapping nodes $O_n = 100$, the number of memberships of overlapping nodes $O_m = 3$ and the average clustering coefficient $C = 0.6$.

Table 1 summaries the detailed descriptions of these datasets, where the community structures are obtained by applying the LFM [22] algorithm.

Table 1. Statistical properties of three real-world datasets and a synthetic dataset.

Datasets	NetHEPT	NetPHY	Epinions	SNOCS
#Nodes	15K	37K	76K	5K
#Edges	31K	174K	406K	36K
Max.Degree	64	178	3044	60
Avg.Degree	4.12	9.38	10.69	15
#Communities	3123	6453	7199	159
Ove. Ratio	2.1%	1.9%	45.1%	2%
Modularity	0.7	0.54	0.41	0.95

- **Baseline methods**

In this paper, we adopt Degree, Single Discount (SD) [8], CoFIM [17] and IMPC [18] as baseline algorithms. Degree and SD are the centrality-based algorithms. Degree selects top k nodes with the maximum degree values, while SD selects nodes according to their degree and decreases the degree of their neighbors by 1. CoFIM and IMPC are the community-based algorithm. CoFIM supposes that an active node first influence neighbors who are distributed in different communities and regards the number of neighboring communities of the node as its influence on other nodes. The IMPC evaluates the influence spread of a node based on multi-neighbor potential in community network.

- **Diffusion model**

The influence diffusion model controls the way of information spread in social networks. In this paper, we use the traditional Independent Cascade (IC) model as diffusion model. For the IC model, every activated node have a single chance to activate each of the inactive neighbors, the propagation probability from u to v is defined as $p_{uv} = 1/k_v$, where k_v represent the degree of v.

- **Evaluation metric**

As a widely used evaluation metric, influence spread is defined as the expected number of nodes which can be successfully activated at the end of diffusion process. In this paper, we use the number of activated nodes as the evaluation metric. To eliminate the contingency of the results, the influence spread value is estimated by executing 10000 times Monte-Carlo (MC) simulations, and the activation threshold of each node is set randomly.

4.2 Experimental Result

4.2.1 Effectiveness Evaluation

In the first experiment, we use four datasets to verify the effectiveness of CCIM algorithm compared with four baseline algorithms. The results are shown in Fig. 2. It can be observed that due to the differences of community structure, different algorithms perform differently on different datasets. SD and Degree are significantly inferior to others on NetPHY dataset, the performance of three community-based algorithms (CoFIM, IMPC, and CCIM) are relatively stable, and CCIM algorithm always finds a higher quality solution in most situations. Although the advantage of our CCIM algorithm is not very obvious on the real datasets, it is significantly superior to the baseline algorithms on the synthetic network. This may be that the community closeness is weak in real networks, but it is stronger in the synthetic network.

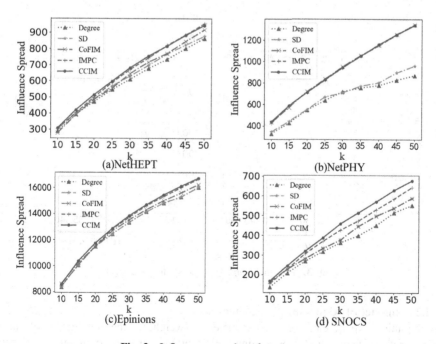

Fig. 2. Influence spread on four datasets

In the second experiment, we employ the four synthetic networks with different $\mu = \{0.2, 0.1, 0.05, 0.01\}$ to further explore how the community closeness impacts the effectiveness of CCIM algorithm. Mixing parameter μ directly determines the community structure, smaller μ means more connections within communities than across communities, which also signifies there are stronger close relationships within intra-community. Figure 3 gives the results on four synthetic networks with different μ, where $\mu = 0.2$ represents weak community closeness, $\mu = 0.1$ represents medium strong community closeness, $\mu = 0.05$ represents strong community closeness and $\mu = 0.01$ represents extremely strong community closeness. From the results, we can obverse that in networks with very weak community closeness (Fig. 3(a)), except for CoFIM algorithm, other algorithms produce almost identical results in all scenarios, our algorithm has no advantage over the baseline algorithms. As the value of μ decreases (community closeness enhancement), the performance of CCIM algorithm gradually exceeds that of baselines algorithms. As a consequence, it is effective to consider the community closeness in solving the influence maximization problem.

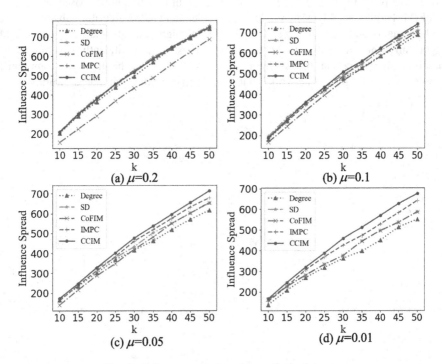

Fig. 3. Influence spread on the synthetic datasets

4.2.2 Impact of Algorithm Parameters

In the third experiment, we set parameter α (weighting the importance of intra-community influence) and β (weighting the importance of inter-community influence) from $\{0.1, 0.3, 0.5, 0.7, 0.9\}$ respectively to explore the impact of algorithm parameters. Experiment on four datasets with the influence spread of $k = 50$ seed nodes.

In Fig. 4, we can obverse that the two parameters have different influence on these datasets. On the NetHEPT dataset, the change in the influence spread value is not obvious as the parameters change, indicating that the dataset is insensitive to these parameters. However, for other datasets, the range of influence is affected by changing these parameters. From the results on the datasets except the NetHEPT, we can see that the value of α is greater than β when influence spread value reaches the maximum. The observation consists with our analysis that the intra-community influence takes on more meaningful roles than inter-community influence in measuring influence. At the same time, the results show that accurately choosing parameters is beneficial to improve the algorithm performance, otherwise, putting too much weight on relevant factors can even worsen the result.

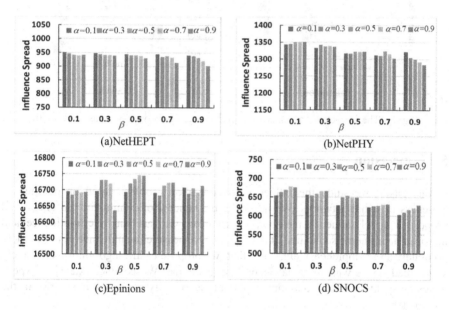

Fig. 4. Impact of parameter α and β on four datasets ($k = 50$)

4.2.3   Impact of Community Weight and Closeness

In the four experiment, we use four datasets to investigate the impact of community weight and closeness. We carry out experiment under three scenarios, only considering the weight, only considering the closeness and both are considered. Set the community closeness to 1, which means ignoring the community closeness and only considering community weight (denoted as *wei.only*). Set the community weight to 1, which means ignoring the community weight and only considering community closeness (denoted as *clo.only*). The *wei.&clo.* represents considering both. From the results in Fig. 5, it is clear to see that the combination of community weight and closeness has the largest influence spread value. It indicates that combining the community weight and closeness make sense in solving influence maximization problem.

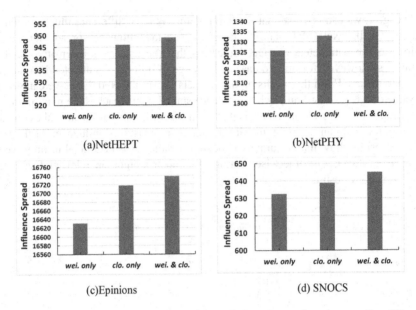

Fig. 5. The impact of community weight and closeness on four datasets ($k = 50$)

5   Conclusion

In this paper, we study the influence maximization problem based on community closeness in social networks. We introduce the concept of community closeness, and propose a novel influence measure, which takes into account micro-influence and meso-influence at the same time. It is beneficial to measure the influence of nodes more accurately and comprehensively. After that, we propose CCIM algorithm to effectively select seed nodes with marginal increment technique. We conduct extensive experiments on synthetic dataset and three real datasets to verify our method outperforms the baselines.

Our approach for influence maximization is only able to apply on the homogeneous network, in which there is one object type and one relationship type. However, the real network is usually heterogeneous network, which has a variety of object types and relationship types. As future work, we will consider how to solve the IM problem by utilizing complex relationships and rich semantic information in heterogeneous networks.

Acknowledgments. This work was supported by the National Natural Science Foundation of China (61762090, 61262069, 61472346, and 61662086), The Natural Science Foundation of Yunnan Province (2016FA026), the Project of Innovative Research Team of Yunnan Province (2018HC019), and Program for Innovation Research Team (in Science and Technology) in University of Yunnan Province (IRTSTYN), the Education Department Foundation of Yunnan Province (2019J0005 and 2019Y0006), the National Social Science Foundation of China (18XZZ005).

References

1. Domingos, P., Richardson, M.: Mining the network value of customers. In: Proceedings of the 7th ACM SIGKDD International Conference on Knowledge Discovery and Data Mining, KDD, San Francisco, pp. 57–66 (2001)
2. Richardson, M., Domingos, P.: Mining knowledge-sharing sites for viral marketing. In: Proceedings of the 8th ACM SIGKDD International Conference on Knowledge Discovery and Data Mining, KDD, Edmonton, pp. 61–70 (2002)
3. Budak, C., Agrawal, D., Abbadi, A.-E.: Limiting the spread of misinformation in social networks. In: Proceedings of the 20th International Conference on World Wide Web, WWW, Hyderabad, pp. 665–674 (2011)
4. He, X., Song, G., Chen, W.: Influence blocking maximization in social networks under the competitive linear threshold model. In: Proceedings of the 12th SIAM International Conference on Data Mining, SDM, Anaheim, pp. 463–474 (2011)
5. Leskovec, J., Krause, A., Guestrin, C.: Cost-effective outbreak detection in networks. In: Proceedings of the 13th ACM SIGKDD International Conference on Knowledge Discovery and Data Mining, pp. 420–429. ACM, San Jose (2007)
6. Kempe, D., Kleinberg, J., Tardos, E.: Maximizing the spread of influence through a social network. In: Proceedings of the 9th ACM SIGKDD International Conference on Knowledge Discovery and Data Mining, pp. 137–146. ACM, Washington (2003)
7. Goyal, A., Lu, W., Lakshmanan, L.V.: CELF++: optimizing the greedy algorithm for influence maximization in social networks. In: Proceedings of the 20th International Conference Companion on World Wide Web, pp. 47–48. ACM (2011)
8. Chen, W., Wang, Y., Yang, S.: Efficient influence maximization in social networks. In: Proceedings of the 15th ACM SIGKDD International Conference on Knowledge Discovery and Data Mining, pp. 199–208. ACM, Paris (2009)
9. Liu, H.-L., Ma, C., Xiang, B.-B.: Identifying multiple influential spreaders based on generalized closeness centrality. Phys. A 492, 2237–2248 (2018)
10. Zhu, J., Liu, Y., Yin, X.: A new structure-hole-based algorithm for influence maximization in large online social networks. IEEE Access 5, 23405–23412 (2017)
11. Kim, J., Kim, S.-K., Yu, H.: Scalable and parallelizable processing of influence maximization for large-scale social networks. In: 29th IEEE International Conference on Data Engineering, pp. 266–277. IEEE, Brisbane (2013)
12. Liu, B., Cong, G., Zeng, Y.: Influence spreading path and its application to the time constrained social influence maximization problem and beyond. IEEE Trans. Knowl. Data Eng. 26(8), 1904–1917 (2014)
13. Ko, Y.-Y., Chae, D.-K., Kim, S.-W.: Accurate path-based methods for influence maximization in social networks. In: Proceedings of the 25th International Conference Companion on World Wide Web, WWW, Geneva, pp. 59–60 (2016)
14. Galstyan, A., Musoyan, V.: Maximizing influence propagation in networks with community structure. Phys. Rev. E 79(2), 056102 (2009)
15. Cao, T., Wu, X., Wang, S., Hu, X.: OASNET: an optimal allocation approach to influence maximization in modular social networks. In: ACM Symposium on Applied Computing, SAC, Sierre, pp. 1088–1094 (2010)
16. Wang, Y., Cong, G., Song, G.: Community-based greedy algorithm for mining top-K influential nodes in mobile social network. In: Proceedings of the 16th ACM SIGKDD International Conference on Knowledge Discovery and Data Mining, pp. 1039–1048. ACM, Washington (2010)

17. Shang, J., Zhou, S., Li, X.: CoFIM: a community-based framework for influence maximization on large-scale networks. Knowl.-Based Syst. **117**, 88–100 (2017)
18. Shang, J., Wu, H.: IMPC: influence maximization based on multi-neighbor potential in community networks. Phys. A **512**, 1085–1103 (2018)
19. Girvan, M., Newman, M.E.J.: Community structure in social and biological networks. Proc. Natl. Acad. Sci. U.S.A. **99**(12), 7821–7826 (2002)
20. Wang, Y., Feng, X.: A potential-based node selection strategy for influence maximization in a social network. In: Huang, R., Yang, Q., Pei, J., Gama, J., Meng, X., Li, X. (eds.) ADMA 2009. LNCS (LNAI), vol. 5678, pp. 350–361. Springer, Heidelberg (2009). https://doi.org/10.1007/978-3-642-03348-3_34
21. Lancichinetti, A., Fortunato, S., Radicchi, F.: Benchmark graphs for testing community detection algorithms. Phys. Rev. E **78**(4 Pt 2), 046110 (2008)
22. Lancichinetti, A., Fortunato, S., Kertész, János.: Detecting the overlapping and hierarchical community structure in complex networks. New J. Phys. **11**(3), 033015 (2009)

Can Reinforcement Learning Enhance Social Capital?

He Zhao[1], Hongyi Su[1], Yang Chen[2]([✉]) [ID], Jiamou Liu[2] [ID], Bo Yan[1], and Hong Zheng[1]

[1] Beijing Lab of Intelligent Information Technology, School of Computer Science, Beijing Institute of Technology, Beijing, China
{2120171104,henrysu,yanbo,hongzheng}@bit.edu.cn
[2] School of Computer Science, The University of Auckland, Auckland, New Zealand
{yang.chen,jiamou.liu}@auckland.ac.nz

Abstract. Social capital captures the positional advantage gained by an individual by being in a social network. A well-known dichotomy defines two types of social capital: *bonding capital*, which refers to welfare such as trust and norms, and *bridging capital*, which refers to benefits in terms of influence and power. We present a framework where these notions are mathematically conceptualized. Through the framework, we discuss the process when an individual gains social capital through building new edges. We explore two questions: (1) How would an individual optimally form new relations? (2) What are the impacts of the network structure on the individual's social capital? For these questions, we adopt a paradigm where the individual is a utility-driven agent who acquires knowledge about the network through repeated trial-and-error. In this paradigm, we propose two reinforcement learning algorithms: one guarantees the convergence to optimal values in theory, while the other is efficient in practice. We conduct experiments over both synthetic and real-world networks. Experimental results indicate that a centralized structure can enhance the performance of learning.

Keywords: Social capital · Reinforcement learning · Network building · Social network

1 Introduction

Human societies are the products of interactions among social actors. The reward theory of attraction, well-established in social psychology, states that people tend to interact with those whose behavior is rewarding to themselves or those who are associated with rewarding events [15]. To study social dynamics, it is thus important to understand the essential constituents of rewards that motivate social networking, and how these rewards impact an individual's decision making. Social networking not only brings an individual tangible rewards such as economic resources, but also intangible benefits in the form of trust, social support, information control, and social influence. The notion of *social capital* was

L. H. U et al. (Eds.): WISE 2019, CCIS 1155, pp. 157–171, 2020.
https://doi.org/10.1007/978-981-15-3281-8_14

introduced to unify these intangible benefits [8]. While undoubtedly a significant portion of social interactions are driven by concerns of social capital, the direct link between social capital and social interaction is often overlooked. In this paper, we tackle this issue through investigating the *network building* process, where an individual in a social network purposely establish social interactions in the hope of gaining social capital.

Our investigation aims to resolve several challenges around the network building process. The first seeks to pinpoint the notion of social capital. A well-known dichotomy has divided discussions on social capital into two categories: *bonding capital* and *bridging capital* [13]. The former depicts the aggregate welfare that an individual draws from its closed social circle in the form of, e.g., trust and social support [3], while the latter captures the individual's capacity to acquire opportunities and information via open links and determines, e.g., status and power [5]. An individual's reward in social networking would be a combination of these two forms of social capital.

The second concerns optimizing the individuals' social networking tactics when establishing social interactions. By this, We would like to identify the optimal decisions subject to the following constraints: (1) Since rewards are typical of hindsight, an individual demands learning from experience via trial-and-error. (2) An individual has limited abilities to establish and maintain relationships. Since if otherwise, trivially she can link to all others to maximize rewards. (3) The individual would have only partial observation about the network and consequently social interaction can only be established with those that are in the surrounding social circle.

The third aims to develop insights regarding how the network structure impacts an individual's social capital. A network may exhibit some salient structural properties such as community structure [10], scale-free property [2] and small-world property [23]. Intuitively, an individual may relatively easily gain social capital in networks with one or multiple centers, as she can always fast approach to these centers or act as bridges between centers. In contrast, a homogeneous network imposes difficulties over making decisions for establishing links, which implies that gaining social capital is hard in such networks.

Contribution. Motivated by the concerns above, we propose the *social capital-driven network building* (SCNB) problem, which involves a social network and an individual within it. The individual has partial observation of the network and can create a limited number of edges, denoting social interactions. As the agent has imperfect information about rewards and network structures, we tackle SCNB problem using the reinforcement learning paradigm. That is, the agent learns to gain social capital via trial-and-error and referring to previous experiences. We highlight the novelty of this work as follows: (1) We present a framework where bonding and bridging capitals are mathematically conceptualized. (2) We propose a fast Q-learning algorithms FQL for SCNB. FQL's efficiency makes it applicable to networks of a non-trivial size. Not only the algorithm leads to quick stability, it also has a performance also compares well with the optimal actions, as computed by a much slower alternative OQL. (3) We conduct experiments on synthetic and real-world networks. Results reveal that centralized network structures enable an agent to gain social capital more effectively.

Related Works. Pioneering works of sociologists advanced the research on social capital. Coleman's serial works lay the foundation for the research on social capital [7,8]. Bourdieu proposes that homophily is the source of bonding capital [3]. Granovetter, Putnam, and Burt state that weak ties are the source of bridging capital [5,11,17].

Game-based research on *network formation* focuses on equilibria among rational agents [4,12,19], where behaviors of agents are subject to restricted predefined rules. Our work surpasses theirs as the learning process captures initiatives of agents. Particularly, authors in [1] propose a micro-founded mathematical model of the evolution driven by social capital, where bridging capital is defined as the betweenness centrality. In this paper, we formalize bridging capital following their work.

Algorithmic research on *network building* problem asks for integrating a newcomer to the center of an existing static or dynamic network via establishing a minimum number of links [6,14,24,25]. Network building problem is computationally hard and thus several efficient heuristic-based algorithms are given in these works. Our work differs from theirs as: (1) The objective of the agent is to gain social capital rather than centrality; (2) We assume that an agent does not have global knowledge of the network, which adheres more to reality; (3) We solve SCNB using reinforcement learning instead of heuristic-based algorithms.

2 Preliminaries

2.1 Social Capital

Rooted in sociology, the concept of social capital aims to capture the benefits attained by individuals via social interactions. Such benefits can emerge in the form of social support, companionship, solidarity, influence, and control over information, which are closely related to network structural properties. As a result, social capital should be measured based on structural properties. However, the structure itself does not define social capital. Instead, social capital arises as a function of social interactions and information conveyed through social relations [7]. Social relations have long been classified based on their functions: While strong ties link homogeneous and like-minded individuals, weak ties bridge diverse and weakly connected groups [11]. Analogously, social capital also consists of two types: *Bonding capital* refers to benefits an individual draws from its closed neighborhood, in the form of, e.g., trust and support, which are brought by strong ties; while *bridging capital* is an incarnation of benefits of accessibility to information and control over information flow, which are largely functions of weak ties. However, so far no consensus has been reached over the formal definitions of social capital. In this paper, we adopt two metrics to measure these two notions in the context of social networks.

A social network captures repeated patterns of social interactions and is viewed as an undirected graph $G = (V, E)$, where V is a set of nodes (agents) and $E \subseteq V^2 \setminus \{uu \mid u \in V\}$ is a set of edges. A (k-length) *path* is a sequence of nodes $u_1 u_2, \ldots u_{k+1}$ where $u_i u_{i+1} \in E$ for $1 \leq i \leq k$. The distance $\mathsf{dist}_G(u, v)$ between u and v is the length of a shortest path between these two nodes. We focus on connected graphs and thus $\mathsf{dist}_G(u, v) < \infty$ for any $u, v \in V$. If $\mathsf{dist}_G(u, v) = d$, then we say that u, v are d-hop neighbors. The *d-hop neighbor set* of $v \in V$ is $N_G^d(v) := \{u \in V \mid \mathsf{dist}_G(u, v) = d\}$.

In the real-world, the sight of an individual tends to be restricted by the large scale and complex dynamics of social networks, resulting in incomplete knowledge of the environment. Consequently, an agent often has a good understanding of its neighborhood but is unfamiliar with distant parts of the network. To capture this fact, we employee the notion of *2-level ego network*, which represents the social surrounding that an agent perceives and maintains.

Definition 1 (2-level Ego Network). *The* 2-level ego network *of a node* $v \in V$ *is the subgraph* O_G^v *of* G *induced by* v, v*'s 1-hop neighbors, and 2-hop neighbors, i.e., the nodes of* O_G^v *is* $V_G^v = \{u \in V \mid \mathsf{dist}_G(u, v) \leq 2\}$ *and the edges of* O_G^v *is* $E_G^v = \{uw \in E \mid u, w \in V_G^v\}$. *The node* v *is called the* ego *in* O_G^v.

Considering distinct differences between origins of bonding and bridging capital, we formalize them using two standard metrics, *personalized PageRank* and *betweenness centrality*, respectively. Bonding capital, as it is often expressed as trust and companionship, measures the degree to which two nodes bind with each other [3]. This can be aptly captured through a measure of "social proximity". In other words, a node gains more bonding capital as it gets closer to others in its own neighborhood. Personalized PageRank index is adapted from PageRank and evaluates structural proximity between nodes through predicting the likelihood of edges between any pairs of nodes [16]. It takes as input a starting node s, and assigns a score to every node u that captures the likelihood of a random walk from s to reach u [21]. Fix a restart probability $\beta \in (0, 1)$, random walk starts from the node s^1; stops moving at each node with the probability of β and restarts from the node s; or continues to walk with the probability of $1 - \beta$ by randomly selecting a node from the neighbors of the current node. The probability that each node is accessed converges in finite rounds of walking. Each entry of the personalized PageRank vector $\boldsymbol{pr}$ records the probability that the corresponding node is accessed. More formally, let $\boldsymbol{a}_u$ be the column vector in the adjacency matrix of G corresponding to node u. Denote by pr_u, the link prediction score between s and u as:

$$\mathsf{pr}_u = \beta r_u + (1 - \beta)(\boldsymbol{pr} \cdot \boldsymbol{a}_u / |N_G^1(u)|), \tag{1}$$

where $r_u = 1$ if $u = s$ and $r_u = 0$ otherwise. Intuitively, assume that s holds certain amount of "goodwill" which is randomly shared with s's neighbors, and whoever that obtains such goodwill can continue to pass goodwill to their neighbors or return them to the node s, in the same manner as a random walk as

---

[1] In experiments, we set the restart probability $\beta = 0.15$.

above. Bonding capital can be viewed as the amount of goodwill eventually received by s.

Definition 2 (Bonding Capital). *Given a graph $G = (V, E)$ and a node $v \in V$, denote by $\mathsf{bo}_G(v)$, the bonding capital of v is defined by summing personalized PageRank indices between v and v's neighbors, namely, $\mathsf{bo}_G(v) := \sum_{u \in N_G^1(v)} \mathsf{pr}_u$.*

Occupying a central position to act as a gateway for information exchange brings an individual bridging capital [5]. Furthermore, betweenness centrality is used to evaluate bridging capital in [1]. The betweenness centrality of a node measures the number of the shortest paths between each pair of other nodes that pass through it, and thus reflects the agent's ability to broker interactions between different groups of agents. Following the work [1], we formalize bridging capital using betweenness centrality.

Definition 3 (Bridging Capital). *Let $G = (V, E)$ be a connected graph. The bridging capital of $v \in V$, denote by $\mathsf{br}_G(v)$, is defined as v's betweenness centrality: $\mathsf{br}_G(v) := \sum_{s \neq v \neq t \in V} \sigma_{st}(v)/\sigma_{st}$, where σ_{st} is the number of shortest paths between nodes s and t, and $\sigma_{st}(v)$ is the number of shortest paths passing v.*

An individual may show different preferences to two types of capital. To cope with this, we employee a *preference weight* $w \in [0, 1]$ to define the *mixed capital*.

Definition 4 (Mixed Capital). *Let $G = (V, E)$ be a network. For a node $v \in V$ and a preference weight $w \in [0, 1]$, the mixed capital induced by w is defined as $\mathsf{mix}_G^w(v) := w\mathsf{bo}_G(v) + (1 - w)\mathsf{br}_G(v)$.*

2.2   Q-Learning

We next briefly state backgrounds of Q-learning that defines a learning method for Markov decision processes (MDPs). See [20] for a thorough introduction. An MDP is a tuple $\langle \mathcal{S}, \mathcal{A}, r, p \rangle$, where $\mathcal{S}$ is the discrete state space, $\mathcal{A}$ is the discrete action space, $r : \mathcal{S} \times \mathcal{A} \to \mathbb{R}$ is the reward function, and $p : \mathcal{S} \times \mathcal{A} \rightsquigarrow \mathcal{S}$ is the transition function, where $\rightsquigarrow$ denotes a probabilistic mapping.

To solve an MDP, we learn estimates for the optimal value of each action, defined as the expected sum of long-term rewards when taking the action and following the optimal policy thereafter. Under a given *policy* $\pi : \mathcal{S} \to \mathcal{A}$, the true value of an action a in a state s is

$$Q^\pi(s, a) := \mathbb{E}\left[R_1 + \gamma R_2 + \gamma^2 R_3 + \cdots \middle| S_0 = s, A_0 = a, \pi\right], \tag{2}$$

where $\gamma \in [0, 1]$ is the *discount factor* and S_t, A_t, R_t denote the state, action and reward at time t, respectively. The optimal value is then $Q^*(s, a) = \max_\pi Q^\pi(s, a)$. An optimal policy π^* is derived from optimal values by choosing highest-valued actions in each state. Estimates for optimal action values can be learned using Q-learning. At each time t, the agent maintains a state-action value Q_t. In a state s, the agent takes an action a, receives a reward r', and enters a next state s'. Then, an action-value is updated using the following rule:

$$Q_{t+1}(s,a) = (1 - \alpha_t)Q_t(s,a) + \alpha_t \left[r' + \gamma \max_{a'} Q_t(s',a') \right], \qquad (3)$$

where $\alpha_t \in [0,1)$ is the *learning rate*. It has been proved that the sequence $(Q_t(s,a))_{t \in \mathbb{N}}$ generated by Eq. (3) converges to the optimal $Q^*(s,a)$ [22] with following assumptions on the learning rate:

$$\sum_{t=1}^{\infty} \alpha_t(a) = \infty \quad \text{AND} \quad \sum_{t=1}^{\infty} \alpha_t^2(a) < \infty. \qquad (4)$$

3   Problem Setup

A question naturally arises as to how would an individual gain social capital in a partially perceived society. Throughout the remainder of this paper, we use v to denote a *learner* in a network $G = (V, E)$, who aims to gain social capital through establishing new social interactions, which take the form of extra edges to G. Formally, for $uv \notin E$, $G \oplus_v u$ denotes the network $(V, E \cup \{uv\})$. We formalize the interaction between v and the network G as a process happening in (finite) discrete time steps $\tau = 0, 1, 2, \ldots$. At each time step, v establishes an edge with an agent selected from its 2-level ego network, resulting in an updated network. This process is formally defined below.

Definition 5 (Network Building Process). *An (ℓ-round) network building (NB) process between $G = (V, E)$ and $v \in V$ consists of a finite sequence of networks $G_0, G_1 \ldots, G_\ell$ and a finite sequence of nodes $u_0, u_1, \ldots, u_{\ell-1}$ such that $\forall\, 0 \leq \tau \leq \ell - 1 : u_\tau \in N_{G_\tau}^2(v)$, where $G_0 = G$ and $G_{\tau+1} = G_\tau \oplus_v u$.*

Definition 6 (Network Building Strategy). *A network building strategy is a function φ that takes as input a 2-level ego network O_G^v and outputs a node $u \in N_G^2(v)$. Any NB process $(G_0, G_1 \ldots, G_\ell, u_0, u_1, \ldots, u_{\ell-1})$ is said to be consistent with a strategy φ if $\forall 0 \leq \tau \leq \ell - 1 : u_\tau = \varphi(O_{G_\tau}^v)$.*

We write $\mathcal{G}_\tau$ for the space of all networks that might emerge at time step τ and $\mathcal{G} = \bigcup_{1 \leq \tau < \ell} \mathcal{G}_\tau$ for all possible realizations of networks during the NB process. The space of v's all possible 2-level ego networks is therefore $\mathcal{O} := \{O_H^v \mid H \in \mathcal{G}\}$. Now we are ready to formally define the SCNB problem.

Definition 7 (Social Capital-based Network Building Problem). *A social capital-based network building (SCNB) problem is a tuple $\langle G, v, \ell, w \rangle$, where $G = (V, E)$ is a graph, $v \in V$ is the learner, $\ell \in \mathbb{N}^+$ and $w \in [0, 1]$. The problem asks for an NB strategy φ^* so as to maximize the mixed capital of $\text{mix}_{G_\ell}^w(v)$ via an ℓ-round NB process consistent with φ^*.*

The SCNB problem has the inherent high computational complexity. The *network building* problem – asking for a minimum vertex set of a static network to minimize a newcomer's eccentricity via linking to all nodes in the set – has been shown to be NP-complete in [14] where several heuristic-based algorithms are given. SCNB is more complicated as the partial observation imposes an extra layer of complexity. Hence the heuristic-based algorithms are no longer effective as they require global information in advance. Moreover, to cope with the incomplete knowledge of the network, an agent needs to learn from the environment by trials and retrieving previous experiences. Motivated by above discussions, it is the most naturally to adopt reinforcement learning to solve SCNB problem, in which an agent learns a strategy via trial-and-error.

4 Reinforcement Learning for SCNB

This section studies reinforcement learning algorithms for SCNB. Let $\langle G, v, \ell, w \rangle$ be a SCNB problem. Learner v iteratively refines a network building strategy φ through replay and trail-and-error. A trial of a complete ℓ-round network building process is called an *episode*. We first show the formulation of reinforcement learning in the context of SCNB problem. Then we propose two Q-learning algorithms for SCNB.

4.1 Reinforcement Learning Formulation

We define the states, actions, rewards, transitions and policies in reinforcement learning for SCNB as follows:

1. **States:** In each episode, for any round $0 \leq \tau < \ell$, v utilizes an *ego-state mapping* ϕ to extract a state S_τ from the current 2-level ego network $O_{G_\tau}^v$.

Definition 8 (Ego-State Mapping). *An ego-state mapping is a function* $\phi : \mathcal{O} \to \mathcal{S}$ *that maps a 2-level ego network to a state in a finite state set* $\mathcal{S}$.

2. **Actions:** An action A_τ is a node from v's 2-hop neighbor set $N_{G_\tau}^2(v)$.
3. **Rewards:** A reward function $r(S_\tau, A_\tau)$ at state S_τ is defined as the change of the mixed capital as a function of taking action A_τ and entering into next round $\tau + 1$, that is,

$$r_{\tau+1} = r(S_\tau, A_\tau) := \text{mix}_{G_{\tau+1}}^w(v) - \text{mix}_{G_\tau}^w(v). \tag{5}$$

4. **Transition:** The transition here is deterministic. Given the current state S_τ and action A_τ, the process transits into next state with probability 1, i.e.,

$$p(S_\tau, A_\tau) = S_{\tau+1} = \phi(O_{G_\tau}^v). \tag{6}$$

5. **Policy:** A policy π takes input as a state S_τ and outputs a action A_τ.

Conceptually, based on state s_τ, v chooses a node a_τ (action) from v's 2-hop neighbor set $N_{G_\tau}^2(v)$ to create a link. Then, v receives a reward $r_{\tau+1} = \mathrm{mix}_{G_{\tau+1}}^w(v) - \mathrm{mix}_{G_\tau}^w(v)$ (change of mixed capital) and enters into the next round $\tau + 1$. We use $Q(S_\tau, A_\tau)$ to denote the action-value of the state-action pair (S_τ, A_τ). Note that since ℓ is finite, trivially we define $Q(S_i, A_i) = 0, \forall i \geq \ell$. For exploration, we employee the standard ε-greedy method as the policy π derived from Q. Namely, choose actions greedily most of the time, but with a very small *exploration probability* ε choose randomly. Formally,

$$A_\tau = \pi(S_\tau) = \begin{cases} \arg\max_{a \in N_{G_\tau}^2(v)} Q(S_\tau, a) & \text{with probability } 1 - \varepsilon \\ \text{randomly selected } a \in N_{G_\tau}^2(v) & \text{with probability } \varepsilon \end{cases} \tag{7}$$

Throughout, we set the discount factor $\gamma = 1$, i.e., the future rewards are not discounted. Thus the long-term cumulative reward in Q-learning is equivalent to the mixed capital after the last round in PONB. Therefore naturally we have the following lemma.

Lemma 1. *The optimal policy π^* in Q-learning for PONB is equivalent to an optimal NB strategy φ^* if the discount factor $\gamma = 1$.*

A strategy φ is obtained after several rounds of learning such that $\forall 0 \leq \tau < \ell : \varphi(O_{G_\tau}^v) = \pi(S_t) = \pi(\phi(O_{G_\tau}^v))$. We next show two Q-learning algorithms for SCNB that are separated by two different ego-state mappings.

4.2 First Try: An Optimal Q-Learning Algorithm for SCNB

We first investigate the optimal Q-learning algorithm (OQL) that directly uses 2-level ego networks as states. More formally, for a SCNB problem $\langle G, \nu, \ell, w \rangle$, OQL utilizes an ego-state mapping ϕ_o such that $\forall 0 \leq \tau < \ell : \phi_o(O_{G_\tau}^v) := O_{G_\tau}^v$. According to Eq. (3) and Lemma 1, the Q-value update rule of OQL is

$$Q_{t+1}(O_{G_\tau}^v, a) = (1 - \alpha_t)Q_t(O_{G_\tau}^v, a) + \alpha_t \left[r_{\tau+1} + \max_{a'} Q_t(O_{G_{\tau+1}}^v, a') \right], \tag{8}$$

where $a = A_\tau \in N_{G_\tau}^2(\nu)$, $G_{\tau+1} = G_\tau \oplus_v a$ and $a' \in N_{G_{\tau+1}}^2(v)$. The following theorem shows the optimality of OQL.

Theorem 1. *The sequence $\left(Q(O_{G_\tau}^v, a)\right)_{t \in \mathbb{N}}$ generated by Eq. (8) converges to the optimal $Q^*(O_{G_\tau}^v, a)$ under the assumptions stated in Eq. (4).*

Proof. We complete this proof by showing that the underlying process of OQL is an MDP. Let $\langle G, v, \ell, w \rangle$ be a PONB problem. Construct an MDP as follows: The state set is the space of the 2-level ego network $\mathcal{O}$. The action set is $\mathcal{A} := \{u \in V \mid \mathrm{dist}(u, v) \geq 2\}$, i.e., all nodes other than v and v's 1-hop neighbors. Note that at each time step τ, the set of eligible actions $N_{G_\tau}^2$ is a subset of $\mathcal{A}$. The definitions of reward function r and transition function p remain unchanged as stated above. It is notable that p degenerates to a deterministic mapping in this setting. The tuple $(\mathcal{O}, \mathcal{A}, r, p)$ is clearly an MDP and hence the optimality of OQL holds. $\qquad\square$

After convergence of all Q values we obtain a near-optimal policy $\pi = \pi^*$ and therefore get a near-optimal NB strategy $\varphi = \varphi^*$ (according to Lemma 1). The procedure of OQL is shown in Algorithm 1.

Algorithm 1. OQL: Estimate optimal strategies for SCNB

Input: An SCNB problem $\langle G, v, \ell, w \rangle$ with $G = (V, E)$
Output: An NB strategy $\varphi = \varphi^*$
Initialization: Set $Q(o, a) = 0$ for all $o \in \mathcal{O}, a \in V$
for *each episode* **do**
    $o \leftarrow O_G^v, F \leftarrow E$
    for *round* $i = 0 \to \ell - 1$ **do**
        $a \leftarrow \pi(o) = \varphi(o)$ ▷ ε-greedy
        $r \leftarrow \mathsf{mix}_{(V, F \cup \{va\})}^w(v) - \mathsf{mix}_{(V, F)}^w(v)$
        $F \leftarrow F \cup \{va\}$
        $o' \leftarrow O_{(V,F)}^v$
        $Q(o, a) \leftarrow (1 - \alpha)Q(o, a) + \alpha \left[r + \max_{a'} Q(o', a') \right]$
        $o \leftarrow o'$

4.3 A Fast Q-Learning Algorithm for SCNB

However, OQL is impractical for most of the time as the space of 2-level ego networks is typically too large to learn from. Therefore we propose a fast Q-learning algorithm (FQL) that aggregates all 2-level ego networks at round τ to a single state. In other words, FQL directly uses the indices of time steps as states. Formally, FQL utilizes an ego-state mapping ϕ_f such that $\phi_f(O_{G_\tau}^v) := \tau$ for all $G_\tau \in \mathcal{G}_\tau$. Hence the Q-value update rule of FQL is

$$Q_{t+1}(\tau, a) = (1 - \alpha_t)Q_t(\tau, a) + \alpha_t \left[r_{\tau+1} + \max_{a'} Q_t(\tau + 1, a') \right], \qquad (9)$$

where $a = A_\tau \in N_{G_\tau}^2(v)$, $G_{\tau+1} = G_\tau \oplus_v a$ and $a' \in N_{G_{\tau+1}}^2(v)$.

The reward distribution is not stationary in FQL as the underlying network $G_{\tau+1}$ induced by a same action a at time τ may vary. Hence $Q(\tau, a)$ is not guaranteed to converge to $Q^*(O_{G_\tau}^v)$ for any $G_\tau \in \mathcal{G}_\tau$. In other words, the cost of a fast speed is losing the guarantee of optimality. However, surprisingly, we observe that FQL often stabilizes faster compared to OQL, which implies that FQL achieves a good trade-off between time and accuracy in practice (see Sect. 5). As the guarantee of optimality is absent in FQL, we obtain a sub-optimal policy π and thus a sub-optimal NB strategy φ. Algorithm 2 shows the procedure of FQL.

5 Simulations and Experiments

We simulate the SCNB processes and test two Q-learning algorithms over both synthetic and real-world networks. As a uniform setting, we set learning rate $\alpha = 0.1$ and exploration probability $\varepsilon = 0.3$, respectively. The discount factor γ is fixed to 1 as addressed in Sect. 4. To capture how a marginal individual embeds herself to a society through gaining social capital, throughput experiments, we determine v as the node with the lowest degree in the corresponding network.

Algorithm 2. FQL: Estimate sub-optimal strategies for SCNB

Input: An SCNB problem $\langle G, v, \ell, w \rangle$ with $G = (V, E)$
Output: A sub-optimal NB strategy φ
Initialization: Set $Q(i, a) = 0$ for all $0 \leq i \leq \ell, a \in V$
for *each episode* **do**
$\quad F \leftarrow E$
$\quad$**for** *round* $i = 0 \rightarrow \ell - 1$ **do**
$\quad\quad a \leftarrow \pi(i) = \varphi(i)$ $\qquad\qquad\qquad\qquad\qquad\qquad\qquad$ ▷ ε-greedy
$\quad\quad r \leftarrow \mathrm{mix}^w_{(V, F \cup \{va\})}(v) - \mathrm{mix}^w_{(V, F)}(v)$
$\quad\quad F \leftarrow F \cup \{va\}$
$\quad\quad Q(i, a) \leftarrow (1 - \alpha) Q(i, a) + \alpha \left[r + \max_{a'} Q(i + 1, a') \right]$

5.1   Football Teams Network: A Case Study

The goal is to test OQL and FQL on a real-world network. We apply two Q-learning algorithms to the FOOTBALL dataset, which represents American football games between Division IA colleges during regular season Fall 2000. Nodes and edges represent teams and matches, respectively [18]. In this scenario, we assume a football team of a college is seeking for a match (creating a link) with another college. The pursuit of bonding capital of a team can be interpreted as exploiting the league that it belongs to. By contrast, the bridging capital can be seen as the capacity to broker two different leagues.

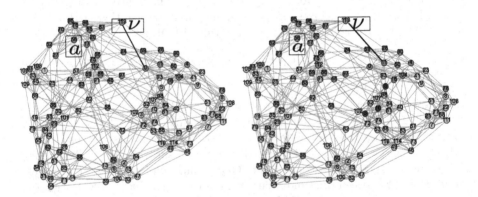

Fig. 1. The agent v and action a are set as nodes 113 and 56, respectively. Red nodes represent v's initial 2-hop neighbors. Green nodes in the left figure represent v's new 2-hop neighbors after linking to node 0 at round 1. Blue nodes in the right figure represent 2-hop neighbors after linking to node 11 at round 1. o_1 is induced by red and green nodes (left figure), and o_2 is induced by red and blue nodes (right figure). (Color figure online)

This simulation is configured as follows. We set the length of NB processes $\ell = 5$ and the preference weight $w = 0.5$. We select two possibly emerging 2-level ego networks (denoted by o_1 and o_2) at round $\tau = 1$, and a node a (see

Fig. 1). We execute 10 independent runs for this experiment. The learning curves of $Q(o_1, a)$ and $Q(o_2, a)$ in OQL, $Q(\tau = 1, a)$ in FQL, and tendencies of social capital are plotted in Fig. 2.

Two facts stand out from experimental results: (1) FQL standouts as $Q(1, a)$ stabilizes considerably faster than two Q-values in OQL, though to a non-optimal value. This coincides with our theoretical results. (2) Thanks to the fast stabilization, FQL surpasses OQL in the speed of enhancing social capital. More surprisingly, FQL stabilizes at a nearly optimal value of mixed capital, as shown in the right part of Fig. 2. Therefore, it is explicitly that FQL successfully achieves a trade-off between efficiency and accuracy in this case study.

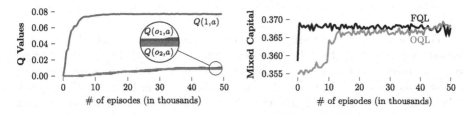

Fig. 2. Results of applying two Q-learing algorithms on football network. Left: Q-values by OQL ($Q(o_1, a)$ and $Q(o_2, a)$) and FQL ($Q(1, a)$). Each curve represents the median over 10 independent runs. Right: Results of mixed capital by OQL and FQL with preference weight $w = 0.5$.

5.2   Random Networks

The objective of this experiment is to investigate how social structure influences the learning speed and effect. We only use FQL in this experiment as OQL requires impractical running time. We conduct simulations on synthetic networks that are generated by standard random network formation model: **(1) Barabási-Albert (BA) model.** Barabási-Albert model generates scale-free networks with a power-law degree distribution, which exhibit in general low clustering coefficient. The process initiates a cycle of n nodes, and from each node, it adds at most $m < n$ edges to others using a preferential attachment scheme. Following the convention, we set $m = 4$ in our experiments [2]. **(2) Watts-Strogatz (WS) model.** The model starts from a regular ring lattice and randomly rewires edges with probability p. As edges are rewired, the network swings from a regular graph towards an ER random graph. When $p \in [0.01, 0.1]$, the graph typically exhibits a high clustering coefficient, demonstrating a small world property [23]. To better reflect the small world property, we set $p = 0.1$ in our experiments. **(3) Erdös-Rény (ER) model.** The ER model builds edges as independent Bernoulli random variables and results in Poisson binomial degree distribution, with low clustering coefficient in general [9]. The model starts with a number n of agents and adds edges between pairs of agents uniformly randomly with probability $p \in [0, 1]$ [9]. Here we set $p = 0.04$. We generate an instance for each model, each of size 500. Table 1 shows the statistics of three random networks.

Table 1. Properties of three random networks.

Network model	Nodes	Edges	Radius	Diameter	Clustering coefficient
BA	500	1491	4	6	0.05
WS	500	2000	6	8	0.49
ER	500	4964	3	4	0.04

The length of NB processes ℓ is set as 5 and the preference weight w is varied in $\{0, 0.5, 1\}$. The values of social capital shown in Fig. 3 are averaged over 10 independent runs. We make two discussions: • A centralized network structure can increase learning efficiency. Stabilization in ER networks requires a large number of episodes (more than 7000). While both types of social capital in BA and WS stabilizes very fast (at ≈ 2500 episodes). • A centralized network structure can enhance the effect of learning. Bonding and bridging capital in BA and WS networks stabilize faster than in ER networks. Moreover, in ER networks, bonding and bridging capital rise by merely ≈ 0.004 and 0.04 after 10000 episodes, respectively, which is considerably lower than in BA and WS networks. This can be explained from the aspect of network structure: BA networks have one and multiple centers; nodes in WS networks are connected densely; while nodes in ER networks are randomly and loosely connected. This captures the fact that an individual can fast learn to access to some center nodes in a densely connected society but fails to remarkably enhance social capital in a chaotic and loosely connected society.

5.3 Real-World Networks

Following the same setting of experiments on synthetic networks, we next simulate NB processes on three real-world networks[2]: **(1) FRIEND.** Friend network contains friendships between users of a social website, where nodes and edges represent users and friendships, respectively. **(2) EMAIL.** This network is generated using email data from a large European research institution, which studies anonymized information about all incoming and outgoing emails between institutional members. There is an edge (u, v) in the network if person u sent person v at least one email. **(3) BIBLE.** Bible network contains nouns (places and names) of the King James Version of the Bible and information about their co-occurrences. A node represents one of the above noun types, and an edge

---

[2] All three real-world network datasets are from the public Koblenz Network Collection. http://konect.uni-koblenz.de/networks/.

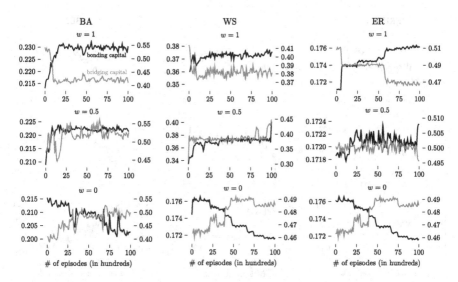

Fig. 3. Results of bonding (left axis and dark lines) and bridging capital (right axis and gray lines) in BA, WS and ER networks during 10000 episodes with varying preference weight w. Each curve is averaged over 10 independent runs.

indicates that two nouns appeared together in the same Bible verse. Table 2 summaries the statistics of three above real-world networks.

The results on three real-world networks are illustrated in Fig. 4. Analogous to the results in random networks, the performance of the learning exhibits a positive relationship with the clustering coefficient, a measure of the extent to which nodes in a graph tend to cluster together. The FRIENDS network has the lowest clustering coefficient, where social capital stabilizes after ≈ 8000 episodes. In contrast, the learning speed in the other two networks is relatively higher, where stabilization can be observed before ≈ 5000 episodes (EMAIL with $w = 1, w = 0.5$; BIBLE with $w = 1, w = 0.5$). This result is consistent with our discussions in the experiment on random networks that a centralized structure can enhance the performance of learning.

Table 2. Properties of three real-world networks.

Dataset	Nodes	Edges	Radius	Diameter	Clustering coefficient
FRIEND	1858	12534	7	14	0.14
EMAIL	1005	25571	4	7	0.40
BIBLE	1773	16401	5	8	0.72

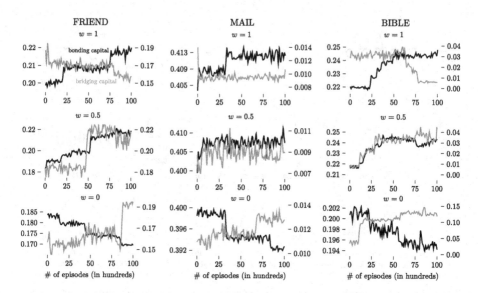

Fig. 4. Results of bonding (left axis and dark lines) and bridging capital (right axis and gray lines) in three real-world networks during 10000 episodes with varying preference weight w. Each curve is averaged over 10 independent runs.

6   Conclusion and Outlook

This paper proposes and formalizes the social capital-based network building (SCNB) problem and develops a Q-learning algorithm FQL for it that strikes a balance between efficiency and performance. The experimental results show that the performance of learning efficiency is relevant to the structural properties of networks. A highly centralized structure can significantly accelerate learning speed and effect.

Ideas and methods proposed in this paper represent a novel research initiative. There are several potential directions for future work. A fairly straightforward expansion is to explore learning algorithms to gain social capital in evolving networks. Another future challenge is to employ representative learning and deep reinforcement learning to our model for predigesting the observation and transferring learned knowledge to other networks. A third future work is to investigate the emergence of social patterns when multiple agents simultaneously learn to gain social capital.

References

1. Alaa, A.M., Ahuja, K., van der Schaar, M.: A micro-foundation of social capital in evolving social networks. IEEE Trans. Netw. Sci. Eng. **5**(1), 14–31 (2018)
2. Barabási, A.L., Albert, R.: Emergence of scaling in random networks. Science **286**(5439), 509–512 (1999)
3. Bourdieu, P.: The forms of capital. In: Handbook of Theory and Research for the Sociology of Education (1986)

4. Brânzei, S., Larson, K.: Social distance games. In: The 10th International Conference on Autonomous Agents and Multiagent Systems, vol. 3, pp. 1281–1282. International Foundation for Autonomous Agents and Multiagent Systems (2011)
5. Burt, R.S.: Structural holes and good ideas. Am. J. Sociol. **110**(2), 349–399 (2004)
6. Cai, Y., Zheng, H., Liu, J., Yan, B., Su, H., Liu, Y.: Balancing the pain and gain of hobnobbing: utility-based network building over attributed social networks. In: Proceedings of the 17th International Conference on Autonomous Agents and Multiagent Systems, pp. 193–201 (2018)
7. Coleman, J.S.: Foundations of Social Theory. Harvard University Press, Harvard (1994)
8. Coleman, J.S.: Social capital in the creation of human capital. Am. J. Sociol. **94**, S95–S120 (1988)
9. Erdos, P., Rényi, A.: On the evolution of random graphs. Publ. Math. Inst. Hung. Acad. Sci **5**(1), 17–60 (1960)
10. Girvan, M., Newman, M.E.: Community structure in social and biological networks. Proc. Natl. Acad. Sci. **99**(12), 7821–7826 (2002)
11. Granovetter, M.S.: The strength of weak ties. In: Social Networks, pp. 347–367. Elsevier (1977)
12. Jackson, M.O.: A survey of network formation models: stability and efficiency. In: Group Formation in Economics: Networks, Clubs, and Coalitions, vol. 664, pp. 11–49 (2005)
13. Lin, N.: Social Capital: A Theory of Social Structure and Action, vol. 19. Cambridge University Press, Cambridge (2002)
14. Moskvina, A., Liu, J.: How to build your network? A structural analysis. In: International Joint Conference on Artificial Intelligence (IJCAI-2016), pp. 2597–2603 (2016)
15. Myers, D.: Relationship rewards. In: Social Psychology, pp. 392–439 (2010)
16. Page, L., Brin, S., Motwani, R., Winograd, T.: The pagerank citation ranking: bringing order to the web. Technical report, Stanford InfoLab (1999)
17. Putnam, R.D.: Bowling Alone: The Collapse and Revival of American Community. Simon and Schuster, New York (2001)
18. Rossi, R.A., Ahmed, N.K.: The network data repository with interactive graph analytics and visualization. In: Proceedings of the Twenty-Ninth AAAI Conference on Artificial Intelligence (2015)
19. Skyrms, B., Pemantle, R.: A dynamic model of social network formation. In: Gross, T., Sayama, H. (eds.) Adaptive Networks. UCS, pp. 231–251. Springer, Heidelberg (2009). https://doi.org/10.1007/978-3-642-01284-6_11
20. Sutton, R.S., Barto, A.G.: Reinforcement Learning: An Introduction. MIT Press, Cambridge (2018)
21. Tong, H., Faloutsos, C., Pan, J.Y.: Fast random walk with restart and its applications. In: Sixth International Conference on Data Mining (ICDM 2006), pp. 613–622. IEEE (2006)
22. Watkins, C.J., Dayan, P.: Q-learning. Mach. Learn. **8**(3–4), 279–292 (1992)
23. Watts, D.J., Strogatz, S.H.: Collective dynamics of 'small-world' networks. Nature **393**(6684), 440 (1998)
24. Yan, B., Chen, Y., Liu, J.: Dynamic relationship building: exploitation versus exploration on a social network (2017)
25. Yan, B., Liu, Y., Liu, J., Cai, Y., Su, H., Zheng, H.: From the periphery to the core: information brokerage in an evolving network. In: International Joint Conference on Artificial Intelligence (IJCAI-2018), pp. 3912–3918 (2018)

A Novel Event Detection Model Based on Graph Convolutional Network

Pengpeng Zhou, Baoli Zhang, Bin Wu$^{(\boxtimes)}$, Yao Luo, Nianwen Ning,
and Jiaying Gong

Beijing Key Laboratory of Intelligent Telecommunications Software and Multimedia,
Beijing University of Posts and Telecommunications, Beijing 100876, China
{zhoupengpeng,zbaoli,wubin,Martyluo,nianwenning,gongjiaying}@bupt.edu.cn

Abstract. With the rapid development of society, economy, politics and science, there is a vast amount of collected daily news reports. How to detect news events and discover the underlying event evolution pattern has become an urgent problem. There have been many existing works to solve this problem, but most just use TF-IDF or LDA features to extract the limited semantic information, and the structural information of documents is also potential to be exploited. In this paper, we propose a novel Graph Convolutional Network based event detection model, named as NED-GCN, for news stream. The proposed model utilizes ConceptGraph to represent a document and fully takes semantic information and structural information of a document into account. Further, a Siamese Graph Convolutional Network (SiamGCN) is presented to calculate the similarity between document pair via shared weights for document embedding learning, and finally the learned document embeddings are clustered to generate events. Experimental evaluation on two real datasets shows that our method outperforms the state-of-art approaches in event detection.

Keywords: Event detection · NED-GCN · SiamGCN · ConceptGraph

1 Introduction

As age advances, users are easily to feel overwhelmed by the explosion of information. Event detection, one of challenging tasks in the information retrieval field, aims at discovering important events from enormous news stream data. Although various existing studies are effective in extracting event, users are still lost in the information forest. In this paper, we target at the task of event detection to help users obtain valuable information from news streams more conveniently, rapidly and efficiently.

Thus far, various news event detection approaches, including non-negative matrix factorization [10,23], probabilistic model, K-Means clustering algorithm,

Supported in part by National Key Research and Development Program of China under Grant 2018YFC0831500 and the National Natural Science Foundation of China under Grant No. 61972047.

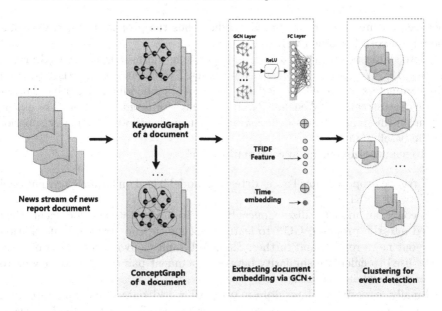

Fig. 1. The pipeline used for event detection via graph convolution network.

Single-pass clustering algorithm, Hierarchical clustering algorithm [9,25] and complex network [17,21], have been exploited to discover news event. However, these previous work on event detection rely on hand-crafted features and most of them just use TF-IDF or LDA to present document, which will lead to problems such as sparse semantic of document feature vector and excessive dimension. In addition, these approaches are not reasonable as they don't take the structure information of documents into account.

In this paper, we propose a novel model to detect news events by tracking news streams, which is based on Graph Convolution Network. There are two entail substantial challenges in event detection. First, due to the diversity of text semantic and the different styles of text representation in news streams, finding a sufficient text presentation method including text semantic content and structure information is the first challenge. Moreover, based on the proposed text presentation method, how to improve its feature extraction ability is the other challenge, which is vital to cluster news reports for final event detection. To tackle such challenging changes, we utilize conceptGraph to represent a text document by an undirected weighted graph [15], which is generated by detecting community from KeyGraph. In the conceptGraph, each node refers to a community (i.e. a concept including several semantically similar keywords), and the edges contain semantic structures information. In addition, we propose a novel event detection model based on Graph Convolutional Network (NED-GCN) to extract the feature of the conceptGraph. Meanwhile, we apply a Siamese structure to Graph Convolutional Network (SiamGCN) to calculate the similarity between document pair via shared weights, thus the proposed Graph Convolutional Network is trained well.

Two datasets are utilized in this paper. One dataset is following Liu and Zhang [15]. We leverage Chinese News Same Event dataset (CNSE)[1] to train the parameters of SiamGCN model for document embedding. The other dataset is the news stream of "Wenzhou Train Accident" for event detection. The experiment on this real datasets demonstrates that our method is obviously superior to the baseline methods.

To summarize, our main contributions include:

- First, we propose a novel event detection model based on Graph Convolutional Network (NED-GCN).
- Second, our model utilizes ConceptGraph to present a news document, then fed into the proposed GCN to learn the semantic and structure information about news report, and further, Siamese Graph Convolutional Network can be used to calculate similarity between document pair via shared weights to train the whole network.
- Finally, experimental results on two real world dataset demonstrate that our model significantly outperforms several state-of-the-art methods in event detection.

The rest of the paper is organized as follows. Section 2 introduces the formulation of our proposed methodology. In Sect. 3, experiments and analysis are presented. The related work is reviewed in Sect. 4. Finally, we conclude the paper with future work in Sect. 5.

2   Preliminary and Background

Recently, various news agencies have sprung up, such as Tencent News, Sina news, toutiao, and so on. The enormous amount of news are pouring into web everyday, which form a large number of events. Following the definition of Topic Detection and Tracking (TDT), we briefly introduce some symbols and basic concepts which are used in this paper.

News Report. A news report is to report a current event or information edited by journalists, including time, location, person, organization, and other important keywords. In this paper, we present a news report document as a concept-Graph $\mathcal{G} = (V, L)$, with nodes denoted as semantic similar keywords, and edges denoted as the relationship between nodes, i.e. $l_{i,j} = (v_i, v_j)$ [15].

News Stream. Let $\mathcal{D} = (d_1, d_2, ..., d_i, ..., d_n)$ be a sequent stream of news report documents, where n is the total number of document in news stream.

---

[1] https://pan.baidu.com/s/1WBo5pGX748rjIsUI86DIZA.

Event. The documents within a topic are denoted as $D = \{d_1, d_2, \ldots, d_i, \ldots, d_n\}$, where i is the time order of documents in news stream. According to Fig. 1, an event consists of one or more documents, such as $E_1 = \{d_1, d_2\}$, $E_2 = \{d_3, d_4, d_5\}$. As the description above, a set of events is a topic, i.e., $T = \{E_1, E_2, \cdots, E_n\}$. According to the definition of event in TDT, each event has its timestamp, places, features, which make the event distinguished from others.

3   Model

In this section, we first present the whole pipeline for event detection, then a novel Siamese Graph Convolutional Neural Network for extracting document embedding is elaborated on.

3.1   Pipeline

Formally, the input of our system is a news stream, and the output are the list of events. As shown in Fig. 1 our model consists of three steps. The first step is a preprocessing process, aiming at constructing a *ConceptGraph* of a document, which combines the strengths of the structural information with semantic information together. Then, a trained Siamese Graph Convolutional Network (SiamGCN) takes the initially constructed ConceptGraph as input and outputs the graph embedding. Besides, we also utilize the same dimensional TF-IDF feature and 1-dimensional time embedding as the supplements of graph features. These three features are concentrated and regarded as the input of the third step, i.e., effective bik-means algorithms are adopted for clustering to generate events.

The core point of our method is the extraction of graph features, which are vital for subsequent event detection. Extracting the discriminative features of a document is not trivial, we argue that if the extracted graph features can distinguish two different graph well, it will be benificial for clustering problems. Inspired by [12,13,15,28], we propose a Siamese Graph Convolutional Neural Network applied to irregular graphs, and select a hinge loss function to train the model.

3.2   Document Embedding via GCN

Graph Construction: Inspired by [15], given an input Chinese document, we aim to transform the document to a graph, called as *ConceptGraph*. First, the Chinese text data is performed word segmentation using off-the-shelf tools such as jieba[2]. Second, the named entities are extracted from the document, then followed by the keyword extraction process. We use the public Chinese processing tool, *e.g.*, LTP [4] for these two tasks. After the former preprocessing finished,

---

[2] https://github.com/fxsjy/jieba.

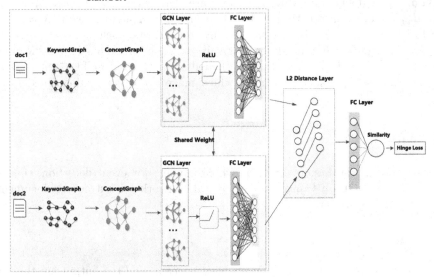

Fig. 2. The framework of SiamGCN for document embedding.

we start to construct the initial *KeywordGraph*, a keyword co-occurrence graph, where each keyword is represented by a vertex. If a pair of keywords co-occur in at least one sentence, then they are connected by an edge. In the constructed KeywordGraph, densely connections are often occurred if the subsets of keywords are highly correlated in the semantics, such a dense sub-graph is called as a *concept*. To extract the concepts, we use the popular *betweenness centrality score* [21] based on overlapping community detection algorithms to extract the concepts. Finally, we assign each sentence to its most related concepts by calculating the cosine similarity between each sentence and a concept, where they are all represented by TF-IDF vectors. Having established the basic graph structure, we construct the final full graph, i.e., ConceptGraph. Specifically, To calculate the feature vector of each vertex, the word2vec embeddings of the keywords on the corresponding sentences of the vertex are computed and the mean value is regraded as the initial vertex feature vector. Further, the TF-IDF similarity between the corresponding pieces of texts on the two vertices is calculated as the edge weight.

SiamGCN: Classical deep learning models are defined for the regular grid-structured data, which is challenging to deal with the irregular-structured graphs. Recently, Graph Convolutional Network (GCN) [11] is proposed to address this gap. For our task, the input to the GCN is the constructed ConceptGraph $G = (V, L)$ with N vertiecs $v_i \in V$, edges $(v_i, v_j) \in L$ with weights w_{ij} and an adjacent matrix $A \in R^{N \times N}$ where $A_{ij} = w_{ij}$. Further, the vertex feature matrix is denoted as $X = x_i{}_{i=1}^{N}$ where x_i is the feature vector of vertex

v_i. Then, we use a multi-layer GCN with the following layer-wise propagation rule [11]:

$$H^{(l+1)} = \sigma(\tilde{D}^{-\frac{1}{2}} \tilde{A} \tilde{D}^{-\frac{1}{2}} H^{(l)} W^{(l)}) \tag{1}$$

where $\tilde{A} = A + I_N$ is the modified self-connected adjacency matrix with identity matrix I_N added, $\tilde{D}$ is a diagonal matrix such that $\tilde{D}_{ii} = \sum_j \tilde{A}_{ij}$, $H^{(l)} \in R^{N \times M_l}$ is the matrix of activation, where M_l is the feature dimension of each vertex in the lth layer, and $H^{(0)} = X$ is the initial features, $W^{(l)}$ is the trainable weight matrix in the lth layer and $\sigma(\cdot)$ denotes an activation function, such as the ReLU. A fully connected layer is followed by the last convolutional layer to map the text feature to the final fixed-sized graph embedding.

To calculate the similarity of two graphs, we apply a Siamese structure to the GCN and construct a SiamGCN network, presented in Fig. 2. The SiamGCN consists of two parallel GCN and fully connected layers which share the same weights, each taking a graph as the input and outputing the corresponding graph embedding. A L2 distance layer computes the square distance of two graph embeddings to combine them, then followed by a single fully connected layer to output the similarity distance.

Inspired by [13,16,30], we use the hinge loss as an objective function for the training of the SiamGCN.

$$\mathcal{L}^{hinge} = \frac{1}{N} \sum_{i=1}^{N} \max(0, 1 - y_i s_i) \tag{2}$$

where y_i and s_i are the ground truth label of the pair (i.e., 1 for matching graphs vs. 0 for non-matching graphs) and the estimated similarity score of the SiamGCN. From the equation, we can see that the output higher than 1 for matching graphs or lower than -1 for nonmatching graphs is not penalized, while outputs within the range $(-1, 1)$ are penalized.

After training model, we use the embedding after GCN $\rightarrow$ FC Layer, and joint TF-IDF embedding, and time embedding to present documents of "Wenzhou Train Accident".

3.3 Generating Events

After document embedding, events will be generated through clustering algorithm. Traditional k-means clustering algorithm is sensitive to the initial value of k, and it is easy to fall into the circle of local optimal solution rather than global optimal solution. To address this problem, we utilize bik-means clustering algorithm [31] to cluster the news reports, which have better effect and faster speed than k-means by using SSE (Sum of Squared Error) as clustering metric. Thus, events will be generated after clustering, and the description of events use the news title of news reports in cluster.

4   Experiment

4.1   Experimental Setup

Datasets: We utilize two datasets in this paper. One dataset is following Liu and Zhang [15], we leverage Chinese News Same Event dataset (CNSE) to train the parameters of SiamGCN model for document embedding. The dataset consists of 12865 positive samples and 16198 negative samples. Further, these samples are split into training set (17438 samples), validation set (5813 samples) and testing set (5812 samples).

The other dataset is crawled from chinatimes.com and ifeng.com by crawler automatically including a number of news reports. In order to demonstrate our model better, this paper selects one topic of news reports, i.e. "Wenzhou Train Accident", for event detection, which is from July 23 in 2011 to January 20 in 2012, including 1160 news reports in total.

Two annotators were invited to read all the news documents of Wenzhou Train Accident respectively, found news events artificially, reviewed the results and showed the event list as the standard answer (ground truth) in this paper.

4.2   Implementation

The proposed SiamGCN is implemented by Pytorch [18]. We use SGD to optimise the network with a mini-batch size of 100, momentum of 0.9 and $L2$ weights regularization coefficient of 0.005 for 50 epoches. The learning rate is initialised as 0.001 and decreases by a factor of 0.1 when loss on validation set plateaus. Besides, a dropout layer with dropout ratio of 0.2 is used at the FC layer. In the setting of SiamGCN, the one GCN layer is adopted with 128 dimension word2vec in each vertex. And the last FC layer outputs the 32 dimension vectors as the graph embedding. Meanwhile, TF-IDF embedding also uses the 32 dimension vectors. What's more, time embedding uses 1 dimension vector, and the impact factor of time is set to 16 to improve the impact of time.

Performance Metric: We evaluated all the competitive methods by Precision, P, and Recall, R, which is measured by $P = \frac{|T \bigcap T'|}{|T'|}$, $R = \frac{|T \bigcap T'|}{|T|}$, where $T = \{E_1, E_2, \ldots, E_n\}$ is the set of real events detected artificially. $T' = \{E'_1, E'_2, \ldots, E'_n\}$ is the set of events detected from our model in this paper.

4.3   Experimental Result

Competitive Methods: To evaluate the performance of the proposed NED-SiamGCN, we compared it with several state-of-the-art methods listed as follows:

- **TF-IDF:** This method is popular in document feature extraction. It is term frequency × inverse document frequency to extract the more important keywords for each document in corpus.
- **TF-IDF**$_{order}$ [26]: This method add time order to traditional method (TF-IDF) to improve performance.

- **JS-ID′F** [27]: This method is Jaccard similarity coefficient × Inverse Dimension Frequency, inspired by *TF-IDF*.
- **JS-ID′F**$_{order}$ [31]: This method improves *JS-ID′F* by adding time order.
- **NED-GCN:** It is our model, we utilize SiamGCN to train the parameters of the model for document embedding, then joint GCN embedding, TF-IDF embedding, and time embedding to present document. At last, bikmeans is used to generate events.

Table 1. Precision (P) and Recall (R) of methods

K	10		15		20		25		30		35		40	
Method	P	R	P	R	P	R	P	R	P	R	P	R	P	R
TF-IDF	0.80	0.44	0.67	0.56	0.55	0.61	0.56	0.78	0.50	0.83	0.40	0.78	0.35	0.78
TF-IDF$_{order}$ [26]	0.90	0.50	0.73	0.61	0.70	0.78	0.56	0.78	0.50	0.83	0.43	0.83	0.38	0.83
JS-ID′F [27]	0.90	0.50	0.80	0.67	0.75	0.83	0.60	0.83	0.50	0.83	0.48	0.89	0.43	0.94
JS-ID′F$_{order}$ [31]	1.00	0.56	0.80	0.67	0.90	1.00	0.68	0.94	0.60	1.00	0.49	0.94	0.45	1.00
NED-GCN	1.00	0.56	0.87	0.72	0.90	1.00	0.72	1.00	0.57	0.94	0.51	1.00	0.45	1.00

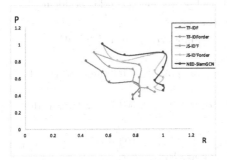

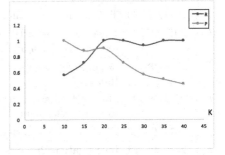

Fig. 3. PR of different approaches.   **Fig. 4.** Effect of different value of K

Table 1 and Fig. 3 show the comparison of different approaches tuning the value of k from 10 to 40. We observe that our model, NED-GCN, outperforms other methods in the task of event detection. The trend curve of precision and recall is shown in Fig. 4 using our model with different values of k. As we can see, when $k = 18$, the precision and recall can arrive the optimal at the same time, Meanwhile, the number of manual annotation of events is also 18. What's more, Table 2 show the event list. These demonstrate that extracting document feature via GCN is significant.

Table 2. The event list in Wenzhou Train Accident

No.	Time	Event
E_1	2011/07/24	The Rear-end collision occurred in Wenzhou MU
E_2	2011/07/24	Medical support
E_3	2011/07/24	Government organized the rescue
E_4	2011/07/25	35 people died in "7.23" MU rear ended crash
E_5	2011/07/25	Experts and industry insiders believed that scheduling errors may be one of the causes of the accident
E_6	2011/07/26	The Minister of Railways called for full rescue and investigation of the MU crash
E_7	2011/07/27	Shanghai Railway Bureau Secretary, Director, and Deputy Director were removed from office
E_8	2011/07/27	Victims in Rear-end accident were each compensated 500 thousand
E_9	2011/07/27	The situation of consuccor
E_{10}	2011/07/27	MU's Rear-end accident in Wenzhou lead to 32 trains' off-the-line and the terminus alternation
E_{11}	2011/07/28	Wen Jiabao held a Chinese and foreign press conference at Wenzhou high speed railway accident scene
E_{12}	2011/07/28	Wenzhou announced the list of 39 victims in "7.23" accident
E_{13}	2011/07/29	The impact on victims of rear-end crash
E_{14}	2011/07/30	Passengers' lost articles were announced in Wenzhou MU rear-end collision accident
E_{15}	2011/08/17	Wang Yongping was no longer a spokesman for the Ministry of Railways
E_{16}	2011/08/22	State Administration of Work Safety: 7.23 MU accident was due to human elements
E_{17}	2011/08/23	Xiao Yiyi was transferred to Shanghai for treatment
E_{18}	2011/08/24	Investigation Progress of 7.23 accident

5 Related Work

According to the original topic detection and tracking research report [2], event detection is defined as discovering news event in news information flow. Clustering is a main technical means to solve such problems. Different topic detection research based on different clustering techniques are introduced as follows: (1) Matrix Decomposition [10,23], data is represented as a web page - keyword matrix in order to learn implicit topics through matrix decomposition. For different purpose, different constraint conditions are added to cost function of matrix decomposition in different research, such as similarity of topics at different time. (2) Topic Modeling [7], since one topic is regarded as one vector and the sum of values in every dimension is one, it can be considered as a point on a simplex in order to give it a prior of Dirichelt distribution. Implicit topics in text can be learned through hierarchical probability model. (3) Non-homogeneous Poison Process [8], variation trend of words is modeled as a non-homogeneous poison process and topics with explosive characteristics can be learned through intensity function in this poison process. (4) Partition and Density Clustering [9,25], web pages with same topics discussed can be classified together by means of distance or density clustering process. Then centers of different classification can be viewed as different topics. (5) Label Propagation Clustering [6,14], first, every web page is classified randomly. In other words, we first find which topic the web page belongs to and then correct the categories based on neighboring pages. We can get different categories of web pages after convergence. This method has the advantage of fast speed, however, it is not stable. (6) Another interesting research is that Hassan [21] transformed clustering problems to community discovering problems by establishing keywords co-occurrence network in order to discover topics through existing community discovery algorithm.

Then, with the rise and development of social networks (e.g. Twitter, Sina Weibo, Facebook, WeChat), social networks has become an important platform for publishing and discussing news event [20]. In order to adapt to new media, some new event discovery algorithms are proposed to consider different information in social networks including (1) Location [29], such as location information in Sina Weibo. Considering location in model can help discover some location dependent events. In [29], location is a new variable that added in topic model to learn regional topics; (2) Entity [24], words appearing in different web pages are regarded as words with same status in general topic detection. However, some proper nouns (entities) among these words such as name, location, organization, specific vocabulary, etc can not only help discover events tremendously, but also they can enrich discovered events; (3) Word Class [19], word class in social media is considered as topics through mining frequent word class to get the topic in web pages; (4) Users' Abnormal Behavior [22], except large quantities of text information in social networks, interactions among users also exist in social networks. Some behaviors such as reply, mention, forward, etc can also be used to discover event. Many simultaneous abnormal behaviors among users in social networks decide whether new events take place; (5) KeyGraph [21], large amount of information in Weibo is transformed into a keyGraph, so that topics can be discovered through community discovery method. Besides, mechanism of assigning web pages to topics is also well-established. But there is no deep analysis of that network; (6) Emotion [3], emotion is the opinion or feelings users expressed to an event or part of the event. Generally there are three kinds of emotions: positive, negative and neutral. It can also assist to exactly discover events. To detect emotional topics, we discover relationships between emotional topics with the help of existing emotional lexicon and Wordnet. Except research focused on single social media above, some research focus on cross-media event detection [5], where events are simultaneously reported by several different media such as Weibo and WeChat. They reported the same event with different degrees and emphasis. Therefore, cross-media mining can more efficiently and completely discover event information.

Though existing research on Web event detection has many outstanding achievements, the result still can't meet the need of practical applications. In [1], the author compared several usual event detection methods and the result indicates that data preprocessing has a great influence on the final result. In addition, most of the existing methods are document representation based on Vector Space Model, which has a limited ability of semantic expression, resulting in inaccurate event or topic. Therefore, web events in the text are manually selected instead of calculated by algorithm. With the mature technology of web event detection in the future, it can be used as preprocessing of the text.

6   Conclusion

The development of Graph Convolution Network brings new changes of event detection. A novel event detection model has been proposed in this paper to discover the hot events from numerous news documents in tracking news streams accurately and efficiently. The document embedding extracted via Graph Convolution Network can obtain more information than traditional model, *e.g.* bags of words, and then clusters documents by bikmeans clustering algorithm. The performance comparison demonstrates the effectiveness of our proposed model. In the future, we want to discover the dependent relationship between events, and explore the propagation mode of news events.

References

1. Aiello, L.M., et al.: Sensing trending topics in Twitter. IEEE Trans. Multimed. **15**(6), 1268–1282 (2013)
2. Allan, J.: Topic detection and tracking pilot study. In: DARPA Broadcast News Transcription and Understanding Workshop, pp. 194–218 (1998)
3. Cai, K., Spangler, S., Chen, Y., Zhang, L.: Leveraging sentiment analysis for topic detection. Web Intell. Agent Syst.: Int. J. **8**(3), 291–302 (2010)
4. Che, W., Li, Z., Liu, T.: LTP: a Chinese language technology platform. In: Proceedings of the 23rd International Conference on Computational Linguistics: Demonstrations, pp. 13–16. Association for Computational Linguistics (2010)
5. Chu, L., Zhang, Y., Li, G., Wang, S., Zhang, W., Huang, Q.: Effective multimodality fusion framework for cross-media topic detection. IEEE Trans. Circuits Syst. Video Technol. **26**(3), 556–569 (2016)
6. Guan, R., Shi, X., Marchese, M., Yang, C., Liang, Y.: Text clustering with seeds affinity propagation. IEEE Trans. Knowl. Data Eng. **23**(4), 627–637 (2011)
7. He, Q., Chang, K., Lim, E.P., Banerjee, A.: Keep it simple with time: a reexamination of probabilistic topic detection models. IEEE Trans. Pattern Anal. Mach. Intell. **32**(10), 1795–1808 (2010)
8. Huang, S., Liu, Y., Dang, D.: Burst topic discovery and trend tracing based on storm. Phys. A **416**, 331–339 (2014)
9. Jain, A.K.: Data clustering: 50 years beyond k-means. Pattern Recogn. Lett. **31**(8), 651–666 (2010)

10. Kalyanam, J., Mantrach, A., Saez-Trumper, D., Vahabi, H., Lanckriet, G.: Leveraging social context for modeling topic evolution. In: ACM SIGKDD International Conference on Knowledge Discovery and Data Mining, pp. 517–526. ACM (2015)
11. Kipf, T.N., Welling, M.: Semi-supervised classification with graph convolutional networks. arXiv preprint arXiv:1609.02907 (2016)
12. Ktena, S.I., et al.: Distance metric learning using graph convolutional networks: application to functional brain networks. In: Descoteaux, M., Maier-Hein, L., Franz, A., Jannin, P., Collins, D., Duchesne, S. (eds.) MICCAI 2017. LNCS, vol. 10433, pp. 469–477. Springer, Cham (2017). https://doi.org/10.1007/978-3-319-66182-7_54
13. Ktena, S.I., et al.: Metric learning with spectral graph convolutions on brain connectivity networks. NeuroImage **169**, 431–442 (2018)
14. Leone, M., Weigt, M.: Clustering by soft-constraint affinity propagation: applications to gene-expression data. Bioinformatics **23**(20), 2708–2715 (2007)
15. Liu, B., Zhang, T., Niu, D., Lin, J., Lai, K., Xu, Y.: Matching long text documents via graph convolutional networks. arXiv preprint arXiv:1802.07459 (2018)
16. Ma, G., et al.: Similarity learning with higher-order proximity for brain network analysis. arXiv preprint arXiv:1811.02662 (2018)
17. Melvin, S., Yu, W., Ju, P., Young, S., Wang, W.: Event detection and summarization using phrase network. In: Altun, Y., et al. (eds.) ECML PKDD 2017. LNCS, vol. 10536, pp. 89–101. Springer, Cham (2017). https://doi.org/10.1007/978-3-319-71273-4_8
18. Paszke, A., et al.: Automatic differentiation in pytorch (2017)
19. Pervin, N., Fang, F., Datta, A., Dutta, K., Vandermeer, D.: Fast, scalable, and context-sensitive detection of trending topics in microblog post streams. ACM Trans. Manag. Inf. Syst. (TMIS) **3**(4), 19 (2013)
20. Sakaki, T., Okazaki, M., Matsuo, Y.: Earthquake shakes Twitter users: real-time event detection by social sensors. In: Proceedings of the 19th International Conference on World Wide Web, pp. 851–860. ACM (2010)
21. Sayyadi, H., Raschid, L.: A graph analytical approach for topic detection. ACM Trans. Internet Technol. (TOIT) **13**(2), 4 (2013)
22. Takahashi, T., Tomioka, R., Yamanishi, K.: Discovering emerging topics in social streams via link-anomaly detection. IEEE Trans. Knowl. Data Eng. **26**(1), 120–130 (2014)
23. Vaca, C.K., Mantrach, A., Jaimes, A., Saerens, M.: A time-based collective factorization for topic discovery and monitoring in news. In: International Conference on World Wide Web, pp. 527–538. ACM (2014)
24. Vavliakis, K.N., Symeonidis, A.L., Mitkas, P.A.: Event identification in web social media through named entity recognition and topic modeling. Data Knowl. Eng. **88**, 1–24 (2013)
25. Wan, L., Ng, W.K., Dang, X.H., Yu, P.S., Zhang, K.: Density-based clustering of data streams at multiple resolutions. ACM Trans. Knowl. Discov. Data (TKDD) **3**(3), 14 (2009)
26. Wei, C.P., Lee, Y.H., Chiang, Y.S., Chen, C.T., Yang, C.C.: Exploiting temporal characteristics of features for effectively discovering event episodes from news corpora. J. Assoc. Inf. Sci. Technol. **65**(3), 621–634 (2014)
27. Wu, C., Wang, B.: Extracting topics based on word2vec and improved Jaccard similarity coefficient. In: 2017 IEEE Second International Conference on Data Science in Cyberspace (DSC), pp. 389–397. IEEE (2017)

28. Yu, J., et al.: Modeling text with graph convolutional network for cross-modal information retrieval. In: Hong, R., Cheng, W.H., Yamasaki, T., Wang, M., Ngo, C.W. (eds.) PCM 2018. LNCS, vol. 11164, pp. 223–234. Springer, Cham (2018). https://doi.org/10.1007/978-3-030-00776-8_21

29. Yuan, Q., Cong, G., Ma, Z., Sun, A., Thalmann, N.M.: Who, where, when and what: discover spatio-temporal topics for Twitter users. In: Proceedings of the 19th ACM SIGKDD International Conference on Knowledge Discovery and Data Mining, pp. 605–613. ACM (2013)

30. Zagoruyko, S., Komodakis, N.: Learning to compare image patches via convolutional neural networks. In: IEEE Conference on Computer Vision and Pattern Recognition, pp. 4353–4361 (2015)

31. Zhou, P., Cao, Z., Wu, B., Wu, C., Yu, S.: EDM-JBW: a novel event detection model based on JS-ID forder and bikmeans with word embedding for news streams. J. Comput. Sci. **28**, 336–342 (2018)

Correction to: Influence Maximization Based on Community Closeness in Social Networks

Qingqing Wu, Lihua Zhou, and Yaqun Huang

Correction to:
Chapter "Influence Maximization Based on Community Closeness in Social Networks" in: L. H. U et al. (Eds.): *Web Information Systems Engineering*, CCIS 1155, https://doi.org/10.1007/978-981-15-3281-8_13

The originally published version of the paper on p. 142 contained several inaccuracies in the content and references. To achieve better understanding the following corrections were made:

Reference 22 has been added as "Lancichinetti, A., Fortunato, S., Kertész, János.: Detecting the overlapping and hierarchical community structure in complex networks. New J. Phys. **11**(3), 033015 (2009).";
Minor typographical errors were corrected on the pages 2, 3, 10, 11, 12;
Page 4: the set of elements in the third paragraph has been changed from "$v \in C_j$" to "$i \neq j$";
Page 8: in the Algorithm 1 the line "6: calculate inter-community influence" has been changed to "6: calculate community influence".

The updated version of this chapter can be found at
https://doi.org/10.1007/978-981-15-3281-8_13

Author Index

Printed in the United States
By Bookmasters